S n o w   W a l k e r ' s
C o m p a n i o n

Garrett & Alexandra Conover

Stone Ridge Press
2515 Garthus Road
Wrenshall, MN 55797
218.384.9856
www.stoneridgepress.com
sparkystensaas@hotmail.com
To Order: 1-800-678-7006

Snow Walker's Companion

Originally published by Ragged Mountain Press, 1995; ISBN 0-07-022892-2
Revised edition by Ragged Mountain Press, 2001; ISBN 0-07-136417-X
First edition by Stone Ridge Press, 2006

Printed in Altona, Manitoba Canada by Friesens
10 9 8 7 6 5 4 3 2 1   First Edition

Editor: Catherine Long
Graphic Designer: Mark Sparky Stensaas

ISBN 0-9760313-3-7

Dedicated to our parents, Don and Linda Brown and Bill and Betty Conover. They were the most liberal, trusting and encouraging of parents in giving us nearly boundless freedom to explore the outdoor world.

&

For porcupines, past, present and future, who, in the act of foraging for inner bark, yield bone-dry standing dead spruce and tamarack through the North.
Countless trail stoves have been fed this finest of firewood, while the bodies and spirits of untold snow walkers warmed.
Our gratitude is boundless.

T a b l e   o f   C o n t e n t s

FOREWORD

A long time ago in Labrador, while trying to learn to be a trapper, I snowshoed 800 miles during one winter. I think I know something about the gear that works and the stuff that doesn't, and believe me, Garrett and Alexandra Conover know the score. As Garrett points out, the long white lakes and rivers, the frozen swamps and muskeg, now become natural highways. "Winter is the travel time."

Camping and traveling in the snowy northern forests, you want to be warm, well fed and happy. In this book the Conovers tell you how to manage it: what kind of tent and stove you should have; what kind of breathable, lined moccasins and mittens keep your feet and hands warm for below-zero travel—where to get them and how to make them. What kind of snowshoes you should buy; how to build the long, springy toboggan that carries your gear—made either from traditional wood, or from high-density plastic sheeting that can be rolled up for stowage in a small bush plane. Alexandra will put you wise to the lightest-weight, most nourishing, tastiest, quickest-to-prepare foods to take on your winter expedition. The Conovers have tested all these under the most rigorous conditions of the winter trail.

For years they've been guiding patrons on summer and winter trips in Maine, Quebec and Labrador. Before that they apprenticed themselves to an old-time Maine guide, a master of the Indian arts. They have since befriended, traveled with and learned from present-day Innu who still revere the old ways. For thousands of years the North Woods have been home to the Innu. As shown by their truly marvelous summertime canoe and their after-freeze snowshoe and toboggan, the Innu know best. Some modern improvements truly are, but not many. The Conovers tell you which ones are, and how to acquire—or make—the rest of the hard-to-come-by items you simply must have. The patterns and instructions are a marvel of clarity and good sense; the photographs and illustrations amazingly instructive and inspired.

As one would expect from long-time guides who attach such great importance to the happiness and welfare of their patrons, we have anecdotes, stories, incidents— a literary flair to enliven the trail. Sometimes you are there in the cozy tent, the stove glowing, bread baking, experiencing the joy of a winter sunrise. The Conovers give us not only the physical details of winter living and survival, but also the spiritual accompaniment that is part of the wilderness experience. And so a how-to book becomes good reading.

I often wonder whether we aren't one-up on the Montagnais and Naskapi. Their wilderness journeys have nearly always been hard and fast, a grind; in other words, work. Ours can be more leisurely and fun, provided (and this is a big proviso) we have the skills and know-how—and the humility—to open our over-stimulated eyes and listen with our decibel-battered ears.

A message is there, and this book will help snowshoe walkers find it.

—Elliott Merrick, North Carolina, 1995

ACKNOWLEDGMENTS

Sharing the Trail

Like any good trail companion, this book is quirky, opinionated and has a sense of humor. At its best we hope it will be thought provoking, fair, gracious to allow for differences of opinion and well reasoned to survive disagreement.

Although we never met, we are indebted to Calvin Rutstrum. His book *Paradise Below Zero* set us on a course we are yet navigating. Although shy on detail and technique, the book has steered countless winter wanderers toward comfortable northern living. Once we personally crossed that threshold we encountered a host of experts who held the keys to various details.

Where Rutstrum suggested possibilities, Craig MacDonald of Ontario has filled in with exhaustive, refined detail. His research among native northerners is broad and deep and with luck will one day appear in published form.

There is Bill Osgood, a member of the intrepid 10th Mountain Division, former librarian at the Center for Northern Studies in Vermont and co-author of *The Snowshoe Book*, who generously shared his time, knowledge and equipment in coaching Alexandra for her first subarctic winter trip.

Francis "Mick" Fahey of Maine passed on to us a wealth of knowledge concerning tent/stove and toboggan travel, from his days traveling with the Penobscot Indians in the early part of this century and from four-month-long timber surveys in winter.

In addition to being a valued friend, Henri Vaillancourt of New Hampshire has contributed enormously to northern snow walking through his skills as an ethnographic researcher, photographer and master craftsman.

Gerald Bessette of Schefferville, Quebec, greeted Alexandra during one of her first trips and provided not only traditional information, but also many stories that still fuel our dreams.

Horace and Joe Goudie of Labrador have given us insight into physical skills as well as a glimpse of a culture and heritage not readily grasped by outsiders.

Paul Duquette is not only a consummate woodsman but has taught us to coax astounding potential out of snow machines in the Labrador bush. His early coaching brought us to a level of capability that allowed us to accompany machine users without being hopeless liabilities.

Tekuanan McKenzie and members of his family have been fantastic instructors both on the reserve in Maliotenam, Quebec, and in the interior Quebec/Labrador landscape that is his home.

David and Susan Swappie from the Naskapi village of Kawawachikamach, Quebec, literally took us into their family and territory and patiently coached us in many skills, including their language.

Elliott Merrick, our favorite pen pal and valued critic, is thanked for slogging through the unedited manuscript and for showering us with all sorts of advice and stories of things northern, and indeed of life in general. [Sadly, Elliott passed away in 1997 at the age of 92; he is deeply missed.]

Our most prized companion of canoe, snowshoe and intellectual trails, Bob Kimber, is also heartily thanked for reading and commenting on the unedited manuscript.

Seamstress extraordinaire Sally Robbins generously provided plans for her splendid anorak. We are also indebted to architect, Maine Guide and former apprentice David Lewis, who provided superb plans for a pyramid and campfire tent.

The guests who have traveled with North Woods Ways over the years are thanked for their many questions, responses to extremes, enthusiasm and exasperations. Several of these friends appear in the photos. Had they not given us the opportunity to lead, we would scarcely have known where to begin or end, what should be taught and what should be left for personal discovery.

Although this is ostensibly a how-to book, it is equally cultural, ethnographic, scientific and philosophical. It reflects the remarkable interdisciplinary and whole-system way of knowing that is the hallmark of College of the Atlantic in Bar Harbor, Maine, from which we both graduated.

Undoubtedly, we have been most immeasurably influenced by our parents, Donald F. and Linda E. S. Brown and Elizabeth O. and William B. Conover. By loving and cherishing deep connections with both nature and people, they modeled balanced ways of being on this Earth; gifts we treasure and continually attempt to emulate.

Finally, as companions to one another as well as co-authors, we are cognizant of our respect for, and reliance on, each other in presenting this book. Although each of us tended to write the first draft of sections that interested us most, we always exchanged drafts for comment, fine-tuning and additions and deletions. The joint presentation is much better than anything either of us could have created independently.

Alexandra and Garrett Conover

Tentbound on a day of screaming wind, 70 miles north of Kawawachikamach, Quebec—Innu country, Spring 1994

Here it is ten years later and well over a thousand snow walking miles later. Under the patient, creative and energetic guidance of Sparky Stensaas, we share new insights, information and photographs in this newest edition. We hope that you can join us on the trail.

Alexandra and Garrett Conover

Along the Big Wilson Stream—Maine, Fall 2005

INTRODUCTION

Late October. Today we saw a flock of snow buntings, or snowbirds as northern-ers call them. As powerfully as did the waves of geese earlier in the fall, this sighting brings us tidings from the boreal regions far to the north of our home in Maine. Perhaps the birds flew hard during the last days of a crisp north wind, pushed south across the muskegs, forests and countless rivers and lakes. Perhaps they crossed the very waterways our canoes recently plied, or overflew segments of a portage route. Now, at the end of the canoeing season, they turn our thoughts toward the coming winter and the joys of the snowshoe trail.

Across northern canoe country, the waters are turning lethally cold. The shift inspires migrants to leave, hibernators to dig in and those who change color to molt and take on the look of snow. For some canoeists it is a time of depression, of resignation to the long wait until open water returns, when maps will be unrolled and dreams of paddle, pole and portage realized.

But for those already addicted, or those just beginning to appreciate the winter trail, the onset of winter is a time of great excitement and restlessness. Freeze-up is something to celebrate, to behold with joy, because it is the key to easy travel in the winter of the northern wilderness. The streams, rivers and lakes that were the canoeist's byways are now highways for the winter traveler. The string-bogs, muskegs and swamps that frustrated summer travelers are now frozen and wind-packed. In their winter guise, these once inaccessible areas are easily traveled.

Aerial study of canoe country reveals an intricate web of waterways parted by low hills. Canada, northern Maine, northeast Minnesota and to some extent upstate New York share these features. Generally, this is a land of drinkable waters, solitude and much of the remnant wildlands of North America. Here nomadic, indigenous peoples developed elegant and sophisticated canoes, snowshoes, toboggans and sleds; here they refined and perfected ways of living and traveling in winter. By adopting these techniques, today's wilderness traveler can enjoy winter in comfort nothing short of extraordinary.

Most books on winter camping deal with the techniques of high-country moun-taineering and/or travel within the relatively small "wilderness areas" that have been preserved politically, and are essentially artificial islands within an otherwise devel-oped landscape. There is little written about long-term living and traveling and the joys to be experienced in the winter wilds of the circumpolar boreal forests. Our hope is that the techniques outlined in *Snow Walker's Companion* will encourage a return to some of the traditions of just such a life.

Those readers who have learned their outdoor skills by subscription to recent philosophies of the low-impact school of thought will initially be shocked at many of the practices described here. We ask that you be patient initially, and then atten-tive to the whys and wherefores of what at first might appear to be blasphemous and heretical disregard for such ethics. We are not interested in the dogma of either side of such issues, yet we are passionate about the middle ground where reason and thoughtfulness may illuminate appropriateness for technique as well as care for the environment of travel. Where contrasts naturally occur we have attempted to define how to think about them with balance and openness, and to give you some tools with which to arrive at your own conclusions.

For those whose passion is boreal northern travel in winter, there is an often-overlooked body of knowledge that allows a life of wonderful comfort and consistency. Although this book focuses on travel by hand-hauled toboggan, many of the skills discussed herein apply to travel by dogsled or snowmobile as well.

Because northern waterways provide a relatively flat surface and overland treks through deep snow between watersheds or around canyons and rapids are relatively short, it is not surprising that native peoples developed toboggans and sleds for hauling gear. Concurrently, the North American snowshoe was refined to levels of sophistication and artistry that are truly astounding.

The snowshoe and the toboggan allow for a level of comfort in winter travel that makes backpacking look Spartan, rigorous and downright unpleasant. Consider that the maximum load for a backpacker is less than 80 pounds, and even that is extreme for most people. In winter, backpacking transfers the load along with one's body weight to one's snowshoes—a prescription for hot, sweaty toil.

A tobogganer, however, can haul up to 130 pounds of gear comfortably, or up to 250 if necessary, and the snow takes the weight without complaint. The load on the snowshoes is then only the weight of the snowshoer and perhaps a camera or a pair of binoculars. The toboggans are long, narrow, flexible and designed to track in the "float" packed by the hauler as he or she walks. Since waterways are more open than deep woods, the snow there is shallower and often wind-packed. Occasionally, on glare ice a toboggan slips almost by itself.

The ability to carry such loads also means snow walkers can enjoy amenities that would be impractical for backpackers. For example, for every four or five people on a trip, there might be one sheet-steel woodstove and a 10-by-12-foot wall tent of Egyptian cotton. This balances out to three to five pounds of stove per person per tent group, and three to four pounds of tent per person. If the trip is only a week or so, there may be one person per tent group who is not even pulling a toboggan. This free person breaks trail for the group and takes shifts at hauling, thus providing equal periods of work and rest for everyone.

The tents, heated by woodstoves, provide an external heat source for eight to ten hours per day. This means that walkers need not keep warm by food intake alone, as one must in cold, bivouac forms of winter travel. Consequently, less food is required per person per day, and this translates into a lighter load, or a longer trip. And that's not to mention the inherent pleasures of lounging in a tent that is 70 or 80 degrees Fahrenheit while the stove is going.

The availability of such warmth not only improves group spirit, but should anything become damp from sweat, condensation or mishap, it can readily be dried by hanging from the ridgeline of the tent, an area that often attains 110 to 130 degrees Fahrenheit.

Once the necessary physical and mental skills are acquired and equipment made or purchased, one is ready to travel the ice-clad byways and enjoy the special rewards of winter travel and living. With experience, one discovers that the skills, at first goals in themselves, are only tools. The greatest rewards are harder to define. For beyond knowledge of cold-weather comfort, natural history, group dynamics, first aid, nutrition and technical skills lies a wider, deeper realm, where the mind can expand like a full, crisp breath to encompass the winter environment.

The experienced snow walker deletes notions of "challenge" and "survival," and accepts the scenery and wildlife as gifts to one's spirit. For those who venture into circumpolar hinterlands is the added potential for meeting indigenous people in their winter camps, or the infrequent nonnative person who has chosen a season in the bush. Beyond sightings of wolves and caribou, shared cups of tea and time spent with friends in snug tents beneath the aurora, is that private terrain where the mind can travel in complete euphoria.

Snow Walker's Companion gives readers a complete education regarding the skills and techniques appropriate to the snowshoe-and-toboggan trail. Although aspects of other forms of winter travel and living are mentioned for comparative or illustrative purposes, it is not our intent to discuss the many other forms of winter camping. Rather, we've kept our focus narrow in favor of details, striving to tell practicing and would-be snow walkers all they need to know to travel with safety, grace and panache.

It may be true that the snowshoes standing by the tent flap are composed of babiche and wood. Yet they are more than that. They are a time machine from the whirling snows of the northern forests, borne by the spirits of countless native people, hide of moose or caribou, wood of birch or larch. Even now they seem to hum in the winter winds, resonating to the invitation of the horizon.

Snowshoes & Footwear

SNOWSHOES & FOOTWEAR

" A snowshoe trail on a sunny day after a light fall of snow is a lovelier thing than I can describe. I often look back at it streaming from our heels, flowing astern ...A darker serpentine ribbon, scallop-edged, filled with tumbled blue shadow markings. And every individual print is a beautiful thing. It is like sculpture and like painting, endless impressions of an Indian craftsman's masterpiece."
—Elliott Merrick, *True North,* 1933

SNOWSHOES

The best examples of the snowshoe maker's art may well be seen among the Attikamek people and the Eastern Cree. These shoes are of such stunning quality and artistry that nothing could be added or subtracted without jeopardizing perfection. Light frames of white birch with thin, tapered larch crossbars support the fine caribou *babiche* (pronounced "ba-beesh"). This strong rawhide is woven not merely neatly and precisely, but with patterns incorporated into the weave. Beyond refined utilitarian beauty and balance are deliberate reflections of the cycles of life. Here is a sense of place, combined with exquisite knowledge of wood, grain, animals, humans and the land.

Even before the availability of steel for crooked knife blades, axes and babiche cutters, which made production easier, these snowshoes reflected a reverence for life that is now all but lost. The babiche from the caribou strings the shoes to make future hunts possible. The wood of the ash, birch and larch trees becomes the frames of possibility. The Indians' knowledge of tools and techniques, their sense of how to be on the land, circles endlessly, passing from mother to daughter and from father to son. Snowshoes thus created, are intricate, infused with profound knowledge and, with amazing grace, allow a person to fly upon the snow.

Although in refined essence a good snowshoe is a great achievement, the people who made them best are humble. The designs they wove into the lacing give thanks; they praise the snow and weather, the trees and animals that gave the component parts and acknowledge a spiritual world beyond our reckoning. Additionally, among some people, the designs reveal with a leaf pattern that the shoe is for a woman, or with a ptarmigan track that it is for a man. With each impression of "an Indian craftsman's masterpiece," a prayer falls upon the snow.

Such snowshoes take our breath away. And well they should, for even as we gasp in awe, if we are lucky enough to find such a pair in a museum or among the people of the northern bush, we know that the older craftspeople are passing away, and that few if any younger people will follow with such care and precision. This is the tradition from which snowshoes as we know them today arose.

Although today's snowshoes cannot match the older versions' sophistication or grace, they contain threads of the old tradition. Modern snowshoes give access to the snow-clad wilds, and if the recreational snow walker is observant and spends enough time on the trail, there is much to be learned. These discoveries become the brightest beads on the sash of our winter wanderings.

Most of us cannot get snowshoes from native craftspeople, and many cannot afford a superb pair made by one of the few nonnative people who have mastered the art. Nonetheless, several manufacturers make wood-framed and babiche-filled snowshoes, and others produce snowshoes in a variety of synthetics.

The economics of factory production delete many of the refinements that were possible when each pair of shoes was made for an individual by family members who had the time and knowledge for exquisite custom building. Volume, standardization and speed of manufacture are the hallmarks of the factory offerings; and thus they are primitive, rough and inferior when compared to the work of the natives. On the other hand, manufactured snowshoes are available, affordable and replaceable, and some are quite serviceable for the recreational nomad. For these last points we must count our blessings and good luck.

Types of Snowshoes

The would-be snow walker's first two questions regarding snowshoes are likely to be these: What type is suitable? And, what are the best materials? The first question is the easiest to answer.

With all the various models of snowshoes it can be hard to know what is best. And since salespeople are hired to sell rather than educate, you cannot always rely on their advice. Look first to the landscape of the area you are likely to travel in, and if possible, find someone who has traveled there.

Regional variations in traditional snowshoes yield a lot of information regarding their intended use. Evolution of design is not accidental and is usually quite specific. For example, the wide, nearly round Beavertail and

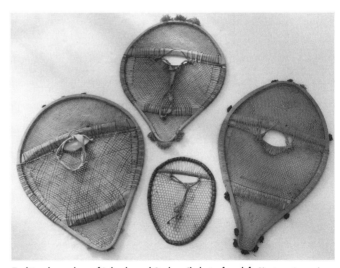

Traditional snowshoes of Labrador and Quebec. Clockwise from left: Montagnais man's shoe, Montagnais woman's shoe, Cree woman's shoe, Naskapi child's shoe (made for a very small child with a bent-willow frame and a simple, coarse weave).

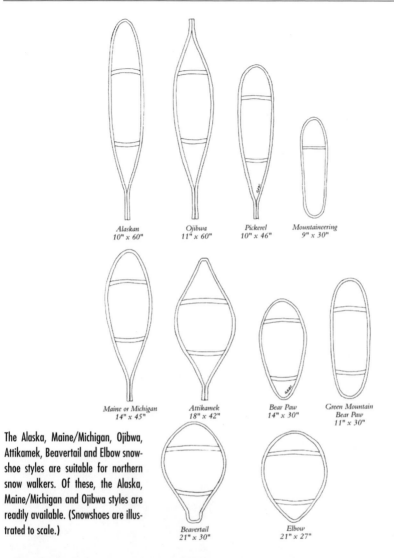

Alaskan
10" x 60"

Ojibwa
11" x 60"

Pickerel
10" x 46"

Mountaineering
9" x 30"

Maine or Michigan
14" x 45"

Attikamek
18" x 42"

Bear Paw
14" x 30"

Green Mountain
Bear Paw
11" x 30"

The Alaska, Maine/Michigan, Ojibwa, Attikamek, Beavertail and Elbow snowshoe styles are suitable for northern snow walkers. Of these, the Alaska, Maine/Michigan and Ojibwa styles are readily available. (Snowshoes are illustrated to scale.)

Beavertail
21" x 30"

Elbow
21" x 27"

Elbow snowshoes of Labrador and Quebec look laughably huge and cumbersome to the uninitiated, but their fine, tight weave is well suited to very deep, fine, frost snow in a land of bitter cold. Farther west, the shoes become longer and pointed at one or both ends, and some have upturned toes. The weave is still fine, and the width may be retained, although the shoes get longer in proportion. Farther west yet, extending to the mountainous wilds of the Yukon and Alaska, the shoes get narrower, very long, with an extreme upturn in the toe. Although river corridors are still the favored routes, the mountainous terrain favors narrowness. People breaking trail ahead of their dog teams found the eight- to ten-inch rise of the upturned toe to be just the thing for breasting deep, new-fallen snow. What was learned from the Athapaskan people who made these shoes now shows up in catalogs as the Alaska snowshoe. In each case, regional preferences serve as an accurate indicator of the best snowshoe for the area.

But what about a shoe for the northern traveler who may show up along the waterways with a toboggan in tow? Is there a snowshoe suited to a wide variety of conditions? Yes, there is. And it is no accident that such a shoe is one of the most popular. Usually called the Maine, or Michigan, snowshoe, it is a true hybrid. It is fairly wide, as commercial shoes go, up to 14 inches, and has a long tail. It may or may not have an upturn of one to several inches in the toe. As offered by the Faber Company of Quebec, it even has (by commercial standards) a fine weave for cold frost snow. At 45 inches long by 13 inches wide, it is not as round as the Labrador shoe nor as long as the Alaska shoe. It handles most conditions moderately well and is the type we use and recommend when specialty shoes are not available.

The challenge is the same everywhere: How can one walk upon a deep, fluffy substrate with a relatively efficient stride? Given the single purpose, the diversity of solutions may seem bewildering. Snow is snow, isn't it?

Snow is snow only to those who engage the least with it. For snow walkers, there are many different kinds of snow. Even as children most of us acknowledged a few varieties. There was "good packin' snow" required for making snowmen, elaborate forts and snowballs. There was "powder," best for skiing; "crust" we could walk atop or sled over with ferocious speed; and "corn," signaling great spring skiing, but also the demise of winter.

Upon growing up, we may have discerned that most of our snow vocabulary had something to do with moisture content and crystal structure, and that these characteristics were related to weather patterns. If, by chance, we grew up to become glaciologists, climatologists, knowledgeable skiers, avalanche experts, hydrologists, nivean naturalists or northern anthropologists, we encountered a staggering body of knowledge about snow. To make a glossary of the terminology alone would require a scribe of unusual dedication.

There is complexity enough in the atmospheric conditions, patterns of deposition, moisture content, temperature gradients, crystal structure and other variables that may affect the snow itself. But that is only part of the picture. Practical matters of interest to someone on the ground will also include the underlying terrain and the history of the season thus far. Moreover, wind, weather, sun and temperature continuously alter conditions; these last factors, especially, are reflected in the diversity of snowshoe types.

Thus, the question becomes a little more elaborate: How can one walk upon a fluffy, deep substrate with a relatively efficient stride, given the terrain, the usual snow structure as it relates to topography and the general atmospheric conditions of the area? For any given region, there may be many solutions to the problem, even before people begin to apply general usage guidelines.

Historically, usage guidelines were basically the same. How could nomadic people best carry on the work of travel and the hunt? In the deep frost snow of the Labrador and Quebec interior, where the land is a maze of lakes, swamps and rapid rivers, the solution was a finely woven shoe that could afford to be flat because it was relatively short. It had extreme width, which required a slight flick outward to pass the other ankle, but that same width would hold a person up no matter how his or her foot was positioned on the shoe. By contrast, in the deep, light snow of Ungava in northern Quebec, a narrow shoe might dive, upending the walker in bottomless powder, whereas round shoes were perfect for brush, open areas, drifts of big lakes and occasional steep, convoluted terrain around river canyons. From the barrens to the thick timber of the deep woods, these shoes handled conditions admirably.

Farther to the west, where snowshoe country is squeezed south by James Bay, the woods get thicker and travel routes more linear. Here, snowshoes begin to get narrower and, to keep a similar amount of flotation potential, longer. The double-ended shoes of the Eastern Cree and Ojibwa appear, as well as the Attikamek's

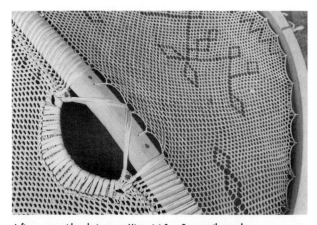

A fine weave with a design on a Mistassini Cree Beavertail snowshoe.

"square-toed" shoes, which taper in the front, but do not come to a point. In the case of some Cree shoes and among the Ojibwa, a curve rises in the toe to keep the elongated, pointed tips from catching under crust, brush and blowdowns.

When one has progressed westward to dog-driving country, snowshoes become lean and long. Running ahead of dogs to pack a float (a trail), or running behind to keep up, favors a shoe that is much more like a ski. Indeed, striding at jogging speed calls for shoes as little as ten inches wide. To maintain flotation for the cold frost snow of the farthest reaches north, the length must become extreme—six-foot shoes are not unheard of. Although travel routes favor river bottoms, there are divides to cross and ranges to traverse in this increasingly mountainous region. Here, for the steepness of a long traverse, the walker needs narrow shoes; width could prove a dangerous handicap.

From such origins come the snowshoes now sold by various companies. The shorter, rounder Bear Paws may reflect the shoes of the eastern forests. The "Ojibwa" model retains slight upturn in the toe and points at both ends. Hybrids such as the Green Mountain Bear Paw arise from the sugarbush and woodlots of

Vermont. It is neither round like a Bear Paw, nor tapered to a split tail in the rear as in the Maine or Attikamek traditions. It is round at both ends, not too wide and not too long—great for hauling sap buckets around in brush or chainsawing next winter's firewood. A slight upturn in the toe resists catching and entanglement.

Another hybrid, the Pickerel or Cross-country snowshoe, is narrow, fairly long and has a split tail and upturned toe. Recommended for beginners and casual snow walkers, these snowshoes are easy to use, cover most bases in a limited way, but do not aspire to excellence. They are good enough to do a little of everything, but will never inspire anyone to try more than a little.

In addition to the hybrids mentioned above, there are specialized snowshoes that solve specific problems. The mountaineering snowshoes popularized by Gene Prater and manufactured by Sherpa are perhaps the best known of this type. Their single function is to give winter mountaineers access to the high country for technical climbing and expeditioning. They are small and usually have a "crampon"-like cleat for handling ice on exposed points. Designed to serve only as access vehicles, these mountaineering shoes are minimalist. Extruded aluminum frames, neoprene filling and plastic clips to attach to the frames are all designed for indestructibility. They come at a high price and, despite their small size, are not lightweight. None are suitable for northern travel, as even the largest are far too small for the frost snow of the northern forests. Although the light, dry snow of alpine areas resembles northern snow in lack of density and fineness of grain, the mountaineer expects to pass the treeline and gain the wind-pack of steep, exposed places where smaller shoe size is a help, not a handicap.

The other highly specialized snowshoe has evolved for racing. Originally, snowshoe racing had something to do with the arts of snowshoeing. Traditional shoes were used because contestants crossed deep snow. They were not allowed to benefit from each other's tracks, and the terrain was chosen so that the track of each contestant would reveal not only stamina, strength and speed, but the finer points of reading terrain, gauging angles of ascent and descent given the conditions, and, of course, the intricacies of natural obstacles such as blowdowns, ledges, open water and anything else that might interrupt progress. In addition to cardiorespiratory prowess, the winners demonstrated considerable skill and knowledge.

In its modern form, however, snowshoe racing has experienced some serious devolution. It now involves sprints of various lengths over snow so packed as to make snowshoes almost irrelevant. In some heats, artificial obstacles are introduced, but the purpose of these seems to be deliberate handicapping and without real significance.

For those who intend to grow into their snowshoes, there are the Maine/Michigan and the Alaska styles. Both have roots in a serious working culture that has not changed much. If wilderness, self-reliance and vast landscapes hold a special grip on you, these are shoes you can fill but will not outgrow.

Materials

In the old days, if you lived north of the Amur River on the Kamchatka Peninsula or along the northern Siberian coast, you would have solid, wooden or framed ski-shaped snowshoes covered with sealskin or the leg skins of reindeer. The fur would point toward the rear for traction and provide a small amount of insulation from the snow below. In North America, there would be the many styles of framed babiche-filled shoes made from a variety of woods and hides. In some areas there would be solid wooden snowshoes made of thin planks in the shape of standard snowshoes, but with no way for snow that falls on top to sift through as in woven babiche-filled shoes.

Today there are many snowshoes available, ranging from the traditional wood-and-babiche to anodized, extruded aluminum frames with neoprene filling. Some are made entirely from molded plastic. Military-issue snowshoes have aluminum frames and a woven wire filling that looks like "hardware cloth." Small-scale producers of snowshoes often fill their frames with braided nylon cord, heavy-test monofilament fishing line, braided plastic line as supplied to the marine and fishing industries and any material thought to resist stretching and water absorption and regarded as adequately durable.

The three most common materials readily available are the wood-and-babiche shoes, wood-and-neoprene laced shoes and aluminum-framed shoes with either neoprene lacing or flat neoprene filling. The latter types are mountaineering shoes and thus not suitable to the North Woods. The other varieties may include one or two models in the form of the Maine/ Michigan, Alaska or Ojibwa styles that will indeed be suitable and fill the needs of the northern traveler.

In general, commercially available snowshoes of either babiche or woven neoprene are not very finely woven when compared with Indian snowshoes. This has to do with keeping manufacturing expense to a minimum and nothing to do with the functional requirements of the finished product. This is why commercially produced snowshoes cost about one-third to one-quarter the cost of a pair of exquisitely handmade shoes. Simple economics inspire most of us to work harder per step on a cheaper pair of loosely woven shoes than to absorb the investment for an exquisite pair. Let us suppose that your knowledge of what you want to do with your snowshoes has inspired you to select the Maine style. A retailer offers that model in babiche or neoprene and the price difference between the two is only $10 and therefore insignificant. In a general way, most salespeople know that babiche may abrade in icy conditions and that the lacing will sag if you have to use the shoes during a thaw in wet snow. Neoprene lacing is more abrasion-resistant, and changes in conditions will not affect its behavior. With babiche, you will have to varnish the lacing and the frames annually and take a little care in storage. Neoprene, by comparison, is low-maintenance, though you may wish to varnish the frames once a year.

So why do traditional babiche-filled shoes still sell in a culture that eschews maintenance and upkeep? It could be that extinction is not far off. Tradition and aesthetics may yet have more appeal than one would assume, but neoprene's low maintenance is clearly attractive.

As an activity becomes more recreational and less of a necessity, one of the peculiarities that occurs is that many of the fine points are lost. When something is no longer engaged in for economy and livelihood and is instead done for fun, it loses the seriousness that demands fine-tuned expertise and economy of means. Thus, people who might snowshoe only several times a year in optimum conditions don't need to know as much as people who will need the equipment for six to eight months as part of their daily lives. The modern marketer needs only to appeal to a generally unknowledgeable public and can thus "teach" them anything in an effort to facilitate sales. In this way, average tastes establish what is offered for sale while the more specialized items tend to become rare and expensive. Snowshoeing is highly subject to this process, and, in the end, traditional babiche-filled snowshoes may slip away. The fussy few will then have no choice but to make their own or pay extravagant prices to increasingly rare craftspeople.

For the serious snow walker, the smaller details that are lost on day-trippers take on larger implications when applied to extended sojourns during which one must live, not merely camp. Wilderness travelers may be recreationists, but once they are a few days beyond easy return to the trailhead, they cross into a world where self-reliance, independence and knowledge rest on attention to detail. This is no place for dabblers and samplers.

It is no coincidence that the most traditional equipment is often the most highly evolved, for its evolution reflects enormous attention to detail. Trips measured in weeks and months quickly reveal the importance of fine points.

In this light, babiche-filled snowshoes stand to gain favor when compared with neoprene offerings. Babiche-filled shoes are often woven in a much finer pattern than neoprene models by the same manufacturer. In frost snow, this gives the same size frame much better flotation while allowing all but the densest thaw snow to sift through the mesh with each step rather than loading the shoe with additional weight. In some cases you may have to seek out a different company to find a finer weave, but at least the option exists. If you plan to travel in the cold snow of the North, it is worth seeking out the finest weave available.

All of the neoprene snowshoes we have seen thus far are composed of wide, coarse strands. Because of this, the weave is inherently bulky and therefore loose. With greater airspace between strands, the shoe sinks deeper in powder than do shoes with a fine weave. Nothing prevents makers of neoprene shoes from using a finer strand and therefore gaining the advantages of a fine, tight weave, but for some reason they do not. It may be related to rubber being heavier than babiche, but if the dimensions were reduced, the additional length of the material in a finely woven shoe would not increase the weight. Of course, the finer the weave, the higher the labor costs, and this is probably the determining factor. The trend toward looser weave as a cost-saving device is certainly evident when you compare new snowshoes with those made by companies that have been in the business a long time. A 50- or 60-year-old pair of snowshoes from the Tubbs Company, for example, is woven five to six times finer than its modern counterparts.

For those of us lucky enough to own Indian-made snowshoes, the gulf between mass-produced varieties and superbly crafted ones is boggling. Most Indian-made shoes are extremely lightweight, the wooden frames being just strong enough for the job. The babiche is cut to strands so fine that many snowshoes are woven with material less than $1/8$ of an inch wide; for some, $1/16$ of an inch would not be considered exceptionally light. Strands such as these easily stretch to full potential before they are woven into the shoe. Consequently, moisture in the snow will not cause even untreated, truly rawhide to stretch or sag. Thus, many native shoes are never varnished yet are remarkably stable despite fluctuating conditions.

All native shoes are, in effect, custom made. Makers factor in the weight, height and stride of the person for whom they are making the shoes. Children are not forced to adapt to outsized equipment but receive new snowshoes of just the right size as they need them.

Evolution has not stopped, either. The snowmobile has had a profound effect on Indian snowshoe traditions. Historically, snowshoes for adults were the same size for both sexes. Movement of the whole band required this. In the age of the snowmobile, women's shoes have become smaller because most of the jobs performed by women take place closer to camp. Snare lines and paths to firewood and water are used repeatedly and become packed. With snowmobiles facilitating long-distance travel, women's shoes can be smaller and therefore lighter, more wieldy and specific to women's tasks.

Men, on the other hand, are still involved with those aspects of the hunt that take place in new, unbroken snow, often over great distances. Even with snowmobiles for mobility, men's snowshoes must still stand up to rigorous conditions.

Once, in Labrador, we helped a Montagnais friend pack a trail through deep, unbroken snow so that he could drive his snowmobile through as soon as we had the float prepared. We followed in his tracks, wearing snowshoes with the finest weave known among commercially available varieties. Yet even in his tracks we sank an additional four to six inches. In new snow, the difference would be even greater and cause a significant difference in energy expended. Needless to say, our envy was extreme. The next time we met, we sported snowshoes made by our friend's uncle and filled with fine caribou babiche by his aunt.

In the end, the decision is equally subjective and emotional. We need tools we can love. We want to please our aesthetic sense as much as our scientific sense. As much as possible, we want all of our equipment to be in keeping with the whole. When it comes to snowshoes, we fall for the natural materials every time.

Size

Beyond choices of materials, there are often options regarding size. Most companies publish charts that correlate size with weight capacity. These charts provide basic guidelines but should never be taken literally. They are invented by salespeople to give the impression that the different models are more specific than they are and that the conditions in which people snowshoe matter little. A far better general rule is this: Flotation has everything to do with tightness or looseness of weave in combination with surface area, and this is in combination with crystal structure, temperature, density and age of the snow underfoot. Persons of differing weights will sink to a lesser or greater degree relative to each other, and nothing is constant with conditions.

For midwinter, cold, dry snow, you will want the largest snowshoe with the tightest weave that you can comfortably control. For transitional seasons, when snow is denser due to thaw and erosion, a smaller, more loosely woven shoe will be fine. If you can have only one pair, select for the part of the winter you will encounter most. If your only purpose is to collect sap buckets in a hilly sugarbush in March, your needs will differ from those of someone who intends to cross Labrador in February. As with choosing a canoe, the more information you have, the more likely you are to achieve a happy match.

FOOTWEAR

As wilderness rambler William Brooks Cabot observed around 1900, "The tale of the winter trail is the tale of one's feet." For thousands of years, native peoples have used a soft, smoke-tanned moccasin for the deep-cold part of the year when the snow is dry (25 degrees Fahrenheit and below). The secret to the warmth

A Naskapi family ready to depart for winter camp in late fall. Beavertail style snowshoes are displayed, as well as waterproof sealskin boots on the adults. (Photo by Paul Provencher in the early 1950s, courtesy of the Naskapi Development Corporation)

of these moccasins is simple. All layers of the footwear are breathable. Since the constant moisture a foot naturally produces passes quickly through "pores" in the moccasins, every layer remains dry. A dry foot is a warm foot. For transitional seasons, these breathable moccasins were replaced with waterproof sealskin boots, called "kamiks," and indeed before the advent of rubber boots, sealskin was used all summer in some cases by people traveling by canoe. Some interior native peoples periodically traveled to coastal regions for materials to make their own waterproof boots or to trade with the Inuit people for them.

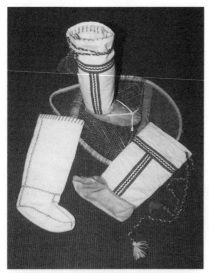

A boot-style moccasin and duffel-cloth liner of the sort favored by the Naskapi and interior Montagnais of Labrador and Quebec.

Historically, both boots and moccasins were lined with dried grass insoles for insulation. Rabbit-skin socks with the fur on were used in winter for additional insulation. With the coming of the fur trade and the introduction of alternative materials, woolen socks were made of blanket material or duffel cloth, and finished knitted woolen socks became an option. With the availability of canvas, winter moccasins underwent a design change. The soft, smoke-tanned leather still covered the foot, but the uppers were made of canvas, or a legging of duffel cloth would wrap the lower shin.

Among native peoples today, sealskin boots are disappearing. They are time-consuming to make and must be softened on a "boot-stick" before each use, as the previous wetting leaves them stiff as boards. With the advent of rubber boots, the sealskin kamiks began to disappear. In wet snow, the Indians now put plastic sheeting or bread bags over their socks, and let their canvas-and-skin moccasins get wet.

An Eastern Cree-style moccasin shown with a felt liner. The snowshoe is an example of the Maine, or Michigan style.

Today you can meet natives on state-of-the-art snowmobiles, but in the interest of warm feet in the heart of winter, they will be wearing traditional moccasins. Such pragmatism points up one of the best-kept secrets in footwear, and proves again that the northern snow walker has everything to gain from tradition.

Meanwhile, back in the world of high-tech footwear, there is literally nothing on the market that is as simple or works as well as the moccasin-and-boot combination. How shoe and boot companies can ignore such basic principles is a mystery. It is even troubling. People like and want warm feet. Why doesn't anyone accommodate that wish?

The military was the last big-scale commercial producer of cold-country moccasins, and since abandoning them some 40-plus years ago, its researchers have come up with a magnificent array of boots and other footwear that do not even come close to the moccasin's elegance, simplicity or effectiveness in continuous use in extreme cold. Contractors have produced only heavy, ungainly systems that work only when the boots can be fully dried each night in a heated building—not exactly the environment on hand for plane-crash survivors or those whose heavy equipment fails in remote areas. There is an impressive array of synthetic fibers and fabrics and boots with airspace between layers of rubber for insulation. But none of the current offerings are breathable, lightweight or offer warmth and dryness over the long haul in conditions where sources of drying heat are not always available.

Anna Trapper of Mistassini, Quebec, making the now-extinct "caribou tooth"-style moccasin, a pattern still being made by a few older women when she was a young girl. (Photo taken in 1980 by Henri Vaillancourt, The Trust for Native American Cultures and Crafts)

The research-and-development branch of a highly respected outdoor company, which counts us as members of an international panel of field experts for testing and opinions, has created a boot featuring "sandwiched" materials that is warm, but fails in all other regards. A pair weighs close to seven pounds, is outsized, cumbersome and does not breathe. Left outside overnight with foot sweat trapped in its marvelous sandwich, it will freeze just as well as military "Mickey Mouse" boots or Sorel boots, or any other type that overlooks the basic principle of breathability. On the other hand, the soles of these boots are not likely to wear out. Composed of heavy rubber with enormous treads, they are so heavy that no one could walk far enough in them to wear them out! For overnight outdoor use, these boots are not only extraordinarily inconvenient, they fail. They are, however, just the ticket for operating heavy equipment, standing around at construction sites or any other work or leisure activity that ends back home where heat will help the interior moisture evaporate overnight.

Any vapor-barrier system traps moisture. This occurs with any material that is truly waterproof, such as rubber, coated nylon and many other laminates. It can also occur in semipermeable materials that are technically "breathable" but in fact breathe too slowly to allow the amount of heat and moisture generated to escape. In both cases, trapped moisture condenses on the inside surface of the vapor barrier, which blocks its passage. If the barrier is outermost, as is the case with most rubber boots, the footwear is very cold—cold because it conducts outside cold to the inside where moisture condenses.

Recognizing this, boot companies have gone to extraordinary lengths to line boots with hydrophobic materials. Water is a remarkably efficient conductor of heat and because of this steals heat from any warm object it contacts. So, rather than elimi-

Two varieties of Steger Mukluks, the only commercially available snowshoeing moccasins on the market.

nate the source of condensation, boot companies have concentrated on inner boots, liners and sock systems that are made of materials that breathe and/or wick water away from the skin. In combination with this, many build an airspace between layers of rubber so that the heat of the foot will warm the inner layer faster than the outer layer can lose heat to the environment. This shifts outright conduction of lost heat to radiation, which is slower, but a loss nonetheless. This is fine for immediate comfort if you are moving around, but what about when you are standing still? What about heat production in an injured foot?

Even if nothing untoward happens and the foot is warm all day, doesn't the condensed water accumulate over the long run, since it can't go anywhere? You bet it does. And when you remove the source of heat at the end of the day, you need a way to dry all those layers out, especially the boot liner farthest from your skin. Socks and inner boots are easy to dry. But most boots have a cloth liner bonded to the rubber of the outer shell. This can't come apart to be dried and is the layer most in need of drying since it was in contact with water, not just damp from high humidity.

Such boots are easily dried overnight in a house with a constant, reliable heat. In a campsite, where heat levels oscillate wildly, wearers have little choice but to sleep with their boots in their sleeping bags just to keep them from freezing; they will not dry. This is exactly what most books recommend, and it should be done with the boots in a stuff sack so your bag stays clean and the moisture your body heat drives out of the boots all night does not chill you. Even if this were not enough inconvenience, sleeping with bulky boots in a small place is anything but enjoyable.

WHERE TO FIND FOOTWEAR & SNOWSHOES

A recurring and frustrating theme in the search for proper winter equipment is the commercial unavailability of the best gear.

One outlet now offers several moccasin models appropriate for the winter trail. Steger Mukluks, a small company run by Patti Steger in Ely, Minnesota, has a fine mail-order catalog. Steger's materials and workmanship are of extraordinary quality (see the address list at the end of this chapter).

Sally Robbins of North Haven, Maine, makes smoke-tanned elk-hide-and-canvas moccasins on commission. Send her a tracing of your foot wearing the socks and felt liner you will wear with the moccasins, and she'll make a pair for you (see Appendix C for moccasin patterns).

Another option is to find native-made moccasins while you are in the North. This should be done in person, not by phone or through the mail. What's more, no matter how accurate your drawing of your foot, the Indian people never believe how huge white people's feet are. Unless they see your foot, it is unlikely that they will deliver the right size.

Also, in the case of the craft co-ops that are beginning to appear across the North, the quality of the offerings greatly varies. Craftspeople have caught on that the tourist trade is not likely actually to use the gear, and some now make moccasins of commercially tanned, not smoke-tanned, leather. Smoke-tanned leather is strong, soft and breathes well. The commercial tanning processes often alter the structure of the leather with chemicals, and often the leather itself is inferior and will not last as long or behave as well. Patti Steger observes that wild leathers such as elk and moose remain supple and rugged, while domestic hides are easily ruined by repeated wetting and drying. Thus, it is best to see your potential purchase, both for sizing and to make sure it is smoke-tanned.

If you make your bindings of soft leather strands, you can get these at any leather or harness shop. A 1/2-inch-wide strip of glove leather three to six feet long will suffice for each binding, depending on which type of Indian hitch you use.

Lampwicking also makes a fine binding material but is available in long rolls only in Canada. Six- or seven-foot strands make a fine binding.

A more durable material than wicking is a tightly woven cotton called "Shaker tape." It is used to fill the woven seats of Shaker style wooden chairs. It stretches very little and wears extremely well (See address list).

Indian-made snowshoes are much harder to come by. With northern native people, there is no transaction without friendship, sensitivity and care. If you exhibit the impatience and demanding nature of white culture, you will be regarded as arrogant and unworthy. On the other hand, sincerity, interest, patience and intercultural diplomacy will go a long way. Without these attributes, you should stay on the format track, plying the native craft co-ops set up for the purpose. Venture further only if invited, or if a person from the village suggests a visit to someone's home.

Unwittingly, in an effort to solve the above-mentioned problems, winter campers embraced vapor-barrier systems more determinedly. The next strategy was to put the vapor barrier in contact with the skin, where the warmth of even a comatose person would keep the barrier above freezing and the insulating layers beyond the vapor barrier would stay dry. A whole generation of people became infatuated with this alternative. They traded a swamp that froze at its outer edges for one that was warm but still a swamp. It is a bad enough system for the feet and hands, but many people applied it to sleeping bags and immersed their entire bodies into soggy, stinking environments that seemed acceptable only because they were better than freezing.

Although vapor-barrier systems "work," they require a lot of fussing, know-how and adjustment if they are to function as best they can. As a short-term solution in extreme situations, the technique may have a place. Otherwise, given the cost in clamminess, marginal comfort at great effort and ferocious body odor, it is hardly a viable methodology.

For some reason, the fact that humans have known how to stay warm and dry in breathable materials for the past ten thousand years or more has not inspired many to ask how and why. And it is not ethnocentric certainty that technology will provide an improvement in the form of some new waterproof material, because native peoples have had waterproof materials for centuries. They chose not to use them in extreme cold. They had reasons not to. In all cold-weather conditions that we are aware of, breathable systems are easier to manage and maintain; have no side effects except good ones; and are safer, cleaner, saner and smarter on all counts. But if existing solutions are forgotten long enough for demand to disappear, then we become easy victims for those determined to sell ineffective solutions. To our knowledge, the last commercial snowshoeing moccasin went extinct in a Moor and Mountain catalog in the mid-1960s. It was not until the mid-1980s, when Steger Mukluks was formed to outfit the Greenland Traverse Expedition and the Trans-Antarctica Expedition with footwear, that anyone made a published claim for breathability as a key to warmth. And for those who will journey on rough sea ice or across the pavement of their local shopping center, Steger Mukluks come with a durable rubber sole that does not extend up the sides of the foot to trap moisture. Long live such a company!

So, starting at skin level, your footwear system for temperatures 25 degrees Fahrenheit and below is this: One or two pairs of wool socks, or a silk or synthetic liner sock if wool irritates your skin (see Chapter 4). Over the sock or socks is either a homemade duffel-cloth bootie, a felt liner such as is used in snowmobile boots or leather/rubber insulated boots. (See Appendix C for duffel-cloth bootie pattern.)

Duffel cloth is essentially felted wool in "blanket" form. It is manufactured in Britain and is available in some northern stores. Duffel cloth is used primarily in mittens, moccasins and anorak liners. Because it is thick and felted and not woven, it is sewn edge-to-edge rather than lapped as in normal sewing, and often a strengthening overstitch with a contrasting yarn embellishes the seams. If duffel cloth is not available, most winter-boot stores carry felt boot liners.

To improve the insulation of the duffel or felt liner, you can insert a felt insole into the bottom, doubling the thickness between the sole of your foot and the snow. Insoles can be bought one size smaller than the felt liners and, if need be, trimmed with scissors to fit. Over these layers the snug but not tight moccasin is worn. (See Appendix C for pattern.)

The sock-felt-moccasin system is entirely breathable, very lightweight and magnificently functional in conditions ranging from 25 degrees Fahrenheit to as cold as temperatures go on earth. At these temperatures, snow is dry, and no matter how hot your feet get through exertion, the layers of insulation block radiation heat, which would otherwise be lost to the snow around the moccasin. Your feet are warm because they are dry.

Not only are your feet dry, but the layers that make up the insulation around them are dry because the entire system breathes. Thus, moisture generated by activity passes through these layers as a gas. The small amount that condenses shows up as light frost on the outside of the felt liners. This can be brushed off with a whisk broom in camp. Because your foot and entire footwear system remain dry, your feet stay warm, even if the level of activity changes. When a morning of snowshoeing and toboggan hauling ends at lunchtime and your feet suddenly go from energetic activity to complete rest, they remain warm and comfortable. Even if the air is well below zero during lunch, you can improve the insulation around your feet by shoving them down deep in the loose snow. A few feet below the powder's surface, the temperature will be nearly 20 degrees Fahrenheit: cold enough to be dry, but considerably warmer than the ambient air temperature.

Not only is the moccasin-and-liner system simple, elegant and foolproof, it is as comfortable and light as can be. The lightest winter boots will weigh in at four or five pounds, while the moccasin system is less than two pounds. You feel as if you are prancing around in bedroom slippers.

When your feet are warm, the rest of your body is warm. The inherent pleasure in this is enough to convince anyone to use moccasins. The real proof of the concept, though, comes from people with circulatory problems. We have had guests who suffer from Raynaud's Syndrome, in which circulation to the extremities is so poor that they turn waxy white and get quite cold. In moccasins, virtually all of these people expected to be cold, yet none were. The only time anyone mentioned cold feet was on extremely cold mornings as we loaded the toboggans. Due to the relative inactivity of this job, one's toes can begin to feel the chill if it is minus 25 to minus 30 degrees Fahrenheit or colder. But since moccasins are so soft, unrestricting and light, a few paces with snowshoes through unbroken snow will soon have one's blood roaring, delivering heat even to the most distant cells, way down in the toes.

Should the temperature rise above 25 degrees Fahrenheit, your body weight will supply enough compression to begin melting the snow, thereby dampening your moccasins. At 32 degrees, the snow is already wet and begins to melt. At this time, winter travelers tend to become gloomy, as thaw makes everything more difficult and time-consuming. Wetness brings inconvenience at best and danger at worst, and managing for comfort and safety becomes more elaborate.

The first course of action under such conditions is to change from moccasins to light rubber boots. Rubbers are not breathable; hence, they are waterproof. They are worn over the same sock-and-liner combination as the moccasins, but they will keep the wet of thaw conditions from reaching insulation and feet. Sweat from your feet, however, is stopped by the layer of rubber, and in some conditions your felt liner can become damp or even wet. Because of this, your feet may feel cold if you stop moving, but at 30 degrees Fahrenheit or above they cannot get dangerously cold and may not even get uncomfortable. In this case, it is preferable to get damp rather than soaked because getting soaked could be dangerous. At night, in camp, it is a simple matter to dry dampened liners and socks.

The rubber boots are single-layer soft rubber with a slight ripple tread on the soles. The best ones of which we are aware are made by the Tingley Company and are often found in hardware and feed stores. They come in overshoe, mid-calf and knee-high lengths, with the mid-calf style being the most useful to a winter travel-er. They are lightweight, can be rolled up small and can be inverted to dry near the tent stove (a wipe of the interior with a bandanna will also dry them). When pur-

chasing a pair, remember to bring the felt liners and insoles you will be wearing with them. As with moccasins, the fit should be snug and wrinkle free, but not tight.

In addition to their use in thaw conditions, rubber boots find daily work once camp is pitched with tent stoves going. Moccasins are hung to dry and any short-term forays out of the tents are made in the rubbers,

Rubber boots with felt liners just inside the door of the tent and ready for use. They are ideal for thaw conditions or sloppy camp chores.

which are easily slipped on and off. This keeps your socks dry when passing back and forth from the hot tents to the ambient cold.

Thus with snowshoeing moccasins and rubber boots, you have covered all condi-tions in a manner that is close to perfect. You have, in fact, mirrored the natives' combination of smoke-tanned moccasins and waterproof sealskin boots.

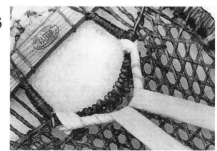

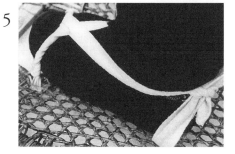

Creating the Indian Hitch binding:

(1) Feed each tail of the binding (lampwicking or Shaker tape) down through the holes in the webbing closest to the edges of your moccasin and the master cord (reinforced load-bearing cord at the rear of the toe hole). Bring the tails back up through the toe hole and flip them back across the toe strap of the binding.

(2) Wind one free tail around the toe strap until you reach the middle of the toe strap.

(3) Place the moccasin under the toe strap so that your big toe can curl over the master cord. Pull on the unwound tail to firmly tighten the toe strap.

(4) Pinch the binding around the master cord and remove your foot carefully, without disturbing the binding. Wind the remaining free tail to the center of the toe strap.

(5) Slip the moccasin back into the toe strap. Tie the tails firmly behind or to the side of your heel. Step in and out as shown on the following pages. Small adjustments can be made by passing the heel loop (still tied) through the toe strap. Add a twist to tighten, back off to loosen. This adjusts the heel-loop tension. To adjust the toe strap, unwind it completely and adjust the tension as before, or unwind one side as in photo 3.

Stepping into the Indian hitch:
(1&2) First slip the loop over your foot and heel.
(3) Back up your heel as far as it will go.
(3&4) Slide your toe under the toe strap. Use the other snowshoe to hold this one in place.

BINDINGS

The inappropriateness of modern boots for snowshoeing appears again when one tries to select proper bindings to fix snowshoes to one's feet. For simplicity, sophistication and total elegance, we need only look to native craftspeople. Their bindings are a single strand of soft leather that works best with a moccasin rather than a boot. Outfit yourself with moccasins for warm feet, and you'll be ready for the best bindings available.

Native bindings provide a simple hinge over the toe of the foot. The toe hole in the native snowshoe is small, so only the toes will fit through with each stride and can likewise aid traction when ascending a steep hill. The hinge is snug, but not tight enough to reduce circulation. Because the moccasin and underlying layers of insulation are soft, the binding depresses the material around the foot so there is no slippage during any part of the stride. If conditions require the use of rubber boots in place of moccasins, you might experience minimal slippage, but not enough to be a nuisance.

The real genius of the Indian hitch is that once it is adjusted to your foot you needn't touch it all season. It is a step-in/step-out binding, so you never have to fiddle with adjustments or bare your hands in the cold. At most, you might have to reach down to align the bindings to step into them. You simply point your toe into the loop that passes behind your heel, back your foot up as far as that loop will stretch and put your toes under the toe strap. To exit, twist your foot so the toe comes out from under the toe strap and then rotate your heel to back it out of the heel loop. Once you get the knack of it, you never have to bend over, bare your hands or even pay attention.

Although this may appear to be a small convenience, seeing it in action will convince you otherwise. It's amazing to watch Indians working around their snowmobiles while getting wood or during a hunt. One minute they are on a machine, the next their snowshoes are thrown down and they are in them instantly. Perhaps they fell a tree with a chainsaw, drag it to the sled and cut it to firewood length. With a twist of the foot they are out of their snowshoes and loading the *komatik* (a sled hauled behind a snowmobile) with the wood on the hard snowmobile float. A few seconds later, they are back in their shoes and off in the deep snow after another tree.

In the cold, efficiency is everything. When working up wood or attending to the kill during a hunt, Indians are in and out of their snowshoes dozens of times, and they need never put their chainsaw, rifle or skinning knife down or even look at their feet to accomplish this.

Such a binding becomes more than a convenience should you fall in deep powder and need to get out of one or both shoes in order to swim them back underneath you so you can stand up. A simple twist, and you are out. The same fall with your feet locked into commercial bindings by buckles is no fun at all. Reaching a bare,

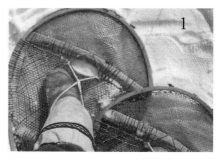

Stepping out of the Indian Hitch:
(1) Back up your heel and twist your toes out from under the toe strap.
(2) Shift your foot pressure forward and to the side so your heel is free of the loop.
(3) Back your heel out of the binding altogether.

hot hand into cold powder to remove buckles by feel is anything but pleasant and could be dangerous. Should some major mishap land you in flowing open water where it is imperative that you get free of your snowshoes, you would have a chance with Indian bindings and next to none with buckles.

Most snowshoes have special holes woven into the mesh to accommodate binding strands, and these holes are almost sure to be too widely spaced for a proper fit. Best to ignore them, and make sure you pass the strands through the mesh at the exact width of your moccasin.

Creating the Alternate Indian Hitch binding:
(1) Lace the lampwick around your master cord.
(2) Snug the toe strap over the toe of your moccasins.
(3) Pass the tails of lampwick behind your heel.
(4) Bring the tails to the front and tie off in a bow.

MOBILITY

Once you have gotten a pair of snow-shoes and rigged them for the trail, a few comments on technique may be help-ful. Basically, if you can walk, you can snowshoe. This is not to say, however, that if you can walk, you know all there is to know about walking on snowshoes. Finesse comes with practice. Once you've become familiar with the weight, feel, balance and gait of snowshoeing, you will find it handy to learn how to turn around without walk-ing in a large circle; back up without catch-ing the tails in deep snow; and gracefully extricate yourself from the falls, tangles and spills into which you will blunder. And once you leave flat, relatively easy going, you will want to learn how to control the descents, ascents or more extreme terrain with safety and élan.

Except with the widest of snowshoes, which require a slight flick outward from the ankle to clear the ankle of your other leg, your stride should be no different than your normal gait. For some reason, begin-ners often think they must spread their normal walk into something wider to walk with snowshoes. This misconception lasts for about 15 paces, after which the liga-ments, muscles and joints of your body begin screaming with pain. The pain tells you not to walk in a manner inconsistent with normal human biomechanics; doing so is a waste of energy.

The sidecut, taper and length of snow-shoes are based on a normal stride. You need lift your foot only enough for the striding shoe to clear the frame of the other, or the loose snow if you have sunk deeply. Never lift your foot higher than you have to. If you will be walking all day, the extra lifting will add up, and you will be unnecessarily tired. It is for this reason

22

that when breaking trail in new deep snow, you shift lead frequently or take frequent rests if you are alone. The trick here is to shift or rest before you get tired, not when you are tired. Prevention is more efficient and benign than recovery.

Many books and articles have pictures of people snowshoeing with ski poles or a single pole. Do not allow yourself to be seduced by this concept. Unless you have a disability that might require poles, avoid them. If you are 78, have titanium hips and knees, arthritis and are stiffer than you were at 20 or 45 or 58, then by all means use poles. But for anyone else, ski poles are only a handicap.

Avoid the handicap of ski poles so you can develop your balance and skill enough to leave the flats, haul water or firewood or engage in any other activity requiring free hands.

Better to learn balance, stride and the use of centrifugal force and gravity to your advantage. If it takes you a week of falling to get there, so much the better, because then you will also know how to get up with grace, economy and speed. When you eventually fall in six feet of cold powder with virtually no horizons in it for support, you won't die or even be inconvenienced. In the end, you want to achieve the necessary grace to cross all terrain easily with energy to spare. Most strategies for ascent and descent and finding the best angles come better through experimentation than instruction. We mention here only two

Proper steep descent involves a controlled slide, keeping your weight on the heel of one snowshoe while cocking the other shoe forward to absorb the impact of irregularities that might other wise pitch you forward into an uncontrolled roll. Keep your hands spread wide for stability and to add friction to slow the speed of the slide.

tricks, which you would probably eventually discover on your own.

To back up on snowshoes, you need to raise the trailing edge or the split tail high enough so that a reverse step will not cause it to dig into the snow and trip you. A quick downward flick of the toe should surprise the snowshoe into rising in the rear. Before it returns via gravity, make your reverse stride.

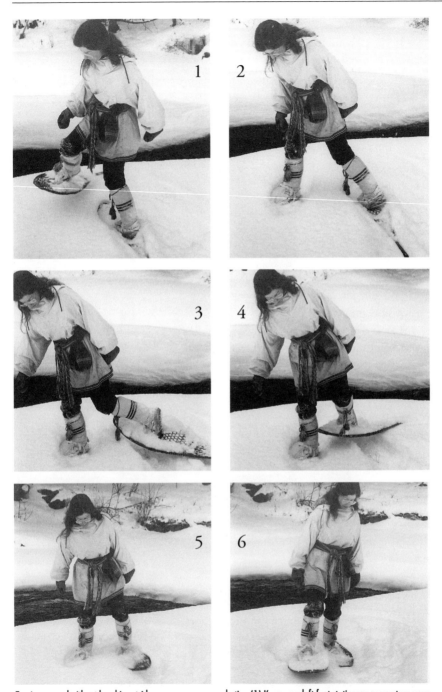

Turning around without breaking stride or unnecessary acrobatics: (1) Keep your left foot stationary as you turn your torso and arc your right foot around without undue lifting or disruption of stride. (2) Place your right foot and transfer your weight to it as you release your left foot. (3) Let your unweighted left foot spin in place and then (4 & 5) continue to turn until it is aligned with the new direction and placed for weight transfer. (6) Left foot fully weighted, and right foot part way through normal stride.

If you can safely descend an extreme pitch (straight downhill, as you would roll if you were a ball) without triggering an avalanche, you can adopt a stance that will allow you to encounter irregularities in the slope or obstacles buried in the powder. By leaning on the heel of one shoe and extending your other leg forward as a buffer and shock absorber, you can slide down incredibly steep faces that might otherwise require circumnavigation. The cautionary points are watching for avalanches and selecting outruns that won't launch you over a cliff or ledge or cause you to collide with trees or rocks at terminal velocity. Just because snowshoes are wide and, in most cases, provide significant friction, does not mean your descent of steep, powdery terrain will be slow. If a group is descending, each person should use untracked snow, as this will keep the speed down. Using someone else's chute doubles or triples your speed. It is best to treat steep descents much as canoeists treat rapids. Evaluate the risks and use sound judgment. A mistake that results in damaged equipment or injury will introduce inconvenience more costly than the energy spent in circumnavigation.

To turn around on snowshoes, all you need do, even with a six-foot pair of Alaska-style snowshoes, is step across the toe of the other shoe, rotate your hips, trunk and shoulders to face the new direction as you weight that shoe, and then rotate the other at ground level the 180 degrees necessary to match the new alignment. This type of turn is fluid, graceful and economical, and can be done without breaking stride. There is no need to lift your foot way up in the air in front of you, attempting snappy off-balance arc maneuvers, as you might with a kick-turn.

Once you develop expertise, you are ready for the trail and the exhilaration of outings that grow from day trips, to weekends, to weeks or months on the trail.

CONCLUSION

As in so many areas, true simplicity is often the result of complicated thought. Such is the case in selecting the best footwear for the winter trail.

For snowshoes, get the finest weave available in a Maine/Michigan or Alaska style. Keep your feet warm in a pair of moccasins, and bind them to the snowshoes with soft leather, Shaker tape or lampwick. And when a thaw threatens dry socks and moccasins, don a pair of rubber overshoes to preserve comfort and joy.

USEFUL ADDRESSES

Moccasins & Mukluks
Steger Mukluks
100 33 East Sheridan Street
Ely, MN 55731
800-685-5857 (800-MUKLUKS)
www.mukluks.com

Moccasins and More
Craig MacDonald
RR 1
Dwight, Ontario
Canada P0A 1H0
705-635-3416 (evenings)

Moccasins and duffel cloth
Labrador Handicrafts, Ltd.
P.O. Box 610
Happy Valley, Labrador
Canada, A0P 1E0
709-896-8500

Moccasins, Anoraks & Wind Pants
Sally Robbins
866 Middle Road
North Haven, ME 04853
207-867-2227

Bark-tanned Sealskin Boots & Mitts
Borealis Crafts
Route 430, P.O. Box 100
Shoal Cove East, Newfoundland
Canada, A0K 5C0
709-456-2123

Smoke-tanned Elk Hide
Eidnes Furs
83363 Highway 3 South
St. Maries, ID 83861
208-245-4753 (Orders: 888-233-4366)
www.eidnesfurs.com

Snowshoes
Faber and Company
180 Rue de la Riviere
Loretteville, Quebec
Canada G2B 3W6
418-842-8476 (866-842-8476)
www.fabersnowshoes.com

SnoTREK
Lebanon, Maine
bentley@Prexar.com
207-324-6367

Snowshoes & Traditional Kits
Wilcox & Williams from Country Ways
6001 Lyndale Avenue South, Suite A
Minneapolis, MN 55419
800-216-0710 (612-861-2262)
www.snowshoe.com

Snowshoe Bindings
(Lampwick: 1-inch x 6-feet)
Craig MacDonald
RR 1
Dwight, Ontario
Canada P0A 1H0
705-635-3416 (evenings)

Snowshoe Bindings
(Shaker Tape: $5/8$-inch x 6-feet)
Royalwood Ltd.
517 Woodville Road
Mansfield, OH 44907
800-526-1630
www.royalwoodltd.com

Chapter 2
Hand-hauling Toboggans

TOBOGGANS

Toboggan traditions appear in the interior northern forests. This is a land of deep snow and intense cold, where even in the best of times, life was never easy. Caribou and fish might come in magnificent numbers or disappear as if they had vanished from the earth. Small bands of hunters and their families were spread over huge tracts of land, and luck and skill were courted and maintained with a strict spiritual attitude coupled with, and inseparable from, highly evolved pragmatism. Reflections of these attributes appear in the weave patterns of the natives' snowshoes, the embroidery on their clothing and equipment, and the carved and painted designs on their toboggans.

The toboggan, or flat sled as it was sometimes called, is the most primitive and basic of sled types. Yet it is ideally suited to its habitat and, for the recreational snow walker, can be a tool of consummate function.

Handmade by the users themselves, toboggans naturally varied in their specific dimensions, but the basic shape and concept remained similar for all. Generally, a ten-foot toboggan would be made from two strakes of birch or larch in the north-

ern reaches of timbered country or from maple or ash farther south. These strakes would be very thin, perhaps a quarter of an inch or slightly more, and held together by crossbars. Overall, the toboggan would be double-tapered rather than straight-sided. At the front, it might be 12 inches wide and flare to 14 inches at the shoulders, a third of the way back from the front. From this point, it would taper evenly to a 12- or 10-inch width at the tail.

Such a toboggan is very flexible, the taper reducing friction and perhaps facilitating turns. Flexibility keeps the toboggan in full contact with the ground, even in very

Each of the toboggans in our fleet is different. Lengths, widths, curves and the number and spacing of crossbars vary. Each of the toboggans on the floor is made of a single piece of high-density plastic.

irregular terrain, and because of this reduces the tendency for such a narrow sled to tip over. The narrowness allows the toboggan to follow easily in the trail, called a float, packed by the snowshoer hauling it as he or she walks.

Thus, when movement is possible in the winter forests, toboggans and snowshoes provide the easiest passage over the widest range of conditions. The toboggan is at home anywhere in the North where the terrain is composed of lake-and-river systems. It will not facilitate passage in hilly or mountainous country, but if the land-scape will allow 90 percent or more of your travel to be on frozen waterways and ten percent or less overland, then conditions are ideal.

Our first trips were made in order to test and practice what our research had revealed, and to learn more. We embarked on a 400-mile loop along several of Maine's most hallowed waterways. We split the distance and took to the ice over two consecutive winters. During the first winter, we departed from Greenville at the foot of Moosehead Lake and finished in Allagash Village after traversing the length of Moosehead, ascending the North Branch of the Penobscot River, and descending the St. John River. The following year, we started in Allagash Village and returned to Greenville by ascending the Allagash, traversing the large lakes in its headwaters, and eventually entering the West Branch of the Penobscot River, which we ascended to Northeast Carry and Moosehead Lake. In the entire 400 miles, we were overland for only 14. Of these, seven miles were height-of-land crossings, and another seven were circumnavigation of open water in rapids, at falls or where there were river-wide open leads (open running water in the ice).

Even with such a high percentage of travel on the waterway (and on a Canadian trip the percentage of land crossing can often be reduced even further), there will be times when hills, canyons and steep rapids punctuate the otherwise gentle relief. Here you will encounter hard, slow going where gain will be reckoned in inches, feet, hours, maybe even days. However, in the big picture of the trip, such hardships are brief and generally interesting. Usually you will be traveling on a winding, wind-packed frozen waterway, each bend beckoning you on to a new wintry vista.

Acquiring a Toboggan

For thousand of years, the frozen North American waterways were winter high-ways for all people. It has only been since the "motored toboggans" (snowmobiles) that these simple but highly refined sleds nearly disappeared from use. The Chestnut Canoe Company used to commercially manufacture hauling toboggans for the Hudson's Bay Company mail carriers. Most trappers and families living on the land made their own. Today, happily, demand for toboggans is back due to an increasing interest in non-motorized winter recreation and traveling in the refined style of the earlier woods people.

One can still make a toboggan with an axe and crooked knife and lash it togeth-er with countersunk babiche. But it is more likely that you'll enlist a lumberyard, a power planer and other woodworking aids, and that you'll screw it rather than lash it together.

You may have to make a steambox as well as a form to create the curve at the front of the toboggan. Purchased hardwood lumber, if you can find it in the necessary lengths, is likely to be quite dry; therefore, steaming will require a real steambox and a good, solid form with lots of purchase points for clamps to bring the wood around the radius of the curve (for details, see "Features & Fine Points of Toboggan Construction" later in this chapter).

Retrofitting

There are alternatives. The easiest is to find a toboggan meant for sliding down hills. A few companies still make these, usually out of good, clear hickory. They often show up in specialty catalogs as well as in the storefronts of northern hardware and sporting stores. The longest of these toboggans are a little short of the ideal length for the trail, but six- and eight-foot sleds exist. The easiest thing is to use them as they come. This means you will have a toboggan that is straight-sided and probably four to six inches wider than ideal, but it is available for under $100 and will work.

Those who are a bit more fussy may want to shave some weight off a ready-made toboggan and give it the "coffin" shape of a traditional trail toboggan. To do this, all the crosspieces must be removed and one or two strakes deleted from the toboggan (most are composed of six to ten, two- or three-inch-wide strakes). The two outermost strakes on each side will then have to be planed to the coffin shape along the edges.

Now the crossbars are too long, and each will have to be recut to length before being screwed on. The shrewd timesaver will cut from one end only, leaving the original ends on one side already shaped with a notch for the running lines to pass under. The ends that have been cut to the new width will all need to have a notch cut into their undersides for the running line on that side of the toboggan to pass through. You may or may not need to drill additional screw holes, as the strakes will now fall in differing locations and the original screw holes may no longer be suitable.

Plastic Toboggans

Another alternative involves high-density industrial plastic, which may be purchased in four-by-eight-foot sheets, and longer. This is the stuff that dogsledders and people who have adapted komatiks to towing by snowmobiles shoe their sleds with.

The longer lengths of this plastic can provide for an eight- or ten-foot toboggan, even after the curve has used up a foot and a half of material. The plastic strip can be bandsawed to shape or sawed with straight edges on a table saw and then edge-planed to the coffin shape.

Although you'll still need crosspieces to hold the running lines in place, you can make the whole toboggan of one piece rather than two strakes. If the material resists taking the bend long enough for the running lines to make it hold its proper shape, the curved part can be heated with a propane torch and bent into a tighter curl. Do not, however, let the torch carry too long in any one spot; keep it moving, so nothing melts or burns. It's also possible just to opt for a fair curve by cold-bending the material and holding it in place with the running lines.

Two advantages come to users of the plastic toboggans. The high-density synthetic is very slippery, and they can be pulled more easily than wooden toboggans. In all but the coldest of frost snow, such sleds slip with ease. Secondly, plastic toboggans can be rolled into a roughly three-foot-diameter circle for transportation inside confined spaces, such as small cars that lack roof racks and for trips in areas where you must fly in and out by ski plane. This is a real advantage, given the space limitations on smaller planes. As a comparative case in point, a ten-foot wooden toboggan fits in a Cessna 185 only after you remove the passenger seat and the door. The door is, of course, put back on, but you must sit on the luggage while only the pilot has the luxury of a seat.

Most plastic toboggans tend to sag into every hollow rather than bridging them as do wooden ones. They track poorly and in general behave more independently than their wooden cousins. If you don't need the roll up

A high-density plastic toboggan can be rolled up for transport in a small space such as a car without roof racks or a small plane.

feature, you can greatly improve the performance of a plastic toboggan by stiffening it with two one-inch by one-inch wooden rails. These hardwood pieces should go topside, parallel and close to the edges of the toboggan, cross and screw into each crosspiece and stop about 16 inches from the end of the sled.

Wood & Plastic Toboggans

Some trail toboggans combine wood and plastic. A standard wooden toboggan may be outfitted with high-density plastic strips running the length of the bottom. Two strips an inch or less wide screwed the full length of the bottom will increase the slip in wind-pack and other hard snow conditions by their innate slipperiness as well as by reducing the bearing area and therefore friction. In deep snow the hybrid will behave as an all-wood toboggan, but under certain conditions it will afford extra ease and joy in hauling. Also, the two strips prevent the toboggan from sideslipping on gentle side-slopes.

Skin Toboggans

In some regions, other means of towing gear overlap with toboggans. The most primitive are the skin toboggans that appear in the Canadian North. Along the coasts, these were traditionally a single large seal skin that was towed headfirst so the hair pointed backward. The edges of the skin were perforated, or the original hide-stretching holes were used to lash the load into the skin with a line that pulled the edges snug. The seal's torpedo shape allowed relatively efficient towing. A person or occasionally a single dog would take such a load.

Inland, skin sleds were made of the leg skins of caribou or moose sewn together. These short-haired sections of the lowest portion of the legs provided a tough skin that would not wear out quickly and used a part of the animal that was not used in ordinary hide preparation. These sleds could be made to any dimension, although most were made small for women, children or a single dog to tow, and the hair was arranged to point toward the rear. Typically, such sleds did not last long and were not a regular part of anyone's nomadic equipment. However, they provided emergency or supplementary transportation when a family was on the move and all the wooden toboggans were already overloaded.

Runnered Sleds

In the southern reaches of toboggan country, and very much related to the presence of white people, a relatively short and narrow-runnered sled evolved. Southern Ontario and Maine have a long tradition of this, and in Maine these "Moose" or "Start" sleds actually eclipsed toboggans. Two factors made these sleds more practical than toboggans.

First, for the most part, the white people who introduced them were sedentary and worked traplines or woodlots where continuous use provided packed trails that needed reopening only after major snowfalls. Second, these sleds evolved in regions where types of snow and general weather conditions varied widely through the winter. While more northern forests might have six or seven feet of undifferentiated, bottomless fine powder, the more southerly reaches of sled country probably hosted less than three feet at any one time. Within this depth there would likely be many strata reflecting thaws or the differing snow densities of each deposition. These conditions allowed for sleds that did not need the extreme float provided by a toboggan. With use generally occurring on packed trails, runners would supply enough float while reducing friction and allowing people to haul much heavier loads than they could on a toboggan.

Because of this, a tradition of eight- to ten-foot runnered sleds developed, and these were up to 18 inches wide. Wood, cargo, game animals, supplies, canoes and anything else that had to be moved through the woods was adapted to this sled. Nevertheless, trappers and nomadic people such as surveyors and timber cruisers retained the toboggan as it was still the most versatile and accommodating cargo carrier under the widest range of conditions.

Craig MacDonald of Ontario is undoubtedly the most knowledgeable practitioner and student of sled and toboggan use, and on many of his trips he accommodates both traditions. Often his groups travel with two or three toboggans placed first in line. As the loaded toboggans slide, they prepare the road for the runnered sled or two that bring up the rear. In this manner, Craig overcomes the aspects of deep, unbroken snow that would otherwise keep runnered sleds hopelessly bogged down.

At the same time, when the party is large enough to make the combination work, such sleds can carry double the weight of a toboggan, making the movement of gear more efficient and delightful.

Craig and his parties have had great success with this combination technique, not only in the denser snows of mid- and southern Ontario, but also in the northern parts of Ungava in Quebec, as well as on the western side of Hudson Bay.

Not everyone has the interest, time or skills necessary to make their own toboggans or, like Craig MacDonald, to revive the Moose sled by making their own and shoeing the runners with high-density plastic. Fortunately, there is a commercially available alternative that has grown out of both these traditions.

Years ago, the U.S. Army contracted with a supplier to make a tub-shaped, fiberglass sled with three shallow, narrow runners on its bottom. Reflecting its Scandinavian roots, it was called the Ahkio sled and was designed to be hauled by a person as well as a dog, pony or snow machine. Drawing from the toboggan tradition, it is high in surface area to float in deep snow. Drawing on the sled traditions, it has runners for wind-pack or tracks packed by people or machine. The sleds were just long enough to sleep in and had an attached canvas box that could be wrapped over the load.

Almost all of the surplus Ahkio sleds have long since been bought up for use as rescue sleds at alpine

An army-surplus Ahkio sled is perfect for hauling firewood or groceries. Some companies are making modern versions of these sleds.

ski areas. However, the past few years have seen a few companies build similar sleds to meet the demands not only of the rescue and mountaineering market, but also of a growing number of recreational snow travelers (see addresses at end of chapter).

Features & Fine Points of Toboggan Construction

Should you build a toboggan of your own, you will invariably face choices. What shape and height should the curve in the front have? Are the crosspieces screwed from the bottom or the top? Are the running lines simply to hold the gear-lashing lines, or do they also help hold the shape of the curve? How many crossbars are required? What is their spacing, and how thick should they be?

There are several tricks of the trade; the rest is really up to you, your sense of aesthetics, and your ability to make things work when things are going slightly differently than you planned or hoped.

The wood-bending process is perhaps the most unfamiliar and daunting. If you are making a toboggan in the field while waiting for winter, you will be using green wood. In this case, you can do the bending with boiling water rather than a full-fledged boatyard steambox. If you are at home in a shop, you will probably have dry or partly dry wood, in which case you will need a steambox. You can consult

boatbuilding manuals that have good sections on steam-bending wood. You can also make the bending easier by planing the section of the planks that will take the curve to a thinner dimension, as this is not a place that will get worn down over time. Another trick is to have three planks prepared, so that if one breaks, you won't have to make a toboggan that is too short. Use pressure and firmness, but don't force the wood beyond where it wants to go.

The curves can be any shape you want. The traditional shape achieved by most native makers, who worked with green wood and did not use forms, is hard to duplicate. It is far easier simply to accept a fair curve that is essentially part of an arc. If you can coax the wood to double back on itself, then you can tie it off to a crosspiece placed directly under the tip of the curve in the vicinity of where the planks go from flat to upswept. A line or short length of chain here will keep the curve from straightening over time.

Wooden toboggans are a thing of beauty. Their graceful curves are not only aesthetically pleasing but functional as well.

The "running" or "ground" lines are lines that run along each side of the top surface of the toboggan and pass under each of the crosspieces. On a sliding toboggan, riders hold onto these lines. On a freight toboggan, the lash lines pass under the running lines to secure the load. If the running lines are also the lines that will pass from the final crosspiece directly beneath the tip of the recurved planks, then they can be responsible for holding the shape of the curve. The advantage of such an arrangement is not simply in the minimizing of lines used; it also causes the recurved section of the planks to act as a flex-absorbing spring.

34

Remember that such a toboggan is flexible and hugs the ground like a flowing snake or a shadow. In irregular terrain or ice hummocks, the toboggan flexes and bends continuously, and this action can loosen the lash lines. If the running lines are also the lines that hold the curve, then the entire unit flexes and absorbs some of the unequal and highly mobile stresses that flow through the lash lines and therefore the running lines.

Running lines that are separate transfer the working of the load in a reduced way, and because of this a day in rough conditions may require periodic stopping to tighten the loads as they flex, shift and work loose.

Crossbars on a wooden toboggan perform several functions beyond keeping the running lines in place. They also hold the planks or strakes together. Typically, a heavier or wider crosspiece will be in place at the tail of the toboggan and also at the head of the curve, where the piece is often called a headboard and may be shaped or decorated. In many cases there is another crosspiece placed low in the curve, where the planks rise from the level. This one may not carry any running lines and may not be there to hold the curve in shape. Its main purpose is to provide an attachment point for either the towing lines or towing poles, depending on your choice. The crosspiece's position low in the rise or the curve provides the towline with just a little lift in addition to supplying a straight-away pull-point.

The spaces for the running lines to pass through each crossbar can be created by clamping two bars back-to-back in a vise and drilling straight down between them; the result is half of a cylindrical hole in each bar. The final step is to bevel the front and rear edges of the hole to prevent sharp corners from abrading the running lines.

With the exception of the specialized crossbars in the curve and at the tip and tail, the spacing will probably fall within the 16- to 24-inch range.

The crossbars must be strong enough so that high-tension lashing of loads will not cause them to snap or pull screws out of the planks. Our first generation of toboggans had crossbars screwed into the planks from above. We feared that if we screwed in from below the metal heads might frost up and cause drag on the bottom. They do not, and this arrangement is far stronger. It is not overdoing things to screw the crossbars on from both top and bottom. Craig MacDonald found that among some native groups the last three crossbars of a toboggan were increasingly V-shaped toward the rear. This gave the last few feet of the toboggan a slight keel and seemed to reduce friction and aid tracking in some conditions.

One final point regarding the crossbars is to bevel and smooth the edges of the notches that provide space for the running lines. At rest, the lines run parallel to the ground, but with a tight lash in place, they will be kinked upward. A sharp edge on a crossbar will abrade and eventually break the lines as flex and torsion slide them back and forth through the tunnels.

LOADING AND PACKING

Just as trimming; a canoe is important in maximizing the blend of function and hull shape, so too is loading a toboggan. Generally, after the toboggan tarp is laid out on the toboggan, attempt to put the heaviest items in the section just behind center on the toboggan, packing lighter on the front and the very tail. The toboggan undergoes tremendous torsion, flexing, twisting and straightening in the course of a day, and a well-packed one will behave best. A toboggan that is not well packed will flip over more frequently, turn poorly and transfer its ills to the body and psyche of the person pulling it. It will, in fact, become a vengeful, seemingly animate entity bent on destroying you.

Loading the toboggan gives rise to numerous options and strategies. The simplest method is to pack gear in duffels and narrow boxes. Each item is its own container and is simply lashed aboard. The only rule regarding the lash lines is that each item has to have two contact points per side. Because of this, the lines cross over each parcel in the form of an X. This prevents anything from twisting in place, getting stuck in brush or snow or falling off.

Lash the entire ground load or first layer of gear completely. The second layer may be affixed with bungee cords or short lengths of line. Remember, though, that if anything must be stacked, it should be only light parcels such as sleeping bags, daypacks or sleeping pads. Stacking a load raises the center of gravity and, if much weight is involved, can make the toboggan tippy. Bows and half-bows are best for all lashings as these can be released with merely a pull. In the cold, you will have little patience for knots you have to undo with bare hands. Make the person who tied them undo them, and they will quickly learn to use bows or other pull-release hitches.

Pull-release knots secure the load to the running lines.

Generally, we use duffel bags of light canvas for personal gear and clothes; sturdy, narrow cardboard boxes for food (as food is consumed, the boxes are burned); and a variety of stuff sacks for such things as tents, wind protection and parkas. Each person also has a daypack lashed on top of the load for easy

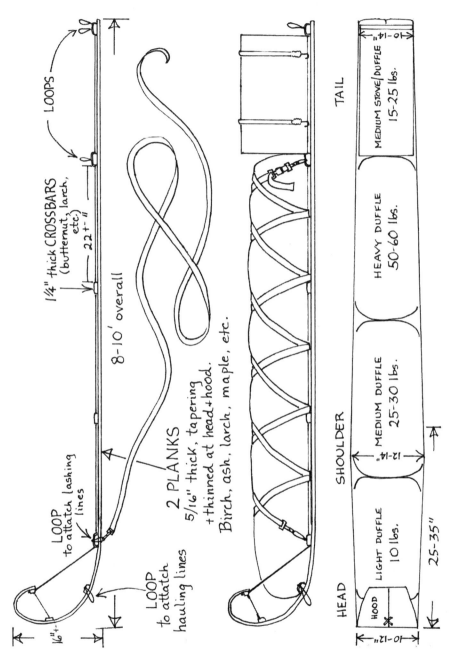

LOOPS

1¼" thick CROSSBARS (butternut, larch, etc.)

22+"

8-10' overall

LOOP to attach lashing lines

2 PLANKS
5/16" thick, tapering + thinned at head + hood.
Birch, ash, larch, maple, etc.

LOOP to attach hauling lines

16"+

TAIL

SHOULDER

HEAD

HOOD

MEDIUM STOVE/DUFFLE
15-25 lbs.

10-14"

HEAVY DUFFLE
50-60 lbs.

MEDIUM DUFFLE
25-30 lbs.

LIGHT DUFFLE
10 lbs.

12-14"

25-35"

10-12"

Hand-hauling Toboggan Parts & Packing Tips

access. Group gear is in a well-marked duffel and contains the first-aid kit, repair kit and other communal gear. It is lashed on in an accessible position, even though it is heavy and must always be part of the ground load. The sheet-metal stoves ride in the open, although some people make a canvas bag for them.

Recently, we have experimented with tanks and tarps. A tank is essentially a canvas box that is custom fitted to the toboggan and is tied on permanently. It is the

right width, has flaps at each end to tuck in under the side flaps and the side flaps are full length and lapped one over the other before you lash the load. Tanks keep snow off the load, keep anything from falling off after working loose and generally keep a load manageably snug and firm. In addition, a stacked load is easier because there is no need to lash the ground load separately. Only items stacked on top of the tank or tarp require separate bungee cords or lashing.

The toboggan in the foreground shows a canvas "tank" folded back from the load, while the other displays stacked duffels. The photo is taken en route during a 57-day traverse of Ungava, and each toboggan is double-stacked full length. Typically the load would be only one layer deep with only a few items stacked.

A tarp is another method of accomplishing the-same thing but is more versatile. Tarps may be sewn of the same marine-grade canvas that a tank would be made from, but they are not as specific and need not be custom made. Essentially, tarps are long, narrow sheets that can be spread over the toboggan before loading and then folded up over the load and tucked in neatly at the ends and along the overlap. One can cover the whole load or part of it, depending on need. Typically, the stoves, which are steel and have corners, are left in the open, where they won't abrade anything. Likewise, the box that contains lunch stays in the open and is easily accessible along with the aforementioned group duffel. It is a simple matter to fold the tarp over a partial load and then load the remainder in the open, preserving easy access. When making camp, the same 6-by-12-foot tarp can double as a groundsheet for one of the tents or cover the food boxes just outside the cook tent in case it snows overnight.

The last things to be loaded are those items for which you need easy access while underway. As in tarpless arrangements, each person has a daypack bungeed or tied to the top of the load, a stuff sack containing wind gear (if he or she is not already wearing it) and a parka to be donned during lunch break. Axes, shovels, ice chisels and firearms, if present, also ride under the crosshatching of lash lines for easy access.

HAULING METHODS

Toboggans are hauled using either soft lines or two poles affixed to the front of the toboggan. The poles run forward about seven feet and have a leather strap from one to the other about a foot from the ends. After years of traveling with both formats, we have seen no clear advantage of using one over the other.

Soft lines are versatile, can be coiled out of the way and don't take up much space. When a hauler winds his or her arms through them, they can take up the small shocks and swaying and rolling of walking, and they soften the pitching of the toboggan on drift-covered lakes. They are easy for beginners to master and can be adjusted readily for length. If overtaken by a toboggan on a downgrade, the snowshoer can step out of the way and control the toboggan as with a brake line.

Poles are a fixed length and a bit harder to learn to handle effectively, but they allow you to back up it you wander into overflow or bad ice, and can slow a toboggan on a mild downgrade by applying reverse pressure. Shocks are absorbed through the poles either by resting your forearms along the part that extends beyond the strap or by resting your hands over the ends. You can even wind your arms through the poles behind you so you can really lean into your pull, but this is accomplished by bending the wrists, whereas in a soft-line system the lines bend around your forearms. For some people, the position is not comfortable enough for long periods. Poles do take up some space, but they can be folded back over the load and even used as brake lines from the side or rear.

A separate short push pole can also be used in moving toboggans. This is used at the rear of the load, giving additional assistance in propelling and steering.

Various hauling placements of the towing strap (from left):
(a) Diagonal over the shoulder and across the chest.
(b) Tumpline fashion across the forehead.
(c) Behind the neck, over the shoulders and under the arms.

(d) Across the upper chest and around the shoulders.
(e) Strap connected to spruce poles worn in the same position as by the figure in the center—behind the neck, over the shoulders and under the arms.

In both pole and soft-line hauling, the basics of wearing the strap are the same. Not surprisingly, the leather strap itself may be identical, whether it connects to loops in quarter-inch tow lines or is tied or tacked to spruce poles. In both cases, the leather is two or perhaps two-and-a-half inches wide and, like a tumpline, distributes the pressure of the load over a wide area.

There are three basic hauling positions. The first is used only for light or moderate loads, and some people never use it at all. The center of the wide part of the strap rests over the back of the neck while the ends pass forward over the shoulders and then rearward to the load under the arms. In our experience, this hauling method puts undue stress on the spine and in particular the knee joints where it transfers torque. This causes discomfort and lameness.

One of the best harness configurations has the strap passing over one shoulder and across the chest diagonally, then under the opposite arm. Again, the weight is distributed over a wide area, and the position of the strap allows for sustained heavy-duty hauling. By simply alternating high and low sides, you can equalize any asymmetry over the day and rest each side, much as paddlers do by switching sides.

The third method is to pass the strap around the outside of both arms and across the upper chest. This holds the most favor with people who are short or short-waisted, although it works for anyone. It is a good method to keep in mind as a rest position to relieve strains brought on by other positions while still hauling. Experienced haulers shift through all the methods over a day, and this seems to provide enough variation to keep the body from tiring of any one position.

The diagonal over-one-shoulder and upper-chest methods are appropriate for heavy loads up to the limits of haulability. For anatomical reasons, women sometimes resist these methods, but, happily, the methods work well for both sexes.

For extreme situations such as steep hills or riverbank ascents, or simply moving a toboggan in marginal conditions, the towing strap can be worn tumpline-fashion with a determined lean into the strap. Such measures are often required to gain a riverbank or height of land or some other relatively short-term goal. You may also favor this method if you have to continue moving in difficult hauling conditions.

TOBOGGAN CARE

We've considered some of what your toboggan can do for you, but what can— and should—you do for your toboggan? You will increase a wooden toboggans lifespan if you apply a good marine varnish to the topside. The outer side of the curve should likewise be varnished until the curve flattens out and becomes the bottom. You will also want to pine-tar the bottom as if it were a giant cross-country ski. Do this by wiping pine tar onto the wood, cooking it into the pores and grain with a propane torch and wiping off the excess with a cotton rag. Carry the pine tar beyond the bottom surface several inches up the rise of the curve in front. If this is done annually, at the start of each season, the wood will valiantly resist moisture in thaw conditions and the base will hold wax well, which will ease the sled's glide.

Ideally, wax should be ironed on for a smooth, perfect surface. Such a surface lasts well, up to a week in most conditions, whereas paraffin rubbed on and smoothed by the heat of your hand or a waxing cork is less durable. Wax applied in desperation along the trail will be rough and wear off within the same day. There is a simple method for ironing wax in the field. Bring the toboggan into the tent while the stove is going and let the surface warm up enough to accept a good coat of wax by rubbing a paraffin block or candle directly on the wood. Meanwhile, have two or more metal cups full of boiling or hot water on the stove. Iron the wax with one of these cups until it cools, then repeat with the other cup. Reheat the first cup while the second cools down during use. Keep ironing until you get a high-gloss, perfectly flat, mirrorlike finish.

With relatively light toboggans, you may not feel much difference in slip unless hauling conditions become marginal. However, with a big load—200 pounds or more—you will be happy to wax and enjoy the results. High-density plastic sleds or runners need not be waxed, but the bigger surfaces of fiberglass sleds between the runners are much improved by a good waxing.

DOGSLEDDING

Although the ease afforded by the toboggan represents a quantum leap beyond the rigors of winter backpacking, a question that is repeatedly raised merits an answer: "Why not use dogs for the hauling?"

Part of this perennial query has to do with stock images of dogsledding. Most published photos show a team on a flat section of sea ice under a bright March or April sun with dramatic cliffs and fjords as a backdrop. Inevitably, on such a stretch of easy going, the sledders ride with their hoods thrown back, admiring the splendid scenery. What such a picture does not convey, however, is the amount of labor involved in all but that brief moment of ease when conditions are perfect.

First, dogs can travel only where snow is shallow, human- or machine-packed or is consistently wind-packed. Second, they need to eat, which requires a region of relative bounty. And third, a dog team requires year-round care, attention and financial commitment.

The sea ice of the high Arctic and, to some extent, the coastal and even interior barrens provide ideal dogsledding conditions. The high Arctic receives little snow. As little as 30 inches fall to the ground each year, and although this may blow around, creating ground blizzards, there is seldom enough to stop sleds or dogs or even require the use of snowshoes. (By contrast, the interior of Labrador/Quebec receives 13 *feet* of snow annually.) For much of the year, the hardness of the wind-pack provides a surface perfect for the slip of runnered sleds and traction for dogs. It is not surprising that, historically, these were the areas where people used dogs for hauling.

Dogsledding poses another set of energy-intensive requirements when taken inland—a region not as suitable as the Arctic. Now there is the frequent need to break trail and pack a float for the dogs and sled in new, deep snow. In the midst of such travail, it is hard to recall those grand moments on the ice when you could actually ride the sleds and the dogs could tick off a 40-mile day as if it were a lark.

In Ungava, hunting dogs were occasionally harnessed into the traces to assist a person in hauling a toboggan. In the Arctic, people frequently lend their strength to teams. Among the Athapaskan people, toboggans were built large and hauled by teams of dogs. Mail packeters and Hudson's Bay Company employees regularly used dog teams in regions where they may have been unknown before. Hybrid toboggan-bottomed, runnered sleds have appeared from Quebec to Alaska, where people had to contend with both wind-pack and deep snow in the interior woods. Modern dogsledders keep this tradition alive by using Lexan and plastic in their hybrid sleds. Likewise, modern travelers have hand-hauled to the North Pole where earlier explorers used dogs, and dogsledded in Antarctica where others have tried hand-hauling.

Often the problems are not so much the mode of travel in a region, but one's expectations of its effectiveness and dismay at its unforeseen inconveniences. Jacques Duhoux and Michel Denis of Adventure Nomade in Quebec are always wrestling with their clients' consternation at the amount of work packing trails ahead of the dogs involves when the route is not on the wind-pack of lakes or along barren ridges. The few guides in Maine who offer overnight dog trips also favor the large lakes and snowmobile trails. Some use snowmobiles to prepack a hard trail for the dogs.

A serious consideration in dog team use is the ability to carry or provide sufficient food. People who wintered on sea ice were there to capitalize on the abundance of sea mammals, providing food, hides, tools, fuel for lamps and dog food. Historically, the use of dogs was common in interior areas only if a major river system nearby hosted seasonal runs of millions of salmon. With some watersheds carrying as many as five species through the open-water season, part of the annual job cycle of people living in the bush was catching and drying the winter's supply of fish. Of this, the greater portion was reserved for the dogs. This made a dog tradition possible deep in the interior of Alaska and the Yukon, where, in some places, more than a thousand miles of river stretched to the coast.

Even in a modern, recreational context, the old equation pertains. Polly Mahoney and Kevin Slater are Maine guides whose love of dogs has taken them to the Arctic as well as the Quebec reaches of Hudson Bay. Toward the end of a recent trip that included both inland forests and the bay coast, Polly and Kevin found themselves running out of dog food. It was late in the season, and the dogs were tired. As their hunger increased, their fatigue and despondency grew, too. A fresh caribou revived their spirits and strength only marginally, and the situation became serious.

However, upon reaching the coast, they were helped by natives who gave directions to some open leads and an abundance of seals. Here the dogs were able to eat something with a high fat content, and the change was astounding. Kevin reported that they reverted to puppylike joy and returned to the trail with the same enthusiasm with which summer-weary dogs respond to the first good fall of snow and the sight of their driver approaching with an armful of harness.

However, most recreational trips are short enough that participants can carry all the dog food their teams will need. Longer forays may be resupplied by packages mailed ahead to outposts along the route or by deliveries by an air charter service.

Year-round care of hauling dogs takes 100-percent commitment. At a minimum, dogs require daily exercise, careful training and a substantial financial output for feeding and veterinary services. But all this is worth it to some. The dog-running people we know think, breathe, dream and wake for their dogs and none seem to mind caring for the dogs all year long for a few months of use in the winter. In the end, the most important factor in the decision to use dogs is one's willingness to accept the work involved.

Tobogganers, by contrast, appear to be a bunch of lazy reprobates. Their sleds require only minimal care and maintenance. Each night in camp and throughout the nonsnow season, the toboggans are stored without thought to continuous feeding, vaccinations or husbandry. In camp, the only needs to address are those of the human participants. Tobogganers have no illusions or grand expectations of their pedestrian life. A high-mileage day for them would be laughably short for a dog driver. Where Sam and Lucy Woodward were up until eleven o'clock every night taking care of their dogs first and then themselves during their 1,400-mile Labrador trip, a group of tobogganers would be asleep by eight or nine o'clock if they wished, and their dreams would be unclouded by envy of night-work. But the Woodwards would have traveled in that day what the snoozing tobogganers would need three to five days to equal.

The illusion to avoid is that either dogsledding or hand-hauling is a lark all of the time. Both involve work, but if you love the work, you're glad to do it, and the glories of the winter trail are a bonus.

Just as the landscape itself informed the people who lived there which methods of winter travel were most economical, so it will inform today's recreational nomad. In this way, toboggans will still occupy the circumpolar reaches of the subarctic forests, and dogsleds will excel on the barrens and sea ice. Overlap will occur naturally where it always has, depending largely on travelers' capacity for balancing work with goals.

However you choose to haul, may the wind be behind you, the temperature range just right and the going easy enough to free your mind and spirit to the glory of the winter trail.

USEFUL ADDRESSES

Plastic Toboggans & Dog Sleds

Chris Evavold
Black River Sleds
3303 East County Road B
Foxboro, WI 54836
715-399-2796
www.blackriversleds.com

Wooden Toboggans

John Harren
Northern Toboggan & Sled
32581 645th Avenue
Warroad, MN 56763
218-386-3005
www.ntsled.com

Michael Gaulin
4 Old Sturbridge Road
Sturbridge, MA 01566
508-347-5976

Fiberglass Sleds & Pulks

Fjellpulken AS
Hagenvn 3
N-2613 Lillehammer
Norway
www.fjellpulken.no

Scandinavian Pulks

Sven Erikson
Bjorneglantan
5500 Rosso 5-45295 Stromstad
Sweden

Toboggans & Lashing Systems

Empire Canvas makes a brilliant system of toboggan tarps, load-lashing straps and piggyback duffels for the top of load for items you need easy access to. The company also sells a full package, including a toboggan, packing system, towing lines and accessories.
Empire Canvas Works
P.O. Box 17
Solon Springs, WI 54873
715-378-4216
www.empirecanvasworks.com

Steambending for Woodworkers

(VHS video)

Northwoods Canoe Co. (Rollin Thurlow)
336 Range Road
Atkinson, ME 04426
207-564-3667 (888-564-2710)
www.wooden-canoes.com

Guide to Traditional Sledding

(booklet)

Craig MacDonald
RR 1
Dwight, Ontario
Canada P0A 1H0
705-635-3416 (evenings)

Chapter 3
Tents & Trail Stoves

TENTS & TRAIL STOVES

"*If you wander out a ways and turn to look back at the tent glowing from the light of the candles within, it seems, in the vast blackness of the Canadian night, like a tiny wayside shrine in which the votive lamp never goes out. The pilgrims inside aren't saying any prayers, of course. They're sipping a dash of rum, wiggling their toes in the heat of the stove,telling stories on each other and themselves, cackling, chortling and rolling around on the floor in total weeping hysteria if the stories get good enough. The tone may be a little too boisterous for proper vespers, but what I hear rising from the warmth and light of that tent is an evensong as full of good tidings as any mortal could hope for.*"

—Robert Kimber, *A Canoeist's Sketchbook,* 1991

TENTS

Perhaps the single greatest pleasure made possible by toboggan travel is the ability to carry a roomy cotton tent outfitted with a sheet-steel woodstove. This combination has long been part of the northern bush dweller's kit and is increasingly evident among recreational travelers. In the early spring and late fall openwater seasons, a tent and stove are not regarded as too much gear either in a canoe or on the portages. On the winter trail, the tent-and-stove combination delivers so much joy that most people come to regard it as a necessity.

The promise of several hours' intense heat in the evening, and a few more hours of it in the morning, has an enormous impact on all aspects of winter travel and life on the trail. The satisfaction of basking in glorious heat after a day in the cold, or waking to a crackling fire that chases the predawn chill from the tent, is obvious and, by itself, worth the weight of the tent and stove. But the benefits are far more encompassing than just this.

Stoveless winter campers typically have only two major sources of heat available to them: metabolic heat, through the digestion and utilization of food, and mechanically generated heat, through muscles that generate heat when active. These forms of heat can only be maintained by eating enough high-quality food and by insulating the body with clothing by day and sleeping bags at night. People who travel with a sheet-steel stove and a tent add a third major source of heat—and this heat has a direct effect on the economics of the other two heat sources. If the tent is heated from six to ten hours a day, that is six to ten hours that your body need not rely on a high rate of metabolism or high level of exertion to keep warm. You are, in fact, relaxed, with few demands on your physiological processes. Thus, a person engaged in cold, bivouac-type camping needs more food, more often, than a heated-tent dweller. Less food means a lighter load, and a lighter load means less work, and less work requires less fuel in the form of food.

A person's morale and sense of of well-being are equally important. The day's headwinds don't feel so bad when you know warm, snug shelter lies ahead. And the cold of night is less frightening when you know that the stove door will soon creak and a match will be struck to tinder and wood. Breakfast and hot drinks are not far off, and you need not get out of your bags until the tent is warm.

Tent Materials

Several companies make canvas wall tents, and a few make "campfire" and "wedge" tents. The main misfortune is that all these companies work with eight- and ten-ounce cotton, which is heavy. It seems that the days of tents made from three-and-a-half-ounce and four-ounce Egyptian cotton or "balloon silk" have faded away, existing only in catalogs from the late 1890s. Even by 1934, the D.T. Abercrombie Company was using six-ounce cloth, where 20 years earlier it listed three-ounce fabric. The balloon silk referred to in many of the old texts is a synonym for Egyptian cotton. It was not silk nor was it used as balloon material. Outdoor writers of the late 1800s raved about it as a lightweight fabric suitable for tents, just as we do today.

Where the modern synthetic tentmaker is interested in a material that breathes well enough to pass the vapor in people's breath while they sleep, the needs of a winter tent with a stove in it are much greater. Not only will four or five people breathe in it all night, but the cooking that takes place liberates volumes of water vapor, as does the wash water. Add laundry and bathing, and the tent fabric must pass even greater volumes of vapor. Cotton, even if waterproofed, does this easily.

After a long day on the trail, the heat of the tent and the evening meal bring on satisfied grins as Labrador wanderers recline among clouds of sleeping bags.

Other important differences between light cotton and heavy cotton are felt in a day's hauling. In Egyptian cotton, our 10-by-12-foot wall tents with their fly weigh in at about 17 pounds and roll into a bundle not much larger than a stuffed sleeping bag. The same tent in ten-ounce canvas takes up two-thirds of a toboggan and can weigh close to 40 pounds.

The crowning irony is that a mill in Arbroath, Scotland, weaves a fantastic 4.25-ounce cloth that is ideal fabric for stunning tents, anoraks and wind pants. The hitch is that the minimum order is 10,000 yards. Even the company's North American distributor does not deal in amounts that would be useful and affordable to people interested in making winter gear. We were exceedingly lucky to import 900 yards by buying the remnants of a larger order that had a nearly invisible water stain on some of the rolls. After selling most of the fabric to finance the deal, we retained a 100-yard roll as our lifetime supply.

Occasionally, sailmakers can order small amounts of the material, and it is sometimes possible to get glorious light stuff through them. The best advice is to plague any and every possible source with questions about the material until demand creates a market or someone discovers a source willing to deal in smaller quantities. If the stuff is manufactured, it should be available.

Don't be afraid to keep pestering potential sources who have said "no" before. When small amounts come up for sale, as they occasionally do, the source will know that your interest is genuine. Be especially dogged during economic slumps: in downturns, people who normally won't deal in small quantities sometimes find it worth their while to consider small sales. Though having a softer finish than desired for tent fabric, 220-count (or more) Egyptian cotton bedsheets can be a creative way to procure material. We know of several fine tents made this way.

If canvas is all you can get, do not despair. If four people occupy such a tent, that is only ten pounds of tent per person, and that will seem a small inconvenience when it is 40 below and you are reveling inside by a humming stove.

TENT TYPES

Four types of tent lend themselves to the winter trail. Three are superb, and the fourth is very acceptable as long as it is sheltered by thick timber.

Wall Tents

The standard wall tent is probably the most common and is the style that virtually all makers of cotton tents provide. They are rectangular, have three- or four-

foot sidewalls, gable ends and, in most dimensions, a reasonably steep roof due to a seven-foot height at the ridge. Because of their rectangular shape, wall tents have large, flat surfaces that tend to catch wind; they do best, therefore, in the shelter of trees. However, if pitched in the open, wall tents can be guyed out, reinforced with interior pickets to

A wall tent and a pyramid tent, pitched at a lake edge in fair weather. With no adjacent trees to guy to, the wall tent is affixed to its own scissor poles.

48

prevent wind from ballooning the walls in, and stretched into an oval configuration at ground level, which may help the sides dump some of the wind.

In timbered country, a wall tent requires three poles. One of these should be quite long and used as the ridgepole. Trim this one carefully with an axe so that no sharp branch stubs project that might puncture or tear the fly. The two other poles may be a little shorter, and these will be the scissor poles. The ridgepole will be tied to a tree at a height slightly less than the height of the ridge of the tent. The tent is then tied on so that its back wall will be toward the tree, which is used as a back pole. After the tent is tied in place along the ridgepole and the fly thrown over the ridgepole, it is time to assemble the scissor poles.

At this point, the tent and fly hang loose on the ridgepole, which is only tied to proper height in the rear at the tree. The front of the ridgepole is still on the ground. The two scissor poles should run parallel to each other and be tied together about four inches back from what will be their top ends. (If this point is 12 or more feet from the base of these poles, you will have a wide enough A-frame to tie the front tent corners to the scissor poles themselves.) Once the top lashing is done, the base of the poles can be spread apart, thus causing the lashing to tighten and bind.

Adjacent trees often do not fall exactly 45 degrees off each wall tent corner. Here a pull point is established in the right place by tying the guyline to the closest tree and then placing a second line to another tree. The tension is then adjusted until the kink in the line is in the proper place for the pull point.

The ridgepole is then cradled between the two ends that extend four or more inches from the lashing, and the legs are spread to a distance that puts the ridgepole at the same height as it is at the rear. With the scissor poles jammed into the snow at the proper distance, the tent will now hang from the ridgepole at just the right height to pitch. The four guylines that emanate from each

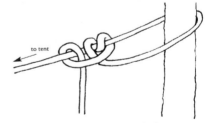

The taut-line (or rolling) hitch.

of the corner grommets on the tent can then be tied off to trees adjacent to the tent site. Should trees not fall in the right place at each corner of the tent, you may have to drive a picket into the snow, or tie to the scissor poles in front.

If your tie points have been selected or created at a 45-degree angle from the tent corners, they will exert equal pull both fore-and-aft along the tent lengthwise as well as pull the tent to full width side-to-side. A tent hung in this way will be tight, true and without sags along its edges. The fly, which was thrown over the ridgepole before raising, is now automatically in place to be guyed out to the same or similar tie points as were used for the tent corners. Or you can tie them to the tent guylines with taut-line hitches. (If you have forgotten to place the fly in advance, you will now have the nearly impossible task of throwing it over an inaccessible ridgepole. If this is the case, spread the scissor poles, lower the ridgepole, do it right and reset everything.)

At this point, the tent is essentially pitched, but you may need to adjust the tension, or the guylines' angles. For this reason, it is wise to use taut-line hitches in all guylines. These are essentially one-way slip knots that can be tightened but not loosened with normal loading. In fact, the greater the loading on the line, the more the hitch binds. To deliberately loosen these hitches, you simply take the load off the line and back up the hitch by pinching it between your thumb and finger. To tighten the line, slide an unloaded hitch forward until all the slack is used. When released, it will stay in place. In this way, you can adjust all the lines in a simple walk around the tent. With luck, none will need to be retied, just slacked off or tightened as needed to true up the tent.

Pitching a wall tent in the open requires more poles. You will need four scissor poles, a ridgepole and a sixth pole to brace the rear scissors fore-and-aft. Otherwise, the whole frame could fall flat, forward or backward. You will also need pickets to guy the corners (the sides, too, if it is windy). These can be driven into the snow, if conditions permit, or buried and packed into the snow as "deadmen." Obviously, the more you can favor the timber, the easier and more economical the setup.

Pole selection can vary from place to place, and many travelers create their own pole system that they can carry with them. In Maine and in the Canadian wilds we cut poles at each site, and leave them carefully leaned into trees for use in the future. Some sets of poles in areas we guide in have been used repeatedly for ten years,

In the southern reaches of toboggan country it is best to use standing dead poles. In Maine there is no shortage of spruce-budworm-killed balsam and spruce saplings, and these are very light, rigid and strong. There are two reasons for choosing dead poles:

One is that in areas closer to population centers it is generally inappropriate to cut green trees, and in many areas it is forbidden by either the paper companies or the agencies in charge of the waterways. Secondly, the temperatures are mild enough so that green wood could flex and bend if it were not frozen solidly, and thus a tent could sag or go out of true.

Farther north where there are billions of trees, few people and almost no use of the areas, green poles and pickets are entirely appropriate. You can cut boughs from the poles for flooring the kitchen area of the tent, and it is always so cold that green wood will never flex or bend.

As you gain experience, you will develop a better and better eye for campsites that require the least preparation and pole cutting. Every once in a while, you might find trees just the right distance apart so that the ridgepole can be tied up at both ends, eliminating the need for scissor poles entirely. Sometimes you can hang the tent from a taut rope between trees and not even need a ridgepole. In such a case, however, you will need an alternative point to anchor the stovepipe to, as this is usually wired to the ridgepole, which is deliberately cut long for this purpose.

Similarly, you'll develop a keen sense of the tent's spatial requirements, and you will always be looking for adjacent saplings and trees to guy the tent to and thus avoid the need for pickets.

The bottom edges of the tent can be staked out by packing the stakes into the snow and then shoveling a small amount of snow along the tent's edges to seal the bottom and provide additional structure and snugness. Many people will sew several foot- wide snow cloths along the sides and ends to facilitate this step.

You are then ready to open the door and arrange the interior. If you always remember to tie the door shut before taking the tent down, it will still be shut when you set it up again. In this way, setup will not spread that end of the tent too wide for the door to shut. Most tents have door flaps that overlap about a foot. This overlap must be maintained in order to baffle any winds that might steal in.

The mention of tent flaps often elicits a question regarding the advisability of zippers. We avoid them. They can fail. They can jam or break, the sliders can wear out and, in the case of synthetic zippers, the teeth may erode or even melt if a spark lands there. By contrast, flaps and ties are not likely to wear out. If they do, you can use your sewing kit to make repairs.

Pyramid Tents

Pyramid tents come in two types. The truest to form is four-sided and pyramidal. These are not bad, but they do have the drawback of exposing flat surfaces to the wind. The better form is often referred to as a pyramid tent, even though such terminology would fail on a geometry quiz. Ours is eight-sided with three-foot walls and an eight-foot-tall apex. Each side is five feet wide, which minimizes the flat surfaces presented to the wind, and the overall rounded shape is good at dumping wind. Since surface area decreases with height, it is very warm and very wind resistant.

We designed our pyramid tent with a fly that is sewn on only at the apex so that it can be pitched at varying distances from the tent roof. In clear weather we pitch it close, with just a few inches' clearance. If snow is likely, we pitch it higher so that heavy snow can sag more without contacting the hot roof. The downside of having eight corners on both the tent and the fly is that there are 16 taut-line hitches to be tied, while a wall tent may require only half that. However, you need only one eight-foot center pole and eight four-to-six-foot pickets, depending on snow depth and whether the tent will be guyed to pickets driven in the snow or buried as dead-men. In timber, you can usually reduce the need for pickets by guying out to adja-cent saplings and trees.

The pyramid tent is easy to pitch by oneself and even easier if the job is shared. After packing down the site by snowshoe, establish the four cardinal pickets, or press any convenient trees into service, and attach the guylines to them. Then put in the center pole and erect the tent to full height. In the snow, place the base of

the pole on a "snowshoe" made of a split piece of wood with the flat side up for a solid base. At this point, you can tie out the remaining four guy-lines, and the tent is up. Now finish the job by shoveling snow onto the snow cloths.

The pyramid can be set up in the open, and, for travel onto the barrens, it is a simple matter to bring along a center pole, and even a selection of pickets. Or, as one often does

Pyramid tent staked out with pickets.

in the barrens, you can use toboggans and other gear as deadmen to guy out the tent. The pyramid's wind-resistant features make it the best choice for the open; in addition, because there is less surface area up in the wind, less heat is carried away through windchill. Also, there is less volume to heat in the apex, so the pyramid is much warmer than a wall tent. In a four-person, 12-foot-diameter pyramid tent, you'll likely leave the door open whenever the stove is going if it is above zero or ten degrees Fahrenheit outside. In a wall tent, because heat must fill the gable ends before it can fill the living space, the door typically stays closed unless the temper-ature approaches 20 degrees outside. (See Appendix D for plans.)

Wedge & Modified Wedge Tents

The wedge tent is essentially nothing more than a steep roof with fairly narrow gable ends. Typically, it is a two-person tent with a centrally located stove. Occupants sleep on either side of the stove with the remaining space between them used as kitchen and common ground. The tent's vulnerability is its large, flat sides that, even when carefully guyed out and reinforced with interior pickets, catch wind and have no way to dump it. Best in timbered country, wedge tents are small, light and easy to set up with either a ridgepole or a rope stretched between trees. Calvin Rutstrum, author of *Paradise Below Zero* and other wilderness living books, favored these tents above all others, reflecting his usual mode of travel, which was solo or with one other person. For that, they are great. A small wall tent, such as an eight-by-ten-foot tent, functions the same way but is a bit more spacious due to the wall height.

Currently a number of tent makers offer modified wedge tents, hybridizing the best features of wall tents and wedge tents. Duane and Margot Lottig of Empire Canvas Works have designed several superbly functioning modified wedge tents. Internal, lightweight aluminum poles make them a delight to use for efficiency in camp set-up. We have happily used these tents on trips ranging from three-day fall hunting trips to two-month winter treks.

Modified wedge tent. (photo by Carol Farchmin)

Campfire Tent

The campfire tent has enjoyed a resurgence of popularity because of the work of the late Bill Mason, the great Canadian filmmaker, canoeist, artist and voice for conservation. It is an old design with a versatile open front that can be pitched to catch the radiant heat of an open campfire or closed by folding in the side flaps and lowering the pitch of the front roof. Over the last century, the design has been modified by just about everyone with a bent for customizing or improving an already good thing. Architect, Maine guide and perfectionist David Lewis has modified the "Bill Mason" tent to have a front panel with a stovepipe thimble that can be buttoned onto the tent, rendering it a full-fledged winter shelter. Because of its large, flat surfaces on all sides, the campfire tent is truly a tent for timbered regions. It is luxurious and dandy as long as it keeps to its proper habitat. And, with the removable winterizing panel, it loses none of its potential for canoe camping, in which it has its origin and primary reason for being. (See Appendix E for plans.)

PITCHING CAMP

Once a campsite is chosen, the first task is to pack down the snow into a large, flat area as a "garage" for unloading the toboggans. This should be central but removed from the tent sites. If the "garage" is too close, stacked gear will impede tent pitching, and you will end up moving gear twice. The next step is to pack down the tent sites, remembering to make the packed areas much bigger than the basal area of each tent. Deep snow makes this easier by covering blow-downs and other lump makers. The shallower the snow, the more you will have to favor flat,

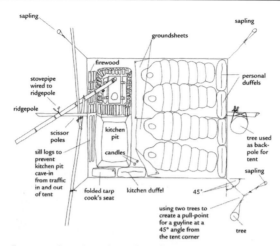

The three schematic illustrations of a 10-by-12-foot wall tent show a number of strategies for setup as well as the placement of items that maximize the efficiency, pleasure and order of a winter camp. The bird's-eye view above shows the layout of the living and kitchen areas. The split-level kitchen pit is shown for a deep-snow camp, as well as the floats for the stove legs, the palisade of firewood that prevents melt-back of the stove pit and the flat firewood that serves as tabletop space to keep utensils out of the snow. Sill logs are in place so that the kitchen pit is not eroded or collapsed by the comings and goings of people.

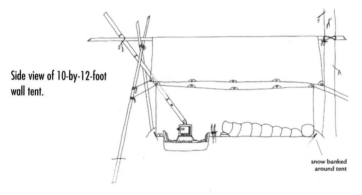

Side view of 10-by-12-foot wall tent.

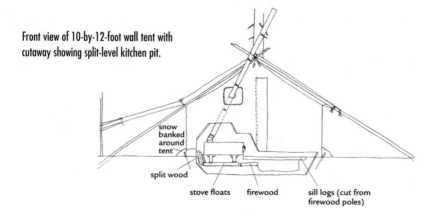

Front view of 10-by-12-foot wall tent with cutaway showing split-level kitchen pit.

clear ground, much as when pitching a summer camp. The whole party can join in the site-packing activity; it generally warms up everyone.

With each of the tent types, there is a floor plan for arranging the stove and the people to maximize the efficiency of life within the tent.

The wall tent provides perhaps the most convenient layout to live in. Basically, the front third of the tent is devoted to the stove area, kitchen and what can be called the "pass-through" zone. This area can be dug down 12 or 18 inches with adequate snow cover, and this sunken kitchen provides a number of benefits. (See illustrations on facing page.)

The rear two-thirds of the wall tent are occupied by the sleeping platform. Since the tents are floorless, this area is covered with rubberized nylon groundsheets before the Therm-a-Rests or foam pads are put down and the sleeping bags unrolled. The rear wall is reserved for each person's duffel bag, which is arranged at the foot of his or her sleeping zone. Heads are arranged toward the stove, and the snow removed from the kitchen pit can be used to level the sleeping platform or slightly raise the forward edge so that people can sleep with their heads slightly elevated.

In a winterized campfire tent, the kitchen can likewise be sunken. The pit provides a well in which to leave rubber booties for exiting the tent, and a place where the cook can sit comfortably and move around. Back on the platform, everyone must sit cross-legged or recline on their gear. Whoever is cooking is constantly moving in and out to the food boxes, getting up and down to monitor the stove, wood and whatever is cooking, and passing things back and forth. Sitting on the edge of the pit, with lower legs and feet comfortably ensconced, is very conducive to the activities required of this person.

With pyramid and wedge tents, the stove is best left at the level of the tent floor. This means that the arrangement of gear is a bit different, and most people working in the kitchen area will do so from their knees rather than a sitting position. The radius of movement is smaller and everything is better kept within reach to minimize getting up and down. In a wall tent, the setup maintains a "pass-through" zone between the stove and the cook. In the other tents, this zone is occupied by the cook, and pass-through is much less convenient and more disruptive.

In the subarctic forests, due to the scale of the landscape and lack of humans, it is appropriate to cut green pickets for the tent poles and thereby gain some spruce branches with which to floor the kitchen area. In small, semiwilderness areas confined by development, and in high-use areas, the use of boughs is not suitable. In these areas, the kitchen pit can be left as snow or floored with extra firewood.

Creating a kitchen pit requires deep enough snow and the right kind of tent. When appropriate, the option will be eagerly seized and, in shallow snow, sorely missed.

ILLUMINATION

The early dark of winter afternoons and the lateness of the sunrise give illumination strategies an importance unfamiliar to midsummer campers. Even those who confine their travels to the longer days of February and March need good light sources for several hours a day.

Natives and other northerners are probably the world's most ardent users of Coleman gas lanterns. Houses, camps, trappers' tilts and hundreds of wall tents are outfitted with wire hooks that make it easy to hang the lamps over work areas. Fancy padded plywood boxes are made to transport the lanterns so that the roughness of the trail and even the flipping of a komatik behind a snowmobile will leave the delicate mantels and glass globes intact.

Personally, we dislike Coleman lanterns. They give a harsh light, hiss annoyingly, have fragile parts and can fail through clogging of fuel lines or problems in other, carefully machined parts that are unfixable by lay people in the field. In addition, the lamps require the carrying of fuel and fuel containers—and plenty of them, as Colemans use fuel quickly.

For years, we carried two small kerosene lamps for each tent. The advantages of these lamps were their quietness and fuel efficiency. They are silent when burning and a gallon of kerosene supplies two lamps for 28 days. The light is soft and warm.

The drawbacks, however, are daunting. Small lamps are hard to find, and modern ones designed for ornamental use are not well made. As with Coleman lamps, the globe is breakable, although kerosene lamps at least have no other breakable parts. In the event of a sled upset, fuel could spill through the wick slot, and the fuel itself has an unpleasant odor. If the wicks are not well trimmed and the level of flame is not carefully regulated, the odor is discernible, and, after years of use, a blackish residue colors the inside of the tent fabric. Who knows the effects of such a residue on human lungs?

To avoid carrying the lanterns, special boxes, fuel, fuel containers and funnels, we happily switched to candles.

Candles are great. They give off a warm, even light, reflected wonderfully by the white walls of a tent. If they break in transport, you can weld them back together by melting wax into the seam at the break. With use, they slowly vanish, so you need not lug the same-weight lamp around, or carry empty fuel containers in your trash. You can even wax toboggan bottoms with them.

The best candles are three-quarters of an inch in diameter, as this seems to provide the best ratio of wax to wick size for an even burn and good light. The eight-and-a-half-inch-tall candles sold under the Radiant label in Quebec are absolutely superb and can be purchased individually in many northern stores or in a box containing three dozen.

Two candles per tent give as much light as two kerosene lamps, and the sloped roof of a pyramid tent reflects all the light like a focused parabola. Even in a more spacious wall tent, if candles are placed near the walls, the light will be reflected and intensified. We select a few kindling splints from the firewood supply each night and affix the candles to them with short segments of snare wire that are just long enough for several wraps and a twist or two to secure the tension. The wire segments are coiled up and carried with the candles; unless lost, they can be used for an entire trip. These kindling-splint candleholders can then be stuck in the snow in optimum positions in the tent and moved around as needed. They are best kept at a distance from the stove as warm wax melts faster. If a candle is 45 degrees off the corner of the stove, it will receive little heat.

Of course, a bit of care must be exercised when using candles. Keep them out of the tent's traffic patterns and other places where feet might kick them. If wax drips, position the sticks over snow and not gear or the groundsheets. As the candles burn down, watch that they don't melt enough to fall through the wire loops to the tent floor.

In addition to candles, you'll also need a battery-powered headlamp. A headlamp with an adjustable angle of beam lights specific areas with ease, whether you are writing in your journal, reading aloud to your companions, cooking or performing any of the myriad neverending jobs around camp. Avoid flashlights; they require a free hand, and most jobs around camp require two hands. You become stupidly handicapped if you must perform them with a flashlight clamped under an arm, held between your knees or gripped with your teeth.

When traveling purely for pleasure, you can time all movement, including camp take-down and tent pitching, to occur in daylight, thus making it necessary to light only the tents. If you must push for some reason, get up in the dark to hit the trail at first light or travel until dark to increase mileage, your lighting needs will correspondingly escalate, requiring extra batteries. In either case, never scrimp on lighting resources or bring a flashlight you already have because a headlamp is expensive. On the trail, it is safe to value even mild inconvenience at about $50 a minute, so a $30 headlamp that will see hours and hours of use is a bargain.

TRAIL STOVES

Tobogganers are most interested in the smallest stove models. The dimensions need seldom exceed 12 inches wide or 14 inches high. A length of 25 or 26 inches can accommodate standard-length, 24-inch pipe inside for storage during transportation.

Although older stoves throughout Maine and Canada often had three-inch pipe, more recent ones use four-inch. After trying both, we find that the superior drawing power of four-inch pipe provides the best heat, especially when burning suboptimum wood.

Stoves range from a simple rectangular box with door and draft intake to models with removable lids, detachable side shelves, legs that fit into brackets, sliding draft adjustment and a damper in the first segment of pipe. Some have rear-mounted pipe collars so that the entire stovetop is available for cooking. Others have a center- or corner-mounted pipe collar, and these provide a hotter surface because the flames are drawn to the surface steel as they seek the top-mounted exit hole. All good trail stoves are end-loading so that whatever is cooking or heating on the surface need not be disturbed to add firewood.

At least one manufacturer makes a folding stove, but these are to be avoided. They leak too much air to be shut down effectively, and warpage due to uneven heating may wreak havoc with the best of hinge systems. Since the pipe, legs, lid, elbows and even a folding saw and slush scoop may ride in the stove during transport, a rigid stove does not waste space, nor can it fail.

Depending on the type of tent and the stove arrangement, you will need one or two articulating elbows. With adjustable elbow angles, you can accommodate variations in setup and terrain.

Leg systems for stoves vary. Indians cut steps into green pickets to hold the stove in a way that it cannot be knocked off the legs once they are driven into the ground or snow. For nomadic travel, it is far easier to carry a leg system that can be set up without fuss. The easiest solution for legless stoves is to fold two pieces of sheet metal into right angles with six inches of material on each side of the angle. Then, in the tent, place the angles across wooden "floats" on the snow with the stove bot-

A woodstove set up in a tent with a bough floor in the kitchen area. The boughs prevent any melt-back around or under the stove, and maintain a very clean kitchen. Crumbs, floor sweepings from the groundsheets and gray water all sift through such a fragrant renewable floor.

tom resting on the apexes of the angles. In transport, the angles fit inside the stove along the edge and thus take up no room. The time saving and adjustability of this leg system is worth every ounce the angles add to your load.

Stoves with removable legs that fit in brackets affixed to the bottom are easily inserted and can be placed on floats split from a piece of wood and laid with flat sides up.

No matter which leg system you use, be sure to lay plenty of boughs or extra firewood under the stove to prevent snowmelt. Otherwise the stove might tip and hot kettles could slide off.

A removable lid in the front of the stovetop is a great feature because you can put a tapered pot down the hole into direct contact with the flame for quick heating. In addition, you can grill things over direct heat should you wish a change from boiling, baking and frying. Fresh lake trout grilled over coals is one of the most delectable northern treats.

In addition to an adjustable draft in the front of the stove, a damper in the pipe is a nice plus. This can be either a real damper on a pin that can be opened or closed by twisting the handle, or a simpler affair made with a flat piece of sheet metal inserted into a hacksaw cut that extends partway through the pipe. A damper will not be missed too much if it is lacking, but if you have one, we can guarantee that you will use it to good effect.

For running the hot pipe through the thin cotton tent wall, many companies sell a thimble made of fiberglass cloth. It is fitted to the diameter of the pipe. The thimbles are sewn right to the tent and can be rolled up with it during take-down and storage. The only disadvantage is that they fray around the edges and must be replaced.

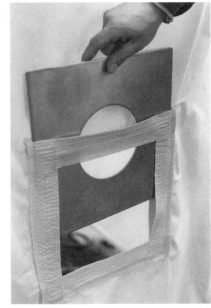

A sheet-metal pipe thimble being inserted into a pocket in the tent wall prior to stove setup.

The other method, which predates fiberglass cloth, is as good now as ever. A pocket is sewn into the tent at the appropriate spot and both the tent wall and center of the pocket have hemmed holes in them. The pocket is sized to take a piece of sheet metal with a pipe hole of the right size cut into it. In windy weather, the sheet metal and pipe may squeak and rattle as they move against each other, but this bit of annoyance is a bargain compared to burning down your tent. For storage and transport, the sheet-metal thimble rides in the stove. While the tent is set up, gravity holds it in place within the pocket. The whole thing is simple and fast.

The final step in stove setup is stabilizing the pipe. A couple of feet of heavy or braided wire attached to small wooden toggles allows you to snug the pipe up to the pipe picket or ridgepole without removing your mittens. In this way, the pipe is made solid at the stove end by the collar, at the top end by the wire and perhaps to a small degree where it passes through the thimble in the tent wall. Such solidity breeds confidence when a night gale arises or one must pitch camp in a windy setting.

Typically, a good stove will be made of 22-gauge steel. This is fairly lightweight, but also reasonably durable. Lighter gauges may yield a fine featherweight stove, but such stoves burn out relatively quickly and need replacement. At the other extreme are stoves with greater longevity but at the cost of additional weight. 18-gauge steel is the thinnest that can be welded with certainty, and fine airtight stoves can be made by people willing to do custom work.

We have had a number of stoves made of 22-gauge that have been going strong for nearly ten years. With all the pipe inside them, they weigh in at 23 pounds. Currently on the market are some state-of-the-art titanium tent stoves complete with airtight doors, side shelves and telescoping stovepipe that weigh 12 pounds or less. Regardless of how you choose to balance longevity with weight and expense, if there are four people for every tent and stove, there will be only three to five pounds of stove per person per tent group. Efficiency prevails.

One factor that influences the commercial availability of trail stoves has to do with the excessively litigious times in which we find ourselves. Trail stoves are a product-liability nightmare and are, in many states, illegal to sell. Manufacturers are caught in a web of regulations and must attempt to protect themselves from that portion of humanity that is comprised of people who would sue the providers of equipment if accidents occur, yet not admit their own stupidity and lack of judgment. Such possibilities are at the root of laws that require stovemakers to stamp absurdities such as HOT WHEN IN USE on their products.

There are no safety features on trail stoves, nor should there be. The assumption is that users are endowed with common sense and know-how. It is also assumed that if infants or small children are around, a grownup or two will watch and train them.

Sale of trail stoves is also illegal on environmental grounds in some areas. The stoves have no secondary gas burners or other pollution-reduction features. There need not be for two reasons. One is that a trail stove often burns secondary gases right in the pipe. On a cold night you can see and hear a jet of blue flame shooting a few feet beyond the end of the pipe as the smoke is burned. The other reason is that trail stoves are not used in great concentration but are spread over vast northern areas. It's hard to regard such minuscule amounts of smoke as pollution.

Regulations applied too broadly have caused many smaller stove companies to fold. Recall, for example, those inexpensive, oval-shaped sheet-steel stoves that nearly every rural hardware store used to carry. For years they were unadorned, inexpensive, functional stoves. Then they became hard to find for a while, and when they returned, a telling change was evident. Now a second sheet of steel riveted to the side carried numerous warnings, regulations and a host of disclaimers. A few years later, the stoves vanished entirely. Suddenly, thanks to a long line of bickering, belly-aching insurance agents, underwriters and lawyers, it was impossible to heat an ice-fishing shack, or a shop or any other small space simply and economically.

With luck, the remaining sources of trail stoves will survive. With even greater luck, new sources may come into being without, we hope, having to go underground. In a pinch, we can, like many sourdoughs and homesteaders, become adept at making our own stoves out of fuel drums, lard pails, honey tins and other discarded sheet metal. But just in case, court a sheet-metal worker willing to do custom work.

Stove Setup

Once you have acquired a trail stove, a few guidelines will help you set it up. First, position it 18 to 20 inches away from the canvas walls of the tent. In addition, the portion of the tent that surrounds the stove area should be well staked and even reinforced with a short picket or two driven into the snow just inside the wall to prevent the fabric from blowing in toward the stove.

Arrange the firewood around the stove so that the wood provides a flat surface that can double as a table-top. A floor of firewood under the stove not only prevents the snow underneath from melting but also provides a warming tray for plates of food. You can even bake the topside of a bannock under there and free up the frying pan for something else. Likewise, the

A stainless steel stove heating coffee on top and baking bread in the attached oven.

wood around the stove prevents snow from melting and simultaneously reflects heat into the living space, where recently chilled campers happily absorb it.

In the case of a tent with a kitchen pit, lean wood upright all along the edges of the pit. This prevents melt-back and is most important along the front edge of the sleeping platform.

If you line the inside bottom of the stove with billets of firewood before lighting the fire, you will prolong the life of the steel. By the time this lower layer of wood burns, there will be enough ashes to insulate the bottom of the stove from the intense heat of the coals. Most stoves are double bottomed, but this extra care will delay the inevitable burnout. The sides of the stove will often glow orange while the fire burns, and the areas with frequent hot spots will be the first to crack and fail.

Over time, trail stoves will warp, wrinkle and change. This is unavoidable in a lightweight stove that has seen long service.

Stove Use

Firewood should be cut in 12- to 15-inch lengths. This is easier to split even when knotty or full of twisted grain, but the main reason is to keep the fire in the forward portion of the stove. As wood is added, coals and partly burned wood get

pushed toward the rear and may need to be raked forward occasionally. With wood significantly shorter than the stove this tendency is reduced. Since the flame responds to the strong draw of the stovepipe, it will heat the entire surface area of the stove, even though the full length of the firebox is not jammed with wood.

Maintaining an even blast of heat is best done by adding two or three sticks of wood frequently, rather than letting the fire burn down and then adding a bunch of wood to fill the stove all at once. It takes vigilance to load a stove lightly and often, and it is hard to be attentive all the time with other things going on, but such care will be rewarded.

Fuel for the trail stove is always needed so splitting and sawing wood are daily tasks.

Otherwise, the stove will get excessively hot during the final blast of the last coals. This will be followed by rapid cooling, at which point new wood will take a few minutes to reach a level of combustion sufficient to throw heat to the far reaches of the tent. Both cooking and the comfort of your companions suffer slightly each time this occurs.

When it is time to remove the stove in the morning, it is handy to have a small amount of firewood left over. Put a few billets in the snow outside to provide a table for the stove once the coals are emptied out. Also, you might need a few pieces of wood to separate the pipe from the collar just before carrying the stove out.

Enlist another person to hold the tent door out of the way, or tie it up so that the hot stove will not contact tent fabric as you pass through the door. Dump the ashes and coals in the snow downwind of the camp, and place the stove on the leftover wood so it can cool in the air without contacting the snow. Snow on a hot stove stresses the metal. If you leave the hot heap of coals and ashes burning at the edge of the site, you have a good place to burn paper trash without risking a bit of paper ash landing on, and possibly burning holes in, the tent fabric. It is also a good place to warm hands that may get cold while taking down camp and loading toboggans, a process that involves baring of hands.

Stoves with legs that fit brackets can be carried and emptied using the legs as handles. Legless stoves can often be outfitted with extremely heavy wire handles for use during the emptying process, or failing that, you can lift the stove with extra pieces of wood and tip the coals out that way. In all cases you may need to touch fairly hot metal, so wear mittens with leather shells. Fancy synthetics will melt instantly and can cause serious injury.

The final note on stove use has to do with where the pipe passes through the tent fabric. People who use tents and stoves are about

A stovepipe wired to the ridgepole of a wall tent. Toggles on the wire make the job easy for someone wearing mittens.

equally divided regarding their preferences. However, the tents of virtually everyone who chooses to go through the roof show galaxies of spark holes in the fly or roof. You would be well advised to favor a thimble placed in the wall or gable end.

CARE OF TENTS & STOVES

The difficulty of acquisition, the expense of raw materials and custom work, and the often unreliable nature of sources of good tents and stoves should give you high incentive to care zealously for your trail equipment.

Tent Care

Although cotton has a nearly unlimited lifespan with proper care, it can be totally ruined in one episode of carelessness. Because of this, those of us lucky enough to have tents made of four-ounce Egyptian cotton are fanatical about proper drying and storage.

The best cotton for the winter trail is loom-state, which means it has no chemical fungicides or fire retardants to weaken the cloth. Even treated tents mildew beyond repair with improper care. Therefore it is imperative that you dry all parts of the tent after each use and store them in a dry, secure environment between trips and over the intervening seasons.

After spending a substantial amount per yard on cloth, and having perhaps paid someone for the sewing, you could easily have a tent valued at more than a couple of weeks pay. Pulling such a tent out of storage only to find that it had been damp when stored or stored in a moist place and is now a gray, rotting mass of mildew, makes suicide attractive.

If you discover only a few spots of mildew, you can wash the affected areas with a mild bleach solution to kill the growth. If the problem covers a wider area, you can put the whole tent in a tub of bleach solution or wash it in mild solution in an industrial-size washing machine. Go easy on the bleach, however—too strong a wash will weaken the fabric.

If you plan to use tents made of lightweight Egyptian cotton in the warmer seasons, you will need to spray the fly with a water repellent at the start of each season. Four-ounce cloth lacks the mass to swell and become watertight the way heavier canvas automatically does. Although there are a number of silicone-based sprays on the market, we have found only Camp Dry, a product of the Kiwi Brands, totally effective. It provides great waterproofing without introducing stiffness, weight or a gunky feeling to the cloth. For heavier canvas cloth, durable Nikwax waterproofing can be soaked or painted on the fabric.

To maintain maximum breathability, you will want to spray only the fly, and leave the walls and roof alone. Since wind pants and anoraks are for stopping wind only, you should not spray them at all.

Heavier cloth may not need to be sprayed, although if you will be using the fly by itself as a rain tarp during canoeing season, you may wish to beef it up anyway. That way, if you must pitch in the rain, take down in the rain and set up again in the rain, the process of rolling and packing for travel will not break the surface tension of the cloth in a manner that might create drip spots. Even treated material should not be touched on its dry side during rain, or a drip spot might be established.

Marketers of nylon would have us believe that such maintenance procedures are a "problem" that nice, lightweight nylon solves. Don't be fooled. Nylon is lighter, but it stretches out of shape when used in flies and tarps, and loses its ability to be pitched tightly. Both waterproof coating and nylon break down through solar exposure within a few years. Nylon burns, melts, holds odors and does not breathe fast enough under adverse conditions to control condensation. What's more, although not as likely, it too can be ruined by mildew and improper storage.

Stove Care

After purchasing or making a stove, there are several things you will want to do before using it in the field. If it is manufactured of galvanized sheet steel, put a few sections of pipe on it and burn a hot fire in it in the open air. The poisonous gases in the zinc will burn off, and the surface will then be ready for a coat of stove paint or blacking. After the blacking, or if the stove comes already blacked, light another blaze in the stove in the same way. This bakes on the blacking and liberates the horribly acrid fumes.

In the course of a trip, not much will happen to a stove. You will want to avoid melting snow onto the hot metal by letting it cool on a few billets of wood before packing it on a toboggan. And in canoe season, you may want to protect it during transport in foul weather by carrying it in a marine canvas sack. It is not the occasional wettings that stress the steel. By far the worst culprit is rust that develops while the stove is in storage. Field use keeps rust at bay, because every time the stove heats up, any moisture evaporates.

Problems arise when the stove is stored between seasons or between trips. A small heap of ashes left in the corners from the last dumping of hot coals may hold moisture and initiate rusting. Damp storage areas encourage the spread of rust. Once the process starts, it continues, and if storage lasts for months on end, erosion and damage can occur.

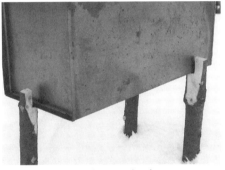

An Indian method of making stove legs from green spruce. Notches cut into the legs ensure complete stability.

Annual blacking of the stove, dry storage or even a light oil coating will all prolong the life of the steel. Blacking compounds are available at any stove shop. We have found wax-based blacking to be superior to stove paint. Butcher's or Rutland brand are known to be very good. Before blacking, scrub the surface of the stove with steel wool. Afterward, and before you use the stove in the field, remember to burn the blacking as described above.

Stove legs made from sheet metal folded at a 90-degree angle. They fit inside the stove for transport, and have been cut away to reduce weight and notchecd slightly for more stability when perched on the floats.

Over time, small cracks may develop in the sides, where the stove most frequently glows when in use. These can be patched for a while with furnace cement, thereby prolonging the life of the stove. As soon as the stove begins to leak too much air and spit sparks out through the cracks, it is time to get a replacement. It is bad enough when a leaky stove shoots a spark that burns a hole in an expensive winter sleeping bag or melts a hole in the pad you sleep on, but these are at least repairable inconveniences. Far more daunting is the possibility of a tent fire and total loss of equipment.

SEMIPERMANENT TENTS

If you are wintering over or planning to spend a long time at one site, there are embellishments that will improve tent living above and beyond anything a nomad can experience.

You may want to pitch camp much as you would for a night on the trail. However, select a site for maximum shelter from all directions since the weather and force of the wind will change from night to night. Plan access to resources with the longer term in mind. Make especially sure that you have access to an adequate supply of standing dead firewood. Often you will find just such a camp in the shelter of green woods, adjacent to an area where a lightning strike has left a swath of fire-killed trees.

Bough Floors

Where a night on the trail will rely on Therm-a-Rests or foam pads for insulation, a more permanent camp is much enhanced by a full balsm fir- or spruce-bough floor. Among native people, a well-laid floor of black spruce tips is a matter of pride and expertise. Unlike more southern species of spruce, the worst of which smell like urine, black spruce is fragrant, and the needle clusters are fine and neat. A well-laid floor is springy, clean and inspiring. Under the groundsheet of the sleeping section there will be no need to change the boughs, but in high-use areas around the stove and kitchen you will want to add a new layer perhaps every week or so.

Bough floors are, of course, anathema to those of us who learned our camping skills in overused areas, fragile alpine regions or parks and so-called "wilderness" areas surrounded by developed or ruined land. The point here is appropriateness rather than dogma. If cutting boughs seems inappropriate, don't make a bough floor. On the other hand, if you are somewhere in the subarctic bush, hundreds of miles from anyone and among millions upon millions of spruces, you probably won't get a ride to hell on a lightning bolt if you use a few boughs. On the contrary, you might feel as though you've arrived in heaven when you recline in the cushy fragrance of a floored tent.

A bough floor is the ultimate in convenience. Bathwater runs through it into the snow below. A sump hole for dirty water can be maintained in the boughs near the stove. Crumbs, crud and detritus sift through and are eventually covered by the new weekly layer of boughs. Visually, the imbricate patterns resulting from the layering are beautiful, sensuous and calming. And of course, the padding, insulation and freshness of a bough floor is nothing short of magnificent.

If you are still troubled by the environmental impact, consider that you select boughs only from the branch tips that are in reach from the ground. The two branchlets below the break will then become dominant and take over the role of the terminal sprig. Your floor is organic, biodegradable, native to the region and no tree was killed to make it. Only the sharpest of observers will detect which trees you tipped, and then only if they should find the same site within the same year.

Permanent Wall Tents

Permanent tents usually have another level of structure. Not only are the tent and fly supported by a spruce-pole framework, but the entire tent might be pitched over low log or wooden walls and have a full-fledged floor, furniture and all the accoutrements of a standard dwelling except that it is smaller and largely fabric.

Until recently, such dwellings were common on northern native reserves, scattered throughout the bush or in the construction camps of northern resource developers. Although less common now with the advent of government housing on reserves, bigger and more powerful aircraft that can deliver modular housing units to construction sites and fewer individuals truly living in the bush, there are still plenty of homesteaders, trappers and oddballs who prefer the wall-tent life.

Since 1987, we have lived in a permanent wall tent for the simplicity, convenience and pleasure of it. Despite our knowledge of the native people we visited each year and others we knew who were tent dwellers, we had never considered living in a permanent wall tent. Something in our culture overruled the idea. Instead, we started out "temporarily" ensconced in our tent while establishing an office space that might include living quarters. None of that happened with any speed, and, in the interim, we realized how comfortable and simple life had become. As years passed and we improved our home tent, we realized that we had no desire for more conventional lodgings. Why disrupt such a good system?

Eventually, we bought land. There we built a facility that contained our office, guiding equipment, a small shop and a meeting-and-food-preparation area for the

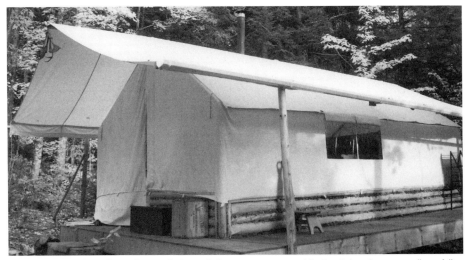

This taut, bright, 12-by-20-foot wall tent pitched on a platform sports an oversized fly that shelters the tent as well as a full-length deck.

67

trips. From there, a trail leads to a river and our permanent home tent. We continue to heat with wood, run one gas light and a three-burner range with propane and illuminate the rest with kerosene-fueled Aladdin lamps. Our neighbors probably find this wildly puzzling. We find it entirely satisfying.

The walk to our phone-free, power-grid-free and annoyance-free tent is just long enough to forget the demands of business. At home, we are in command of our destiny, limited only by our choices and dreams.

The walk in the reverse direction is just long enough to plan the day and readjust ourselves to the superstructure of the mainstream and the requirements of business. We play the game to the degree we must, but that length of trail is important. It is the zone between our public and private lives, between the world as we want it and the world as society decrees it. Like coyotes whose home range includes the edges of towns, we live both close to, and yet remote from, the "civilized" world.

Most permanent tents reflect the nature of local materials as well as proximity to the services and products of towns or outposts. There are tents in the Canadian and Alaskan bush that are supplied by airplane and have generators, refrigeration and all the comforts of home. Fly-in fishermen and hunters stay there quite luxuriously. Considering the near-town location of our tent, we are, by comparison, rather primitive.

The floor is plywood, and the low log walls all around are chinked with moss. The tent is pitched so that the bottom edge of the canvas walls covers the top log along which the whole system is tacked. Thus the four-foot tent walls are increased to five and a half feet when log walls are factored in. There is partial internal framing with spruce poles, as well as an external frame that supports the fly system.

In addition to a regular cotton fly, we place a woven synthetic fly over this during the winter, which slips the snow whether we are home or not. While we are up north for several months each winter, we need not worry about the snow-load at home.

Two disadvantages of the synthetic fly are its noisiness in wind and rain and its tendency to deteriorate enough in a single year to require replacement. It is easy enough to replace, but the throwaway syndrome that surrounds the world of synthetics is troubling.

At first we used our ears and noses for windows and went outside if we wanted to see. Then we got a roll of that heavy clear plastic used to cover storm windows, and, with a pocketknife and needle and thread, went about the tent and installed windows. These proved to be very durable and wonderful.

Unlike nomadic tents that are served by small and simple trail stoves, a permanent tent needs a much larger airtight stove that can be regulated with some precision. Weight matters only in the initial move, so a larger, heavier range can be lugged to the site in pieces or brought in over the snow. Our stove is big enough to hold a load of logs all night. A sheet-metal shield protects the log wall adjacent to the stove. Tent dwellers tend to keep their homes hot compared to people in houses, and winter visitors often wilt in the heat. We, of course, plunge into hypothermia when we visit their homes and embarrass ourselves by leaving our coats on and begging for hot tea by the gallon.

TENT LIVING

Ease of heating is entirely related to the smallness of space. Since the canvas has an R-factor at or near zero, overall insulation is not a primary concern. Rather, we insulate in a site-specific way: the bed is well insulated and in winter has a down comforter over the blankets. Snow is banked up to the top of the log walls, but other than that, temperature is maintained by stove management.

Tents lose heat fast after the fire goes out, but they heat up fast when a fire is lit. When we're home in winter, the fire rarely goes all the way out. It may be shut down to maintain minimal warmth if we are at the office all day, then boosted up for meal times and the evening. At bedtime, we shut it down so that we don't bake as we sleep. A large kettle of water on the stove humidifies the atmosphere. By adding cloves, cedar boughs and a variety of herbs or spices to the water, we can create a festive, pleasant aroma.

When you leave a tent for more than a day in winter, you simply empty all water containers and leave. Upon return, you refill them. In the time it takes you to walk to the water hole and back a few times, the stove warms the tent. In a building, it can take several days to heat the structure enough so that warmth is reradiated back into the living space and the place really feels warm. A tent takes 20 minutes to bring to warmth and another 20 to reach 80 or 90 degrees Fahrenheit, although we

The clean lines of peeled spruce poles and white canvas add to the snugness of a permanent wall tent.

69

typically damp the stove down before it reaches such tropical levels. Since there are no water- or drainpipes anywhere, we are never greeted by burst pipes that require time or other people and great expense to fix.

Fall, winter and spring, when the weather is cool enough to call for stove heat for at least part of the day, are the tent dweller's best seasons. Most people imagine us suffering in the dark of winter, but that is really the time of coziest and easiest living. People who try to heat large dwellings while struggling to save money on fuel are one of the North's great paradoxes. They live in long underwear, under layers of sweaters, as if there were virtue in suffering. Meanwhile, people in tents lounge in scantily clad bliss like a bunch of sybarites.

A rechargeable 12 volt power pack, in combination with an inverter that changes DC to AC, runs any twelve-volt appliance you might have. The power pack can be recharged on long drives via the cigarette lighter in your vehicle, or with accessories, via solar panels or an AC wall socket in a building connected to the local power grid.

For the tent dweller, summer is not as comfortable. The reason is humidity. Tents let the humidity in, and even if it is too warm, a siege of rain may inspire the lighting of the stove to drive the moisture away. We have to remove books the minute we are done reading them, and, of course, certain kinds of food cannot be stored too long. On days of crisp, windy high pressure, it is good to fluff things up and get some air into everything. Blankets and sheets hung outdoors on such a day come back in smelling like sunshine.

In a permanent tent, furniture, shelving and hanging hooks take on an importance that only sailors of small boats can appreciate. Organization, minimization and neatness all count. People content with disorganized heaps of stuff should avoid living within such confines. By the same token, people of a persnickety bent are much rewarded. Everything is close at hand, easy to clean and arranged for maximum yield with minimum complication. You are not neurotic just because you favor keeping things in place. When you arrive after dark, you grab matches and light lamps as if you had splendid night vision. You needn't grope for flashlights to scare off the raccoons and bears, because lights are always kept in place on the bed shelf. Everything is known the way the location of fire extinguishers should be known and thus is easy to locate and use.

Long-term tent dwelling requires a bit of care in other ways, too. Since you can't lock a tent, you will want to store valuable stuff elsewhere or in a special lockable trunk at the tent site.

To keep food from spoiling in summer, you need to have a cold-storage system. This can readily be provided through use of a spring box, icehouse, old-fashioned icebox or root cellar containing blocks of ice. The challenge of winter food storage is to keep it from freezing. Apples, oranges, potatoes, carrots, cheese and butter (in tubs) all can be stored in a gunny-sack below the ice, immersed in a local pond or lake. The water stays a constant 36 degrees Fahrenheit at a nine-foot depth. Be fore-warned that bruised foods eventually will spoil as the water gradually permeates the skin. Only store undamaged goods underwater. Or, you can store food underground, heated by the earth's constant 55 degrees Fahrenheit. If your root cellar is adequately insulated, the temperature will probably remain in the 40-degree range all winter.

In addition to guarding against spoilage, you must also be concerned with food odors that can attract everything from mice to bears. We have several metal food boxes and a screened, mouse-proof hutch for fresh foods. Dried foods are stored in large jars that keep humidity out and odors in. For the most part, our animal-proofing works—except for unusually persistent raccoons and, of course, bears. Bears can easily liberate foods from their containers and lay waste to your tent in the process. We have been lucky. We scared off the only bears that have visited us, and they did not come back. Problem bears in the bush often must be dealt with by lethal means.

But successful animal control is more a matter of cleanliness than luck. Although our cutting board must reek of garlic and onions, it and all other kitchen surfaces are wiped down after each use. Dishes are washed promptly after meals, and compost is burned or removed to a spot quite distant from the tent. Except in winter, when we can keep things frozen in containers outside, we rarely have more than three or four day's worth of fresh food on site.

Clothing storage must also be mouse- and moth-proof, and we keep our clothes, extra bedding and any cloth items in bureaus with close-fitting drawers and blocked-off backs and bottoms.

While tent dwelling affords considerable freedom and independence, regulations apply. Even trappers in remote regions have to register their lines and list their tents and cabins. In the middle of the Labrador bush, it is amusing to see a Crown Land Permit prominently posted next to a heap of peeled logs being readied for a tent frame or small tilt, as if authorities might helicopter in to check.

In towns, research local zoning and state ordinances with great care. Your tent dwelling may not seem to fit existing categories, but this may not exempt you. A little advance checking can save a lot of grief.

Beyond the rewards of convenience and practicality, dwellers in permanent tents also gain in an aesthetic way. In a tent, you live in close association with the land-scape. Even before dawn, or before you open your eyes, the pressure and smell of the air is your weather report. You can hear the world around you as keenly as if there were no walls or roof between you and your surroundings. We situated our home next to mild riffles in the river that make just enough noise to block sounds of vehicles on nearby roads, yet are quiet enough that we can hear approaching footsteps and the sounds of wildlife. Both of us would feel deprived if we did not have to fetch water, a task that provides glimpses of the river and opportunities to reflect. The necessity of hauling wood and water and supplies keeps us balanced and engaged with the basics of living. Small as these rituals may be, they constitute a calm and solid basis for dreams and doings, and the happiness that arises when the two are one and the same.

Although not for everyone, a permanent tent can provide an inexpensive, enlightening and rewarding way to live.

FINDING GOOD TENTS AND TRAIL STOVES

If you want good trail equipment but don't know where to start, try these addresses. They will at least provide a jumping-off place, if not the actual goods.

A word about 4.25-ounce Egyptian cotton. It is exceptionally light and gains strength from a thread count that exceeds 220 per inch. Because of the tight weave and fine finish, it is windproof and makes fantastic anoraks, wind pants, tents and tarps.

Ideally, you want material that is "loom-state," which means nothing has been done to it. No chemical fungicides or fire retardants have been applied, nor has it been preshrunk. Before you sew anything with it, wash it in hot water. This will take most of the instability out of the fabric and allow shrinkage to occur if it is going to.

As with any cotton, you will want to wear a dust mask while sewing; the action of the sewing machine needle liberates fine dust particles. At least loom-state dust particles do not carry chemicals that can wind up in your circulatory system.

A common fungicide ingredient, pentachlorophenol, has stirred health concerns among people who work with treated cotton, and one of our sources no longer carries the material as a result.

All commercially made tents are treated with a fire retardant and fungicide in keeping with product-liability laws. Because of this, official companies may refuse custom work with loom-state materials. If you puzzle over laws that compel manufacturers to expose both workers and consumers to potentially dangerous chemicals in the name of safety, then you may want to consider sewing your own gear of loom-state cloth as a matter of principle, as well as to acquire stronger, better, safer and less environmentally damaging products. One might ask, quite innocently, just who or what such laws are designed to protect.

USEFUL ADDRESSES

Wall Tents and Trail Stoves

For those willing to accept standard tents in heavier cotton canvas, the following companies, many of which also carry accessories such as trail stoves and fiberglass pipe thimbles, are best:

Alaska Tent and Tarp Company
529 Front Street
Fairbanks, AK 99701
907-456-6328
www.alaskatent.com

Beckel Canvas Products
2232 Southeast Clinton
Portland, OR 97202
800-237-3362
www.beckelcanvas.com

Cabela's
812 13th Avenue
Sidney, NE 69160
800-237-4444

Frost River
5555 U.S Hwy 2
Duluth, MN 55810
800-375-9394
www.frostriver.com

Peter Marques of Tentsmiths makes tents in standard weights of canvas, percale and has fabricated some from Egyptian cotton.
Tentsmiths
Box 1748
Conway, NH 03818
603-447-2344
www.tentsmiths.com

Empire Canvas sells several sizes of the Snow Trekker Tent. These come with lightweight poles and are superbly designed with the winter camper in mind.
Empire Canvas Works
P.O. Box 17
Solon Springs, WI 54873
715-378-4216
www.empirecanvasworks.com

Montana Canvas makes very high-quality tents in heavy canvas for permanent tent homes. They can do custom work with windows, screening and design.
Montana Canvas Company
P.O. Box 390
Belgrade, MT 59714
800-235-6518

Craig MacDonald is a source for Egyptian cotton as well as stoves and other equipment. He also offers excellent literature on trail skills and techniques for a small fee. For information on stoves, ask for the catalog entitled "Odawban Camping Equipment."
Craig MacDonald
RR 1
Dwight, Ontario Canada P0A 1H0
705-635-3416 (evenings)

Tent Plans

pyramid or campfire tent
(see also Appendices D & E)
David Lewis
183 Rankin Road
Buxton, ME 04093
207-929-4107
fdlmsl@sacoriver.net

Trail Stoves

(steel or titanium)

Don Kevilus makes exquisite trail stoves in steel or titanium. The Ultra Light I, for fringe season canoeing, is 10 x 10 x 18 inches and weighs 8 pounds. The 11 x 11 x 22-inch Ultra Light II will heat a 10-by-12-foot wall tent for winter travel, and weighs only 12 pounds, including legs, pipes, elbow and side shelves.

Don Kevilus
Four Dog Stove Company
25909 Variolite Street NW
St. Francis, MN 55070
763-444-9587
www.fourdog.com

For the home fabricator and tinkerer, or for general interest there is a splendid book by Ole Wik entitled *Wood Stoves—How to Make and Use Them*. Ole is highly regarded for his bush skills, and the sections on stove alternatives are of great interest to the scavenger/recycler/inventor seeking to turn "found" objects into stoves. First published in 1977, Ole's book is now out of print. It should be available through used book dealers or internet sites.

Radiant Tent Candles

Mailloux Baillargeon, Inc.
230 Rue Saint-Pierre
Saint-Constant, Quebec
Canada
514-861-8417
(Craig MacDonald sells these as well)

Off-the-Grid Items for Home

Real Goods
360 Interlocken Blvd, Suite 300
Broomfield, CO 80021-3440
800-762-7325
www.realgoods.com

Lehman's "Non-Electric Catalog" serves the Amish communities as well as others with a commitment to simple, durable goods that foster independence. Their catalog contains many items useful for remote nomadic and any off-the-grid living situations.

Lehman Hardware and Appliances
P.O. Box 41
Kidron, OH 44636
888-438-5346
www.lehmans.com

Cotton Waterproofing

If you can't find Camp Dry waterproofing spray at your local camping store, try the manufacturer:

Kiwi Brands, Inc.
447 Old Swede Road
Douglassville, PA 19518
800-523-1210
www.kiwicare.com

The Nikwax product called "Cotton Proof" is a good waterproofing for cotton tents.

Nikwax USA
P.O. Box 1572
Everett, WA 98206
800-335-0260
www.nikwax-usa.com

Chapter 4
Clothing for the Elements

CLOTHING FOR THE ELEMENTS

Just as the tent provides a breathable yet windproof envelope that holds the heat of the stove, a winter traveler's clothing provides a breathable envelope that holds and maintains the heat of the body. Unlike a tent, however, clothing introduces insulation, variability in layering and other complexities.

Where a stove functions by simply overpowering a small space with great heat, the human body generates heat at a much lower but steadier rate. Body heat can still overpower its envelope of clothing on occasion, thus needing to be vented, but on the whole it purrs along at a rather consistent level with periodic oscillations but few wild fluctuations.

The body "stove" is as fussy as the tent stove about its maintenance and fueling. Instead of timely introductions of appropriate wood, the body requires timely stokings with an appropriate balance of foods and lots of water. When you understand basic physiology, dressing for ambient conditions is easy. Similarly, understanding clothing as it relates to physiology makes it easier to maintain the "stove" effectively. With sound management, the microclimate around the body stays within a range that maximizes comfort as well as physical and mental output. To disrupt either the clothing or the food part of the system is to invite breakdown.

Overview

What is the optimal ankles-up outfit for the winter trail? Our preference is for breathable materials and natural fibers, although synthetic piles and fleeces are also suitable. Since we will not be able to mask our opinions about synthetics, we'll express them up front, trusting that you will accept them as points to consider, not as dogma.

One of the great ironies of outdoor life is perfectly symbolized by the pervasiveness of synthetic outdoor gear and clothing. Virtually every catalog that caters to the serious outdoorsperson is filled with fabrics made by petrochemical industries. A few catalogs carry token amounts of wool, silk and cotton, but for the most part it is difficult to get high-quality, natural fiber materials.

Synthetic clothing is junk. It begins as junk, and it stays junk all the way to the landfill. It is, in fact, a double negative. It wears out readily, yet it may never decompose once discarded.

A recent advertising campaign that appeared in outdoor magazines showed an attractive woman resplendent in her petrochemical finery, feeding a sheep in a scene of pastoral purity. "Let 'em keep their coats this winter," the ad copy said, implying that shearing hurts sheep and that petrochemical clothing has no negative impacts (the photo, of course, showed no oil derricks, sprawling refineries, laboratories or production facilities). A nice, rosy picture, except that the whole advertisement is pure malarkey. Such attempts to mislead promote a mediocrity of thought that should appall literate souls. To their credit, many manufacturers have been introducing pile and other synthetic garments made from recycled materials and we applaud such efforts.

To be fair, we should note that natural fibers and products made from them are not completely innocent. There is overgrazing and other improprieties in sheep raising. There are horror stories about pesticides, monocultural farming, damaging irrigation schemes and soil abuse in the growing of cotton. Woolen mills contribute their share of pollution in the production and dyeing processes. And, on a human level, history reveals all sorts of abuse of wool and cotton workers. Still, it is at least possible to produce natural fiber products responsibly, and the raw materials used are renewable. Compared to petrochemical clothing, natural fiber products are the more benign.

Aside from the political and social factors, there are also functional reasons to choose natural fibers. There is nothing in the synthetic line offered to the northern winter dweller that can't be equaled or exceeded by a natural fiber. Many synthetics function poorly when dirty. If anything is going to get dirty, it is outdoor clothing that will see long, hard use in the wilds. Although much improved by blocking agents, solar breakdown of synthetics vastly reduces the lifespan of the materials or their laminates and coatings. All synthetics melt and burn. Just ask the doctors and nurses of any burn-trauma center. They will tell you how much more seriously injured burn victims clothed in synthetics tend to be compared to those who were wearing natural fibers. Long-term burn management is an element of backcountry medicine regarded with dread by even the most experienced caregivers.

Wool clothing is de rigueur on the winter trail. It is rugged, breathable, long-lived, warm, comfy and stylish.

Just enough people in the camping community have jumped back from a gas stove flare-up minus their eyebrows and eyelashes to show that campers are not immune to burns. Just enough others have watched a sleeve or tent vestibule vaporize with terrifying speed to keep any of us from assuming that this sort of thing doesn't happen in the wilderness.

On our own guided trips with tent stoves, we have seen hats that fell from the drying line vanish, a sleeve onto which a candle fell bubble into globs of molten yuck and countless small meltdowns involving parts of sleeping bags, underwear, shirts, socks and other synthetic items.

Compared to synthetics, it takes natural fibers a long time to scorch and eventually burn. And even if they do, you can still repair the item by darning or patching.

Of course, from the marketer's standpoint, well-made natural fiber items last too long. You can't make money selling durable goods, and that, of course, is why style marketing has overtaken quality, which speaks for itself. (Only the C. C. Filson Company has made a virtue of longevity, and the result is a magnificently fine line of cottons and superior wool clothing.) Synthetics last well enough to avoid much complaint from consumers because they are rarely used hard or long. A weekend outing under optimal conditions does not stress clothing the way living in it month after month, year after year, does. Outdoor catalogs cater to professional people able to afford recreational equipment but less likely to make the time to use it. They use their equipment sporadically for the most part, and that gives the equipment the appearance of durability. Anyone can have a 20-year-old item if it is worn only ten days per year.

Manufacturers change styles with remarkable speed and spend enormous amounts of money to keep things "new" and "improved." For the moment, fashion is playing our insatiable infatuation with high tech for all it is worth, which, even by casual accounting, seems to be quite a lot. Never have so many people been in possession of so much that they don't need. Through careful marketing, the need to look the part has exceeded the practical needs of actually living the part.

To learn which clothing really functions and lasts, look to the people who work in the wildlands under sustained hard conditions. You won't find many walking catalogs. Instead, you will find a lot of battered wool, dirt-caked canvas and items recycled by patches upon patches. North Sea fishermen, loggers, miners, oil riggers, trappers and others who live and work in uncompromising conditions don't seem to care much for the usual catalog fare. This may have something to do with socioeconomic class, but it also has a lot to do with the workers knowing what lasts.

Another seldom-mentioned aspect of layering with wool is the very wide range of comfort it affords. This is because it is so breathable yet sacrifices no insulation value. After decades of observing our guests who provide us with working examples of the full range of options and combinations, we have been able to "experience" all sorts of things that we would not be bold enough to experiment with firsthand, particularly when already comfortably in possession of a system that works.

Most guests who have synthetic long underwear are too hot when active. Frequently, these folks wear their wind pants over longjohns without pants. At lunch and for rest stops, they can't recline or sit in the snow because there is no thick layer to insulate the snow from their body heat. The snow then melts, gets things wet and conducts heat away. Synthetics breathe relatively slowly so that they trap moisture that although warm enough when heated through sustained activity, cools rapidly with a shift or stop of that activity. If the wind protection is also synthetic, the situation is even more damp and uncomfortable. This quick overheating when active is always the first step to chilling and getting cold. Even when things are going as well as they can, it is due to excessive fussing, and making use of all those elaborate zippered vents in the armpits and backs—gussets and side zips that appear nowhere else but on synthetic windshell clothing. Trapped moisture is exactly why the labs producing synthetic insulation layers have gone to such extreme lengths to ensure that very fast wicking properties are part of the fabric.

Those clad in wool, by contrast, can easily shift from work to rest with minimal chilling. Wool layers have much more effective breathability that leaves little moisture to contribute to rapid cooling. Because of this wider comfort range, heavy mackinaw pants are seldom too hot. They are also thick enough so that kneeling, sitting and reclining in the snow produces little heat loss through conduction and little snow melt at contact points. The result is that wool-wearers stay warm, and their wind pants, made of light, tightly woven cotton, stay dry.

This holds true for all the little chores of camp setup and takedown, where you are frequently kneeling in the snow. Snow slips off the fine weave of cotton wind gear, and the thick underlayer of insulation minimizes melt-through, unless the snow is near the melt-freeze point anyway. Such fuss-free comfort means you are free to enjoy the break or lunch or concentrate on the task at hand.

Next time you see a lunch-stop shot in someone's slide show, you'll be able to pick out who has what for underwear as if you had X-ray vision. Those flopped comfortably in the snow are probably wearing layers of wool, and those standing with hunched shoulders and pinched expressions are probably desperately trying to heat up moisture trapped in a layer or two of synthetics.

Each year, news of the latest in synthetics is covered exhaustively in outdoor magazines. The outdoor magazine trade is almost entirely funded by advertising contracts with purveyors of synthetics, and few editors are brave enough to offend their backers. Most of what follows concerns the virtues of natural fibers, as they are rapidly being forgotten. A whole generation of outdoor enthusiasts has grown up in the age of synthetics and has no way of knowing whether alternatives exist or what they might be.

THE BASIC SYSTEM

Beyond underwear, bandannas and such things as sock and hat liners, your kit for a northern trip is spare. You will need two full sets of longjohns, two light wool shirts and two pairs of wool pants so that you'll have something to wear on laundry days or in emergencies when you need dry clothes. For layering, you'll need one medium- and one heavyweight wool shirt, and for wind, an anorak and a pair of wind pants. A thick down- or synthetic-filled parka covers lunch, rest stops and emergencies, and serves as a quilt over sleeping bags. Moccasins, rubber boots, liners and socks for the feet (see Chapter 1), mittens for the hands and a good hat complete the system.

This system remains the same whether your trip lasts a week or several months. On a longer trip, the only difference is in the number of times you launder your primary and secondary layers.

While high-elevation mountaineers may require synthetics for lightness, ease of drying with no source of heat and functioning in sustained marginal conditions, the northern dweller seldom encounters such requirements—certainly not on a voluntary basis.

The Primary Layer

What you choose for panties, undershorts or breast support is up to you. Even in the no-cotton-in-contact-with-skin world of winter camping, it is "legal" to wear cotton underwear. Cotton undies are comfortable and, relegated to such a small surface area, are neither inconvenient nor dangerous.

Long underwear is the important layer, because it provides insulation. When selecting long underwear, consider comfort, odor retention and washability. You are likely to be in it not just 24 hours a day, but perhaps for days or weeks on end.

Mention of woolen long underwear conjures images of thick, bristly, unbrushed, material that feels like it may have thistles, strands of barbed wire or whatever else the sheep rolled in still in it. Fortunately, all the woolen long underwear we have used is very fine, very comfortable and superbly protective.

Ullfrotte of Sweden and two firms in Canada make fantastic woolen longjohns. Both Windsor Wear and Stanfield's of Nova Scotia offer a soft, finely woven wool longjohn that sets the standard for warmth and comfort. Both offer a heavy option that is almost bristly, but very warm for extreme conditions. The heavy stuff must be washed first to soften it up for comfort. The lighter varieties come in a durable yet soft, gossamer fabric so fine that you can almost see through it. Ullfrotte makes men's and women's styles in various colors, all with long, lumbar-warming tails. Zip necks are also available.

By virtue of its softness and the airspace within its weave, long underwear holds body heat at skin level while passing all moisture through as a gas. If you exert to the point of sweating, the moisture wicks to the outer surface, away from the skin. There, moisture does not cool the skin by conduction, although there is probably slight cooling by evaporation.

If you wear long underwear full time, perhaps for days or weeks, it is beneficial if the material does not hold body odors. Wool does not. It absorbs odor slowly and does not seem to magnify it. Rather than worsening as the days go by, odor stays at the level reached within the first few days of wear.

Wool has other advantages, too. It does not readily melt or burn should it contact the stove or should a candle fall on it. It is easily darned and patched to prolong its life almost indefinitely. And it washes well, both in the field and by machine. The relative drying speeds of different materials are of little consequence because a tent's drying areas are so hot. (A typical ridgeline temperature in a wall tent while the stove is going is about 130 degrees Fahrenheit.)

Still, there are people who, to varying degrees, are allergic to wool and can't use it against their skin even in its softest weaves. Silk longjohns provide a wonderful liner to prevent wool contact. Silk is available through many catalog companies, including Wintersilks, Inc.

The world of synthetic long underwear is packed with offerings in a dizzying array of polymers and fibers that are further confused by a variety of different brand names. Presumably the idea is to keep the consumer from finding out that despite some differences these fibers are all similar, and that the mystical properties touted by the advertisements are all essentially the same on a practical level.

Synthetics are warm, dry quickly, wick moisture away and are breathable to varying degrees. The early generations of synthetics were notorious for the vengeance with which they held and perhaps even magnified body odors. Laundering with dangerously powerful detergents could not erase the stench. For some reason, the public accepted this as the price of "improvement" over natural fibers. Recently, most companies have announced stink-reduction breakthroughs. There are many claims of improvement, but an improvement can be a far cry from a solution.

We favor a long underwear set composed of a separate top and bottom. Union suits are inconvenient in the field and suffer from an inability to mix and match parts. For example, you might choose to launder the tops about twice as frequently as you would the bottoms. Furthermore, fiddling with a drop seat beneath an anorak in a high wind just to go to the bathroom leaves a lot to be desired, especially when compared to the quick drop-down and pull-up of regular pants.

For the top, be sure to choose a cut that has tails long enough to lap over your hips completely and thereby eliminate drafts. This effectively deletes the claim that one-piece suits are warmer.

As longjohns age, the sleeves may develop a tendency to work up the forearms during routine activity. If you get tops with long enough sleeves, you can cut a hole through the cuff in line with your thumb. By inserting your thumb through the hole, you can hold your sleeve to full length with security, comfort and freedom of movement. If the legs tend to climb your calves, you can sew onto the cuff a stirrup that passes under the arch of your foot.

The other element of the primary layer is socks. As with long underwear, socks come in different weights of wool, silk and a variety of synthetics. Common combinations are a pair or two of wool ragg socks, or a silk sock under a bulky wool sock or any suitable combination of the synthetics. At least one layer should be bulky and full of air to maximize heat retention. All socks should be breathable in the extreme, and some synthetics are not. It is unlikely that you will wear more than two pairs at any one time, and many people will be content with one bulky pair. (For more information on socks, liners and insoles, see "Footwear" in Chapter 1.)

Secondary Layer

This layer is essentially shirt and pants. The shirt should be lightweight wool cut large enough to fit over the longjohn top. A light wool dress shirt of up to 13-ounce cloth is suitable for this. If you can't find a light one, a medium-weight up to 18 ounces will be fine.

Wool pants can be heavy. The best available are the Filson Mackinaw Pants, which are constructed of a tightly woven 24-ounce cloth. They cost more than $100 a pair, but they last three times as long as the next best option and thus are actually cheaper. Johnson Woolen Mills carries Malone Pants made of 28-ounce cloth and Bemidji Woolen Mills makes the Lumberjack pants that are 30-ounce wool. Both are nice and heavy but more loosely woven. Both are a reasonable buy but, compared to Filson pants, wear out relatively quickly. The loose weave is less wind-resistant and can pack up with snow.

Frost feathers on the outermost heavy wool shirt reveal the importance of breathable insulation. At minus 29 degrees Fahrenheit, even the relatively light work of sawing firewood raised heat and moisture, which should be vented as a gas.

There are a number of lighter woolen pants, and those with a tight whipcord weave are very good. Since they are lighter, there is less insulation, but they are entirely suitable. The tighter weave and harder finish of such pants make them more abrasion-resistant and they slip snow much better than the fuzzier thick weaves. In addition to winter service, they function well as northern canoeing pants, and the tight weave holds less dirt and grime.

Any of the synthetic pile or fleece shirts and pants are comparable in insulation value. We don't know what the longevity is, only that wear will show first in the knees and crotches of the pants, just as it does with wool. The finish on most synthetic garments is very soft and prone to snagging and catching. While wool can be worn as an outer layer when there is no need for wind protection, it is better to cover pile garments with a shell material, both to prevent catching in brush and to prevent snow from filling the weave and catching on the fuzzy little filaments that sprout with wear.

Additional Layers

A complete outfit requires two more wool shirts, preferably one medium- and one heavyweight shirt. The medium-weight shirt must be large enough to be worn over the lighter one without tightness or binding. Likewise, the heavy shirt must fit over the medium shirt. Or, one may choose a wool vest for the medium layer. This keeps your torso snug while ensuring freedom of arm movement. In cold conditions, you may wear all three at once, and you will need full range of movement. A medium shirt is generally 16- or 18-ounce cloth; a heavy wool fabric might be 20-, 24- or even 26-ounce cloth. In addition to the air trapped within the weave of each layer of cloth, you will have airspace between each of the layers. The result is warm, breathable bulk. Again, layers of the synthetic options provide the same service.

At this point you have a full set of working clothes. Much of the time, you will wear considerably less to avoid overheating.

WIND PROTECTION

The wool items mentioned thus far are for insulation. Even those with a tight weave will not do well in a wind of any power or duration. For wind, you need a tightly woven or coated fabric, and it need not be heavy. The best but least available option is to have an anorak and wind pants made from the four-ounce Egyptian cotton that tents are made of. This cloth is completely breathable yet stops wind.

Gore-Tex, nylon and coated nylon all stop wind admirably, but none are breathable in a practical sense. The two varieties of nylon don't breathe at all. And although Gore-Tex and any of the other "breathable" laminates technically "breathe," they do not do so fast enough during exertion and in effect behave as a vapor barrier. Proof of this is the layer of frost that coats the inside of these materials whenever they are used as wind protection in winter. Fortunately, this is not a problem since your layering system underneath the wind shell will keep the frost at enough of a distance to preserve your comfort even if a layer gets slightly damp. Most of the frost can be shaken out of the garment before entering the tent, and there the heat of the stove will quickly evaporate the rest. The only measurable inconvenience is that these garments need drying time and space, whereas cotton wind shells do not collect moisture in the first place.

Synthetic wind protection is readily available through all catalogs. Most of it is functional since it is built for the extreme exposure climbers encounter. It is thus suitable for the similar wind, blowing drift and low temperatures that northern travelers encounter.

Keep in mind that anoraks involve a lot of careful design. The best designed ones are those that were developed in the areas most crucial for function: the subarctic and Arctic regions. Fortunately for snow walkers, modern companies have imitated these classic designs (see addresses at end of chapter). However, those available in most catalogs all stop wind, but as climbing gear first and foremost, they are cut too small and too tight and often have a zipper front.

The best wind pants have full-length zippers on the outside of each leg, which allows them to be put on or taken off without removing skis, snowshoes or footwear.

The best anoraks are made in pullover format, are quite voluminous and long, and have large sleeves. If the sleeves are large enough, the arms can be withdrawn while wearing the garment. This allows you to do two important things without exposing yourself to the wind. Completely inside the shelter of your anorak, while the temporarily empty sleeves flap like flags in a gale, you can add a shirt if you are too cold, or delete a shirt if you are overheating. This may seem a small detail, but if you are in open country or on a huge lake with no access to shelter, you can thermoregulate with virtually no exposure. Likewise, you can squat down completely inside your anorak if the skirt section is big enough and go to the bathroom in the same conditions. The anorak in such cases functions as a small portable tent. Even a breeze at 20 below zero will make these features highly desirable. A gale at the same temperature will make them a necessity.

Even on the coldest days, thawed water is available when the water bottle is carried between the primary and secondary layers of clothing.

An anorak should have a good, deep hood; the best of hoods have a ruff of natural fur around them. Natural fur such as coyote, wolf or wolverine slips the frost from your breath very well, whereas synthetic furs don't. The long hair of such a ruff traps calm air around the face and thus keeps a warmer microclimate near the skin. If you are reluctant to support the fur industry, you might find at a thrift shop an old coyote or European badger coat that will yield a number of hood ruffs. Such recycling also saves an enormous amount of money.

A bellows throat gusset that can be closed up in a powerful headwind or vented in milder conditions should be part of the anorak design. Just below the gusset, it is handy to have a large, deep pocket that can accommodate a compass, maps or other small, light objects that you might need during the day. Such pockets should have a good storm flap to block blowing snow.

Our Egyptian cotton anoraks have diagonal slash pockets, each of which has a second flap that allows access to the inside of the garment. In this way you can reach your shirt pockets and any items, such as snack food, that might be there. (Appendix C offers instructions and patterns for making an anorak designed by Sally Robbins.)

The most important point in favor of having pockets all the way through to the layers underneath is that they allow access to a water bottle stashed in the warmth between shirt and longjohns or first and second shirts. By slipping the bottle from beneath your shirt layers and out through the slash pocket slits, you can drink your own water or share with someone else who may have run out. The lanyard that holds the bottle loops around your neck and must be long enough to wend its way to the outside of your layering system. Not only does such a system promote adequate hydration, but the vision of your companions pausing to nurse themselves and each other like some band of nivian primates makes hilarious photos.

The pleasures of the winter trail are best perceived while snug in a well-managed layered system of clothing, covered by a light, breathable, windproof anorak.

It is wise to have a closable gusset at the end of each sleeve. Velcro or buttons work well, although Velcro works poorly when filled with powder snow. Depending on the type of mittens you have, you may need the sleeve fully open to cover the mitten cuff. Or, if your mittens have gauntlets that cover the forearms, you may want the anorak sleeve to go inside the gauntlet by snugging the wrist closure tight. In any case, sleeve gussets let you vent the sleeves in mild conditions, or close them up tight when the wind and cold are brutal.

To go along with a full-volume anorak, you will need a sash six or eight feet long. In addition to choosing a colorful one that looks dashing and voyageuresque, the sash actually has many uses. In extreme conditions, it snugs the anorak close to your inner layers and prevents the air exchange that would occur at the throat gusset, sleeve ends and via the skirt edges below. Trapped air is simply lightweight insulation that you can use, but you don't really carry it with you as equipment.

(By contrast, in mild conditions that still require a wind shell you can leave the sash off, open your gussets and perhaps throw your hood back. The normal movement of walking will suck and whoosh and circulate air through the space between your wind garment and the layers beneath. This vents moisture and cools you by introducing fresh cold air all the time. Many people refer to this process as the anorak's "chimney effect.")

When working with extreme loads or in hauling conditions that require great effort, the sash can be tightened and function as a belt that confines your stomach muscles during great strain. If your sash is wide and made of wool, you can create a scarf or cowl around your head and hood to double protection in extreme cold or violent wind.

Finally, the sash creates a belt to hang stuff on while simultaneously making a pocket of the entire anorak. If you are overheating somewhat, but not enough to shed a full layer, you can use your head and hands as radiators to get rid of excess heat. Removing your hat cools down your whole body; the same goes with removing your mittens. For a short cooling spell, you may choose to simply carry the items in your hand. For a longer session, it is convenient to hang your hat by tucking it under your sash, or to pin your mitten cuffs together with a blanket pin and hang the mittens, one over and one under the sash. Of course, in mild conditions much above zero, you won't be wearing your sash or anorak, and in such a case you can tuck mittens and hat under the lash lines of the toboggan.

HEADS & HANDS

The entire system of clothing and thermoregulation is designed to maximize comfort and output. Everything you know about proper food intake, hydration and layering has to do with keeping your body functioning at its peak. If this is done well, you needn't think about circulation, oxygenation and metabolism. Your head and hands, both vitally important on the winter trail, can then do their best work.

Head and hands share several similarities. Both function best when circulation is at its peak. Both are highly vascular, requiring a lot of oxygenated blood. Both are extremities located some distance from the body core, and both are great radiators of heat due to their extensive vasculature and capillary networks close to the skin.

Because of this, the winter walker must think carefully about mitten types and hat/hood/scarf combinations. Again, breathable is best. The primary layer requires some bulk to trap air for adequate insulation. Beyond that, one can choose additional insulation layers and a shell material as needed.

For maximum warmth, wear mittens, not gloves. Gloves keep fingers separated and therefore cool. Insulated gloves also severely limit dexterity.

HYPOTHERMIA & FROSTBITE

Hypothermia is the dropping of the temperature of the body core. Chilling starts slowly but is detectable to informed observers and easily reversed. If the early stages are not responded to, a serious escalation may occur, and a full-scale medical emergency will exist.

Head and hands can lose heat rapidly, and one of the body's responses to unchecked heat loss is to protect the core that houses the vital organs. By automatic constriction of the vasculature to the extremities, the body curtails the flow of warm blood to the limbs, hands, feet and head from whence it would return to the core in a chilled state and further reduce the core temperature. This mechanism allows the body to survive even if feet or hands are literally frozen solid.

In an emergency, the body "knows" that it can't afford to wait for a distant brain to catch on and correct the situation. Compared to the heart, lungs and other organs within the core, the brain is considered dispensable. Unfortunately, judgment and motor skills are what are needed most to reverse the onset of hypothermia, and these are the first functions that fail. As mentation drops, the victim can no longer recognize the decline or perform the functions necessary for recovery. Without companions to observe a sudden lack of coordination or inability to answer simple questions, the person is doomed. You have two chances in a group—one if you are solo. If you are alone and miss the signs that occur early enough for self-recovery, you are out of luck. If you are with a group, your companions can still help if they catch the symptoms in time.

Frostnip is the surface freezing of skin (first-degree frostbite). On the winter trail, this is most likely to occur on noses, cheekbones, earlobes and fingertips. Windchill is the usual mechanism for frosting the face, while most finger frosting is the result of conduction through direct contact. Touching metal with a bare finger can create a white frost spot.

Everyone is likely to experience frostnip a few times while learning to manage layering systems effectively. It is part of the pathway to becoming smart, preventive and vigilant and is initially forgivable among beginners.

The cure for frostnip is simple. Thaw the frost spot. This can be done by placing a warm fingertip or whole hand over the affected area until the skin returns to normal flush. It takes a matter of seconds. Never rub the area, as ice crystals can rupture cell walls. And never, ever, rub snow on the area.

If frostnip goes undetected and underlying tissue becomes frozen (second-degree frostbite), then you have a more serious problem. After warming the area, it is likely that a fluid-filled blister will occur. Such frosting is treatable in the field but will be accompanied by sensations of itching, burning or pain and the skin will invariably turn brown and slough off. Keep the area clean and watch for infection.

If an extremity such as a foot freezes solid (third-degree frostbite), do not thaw it in the field. A trail first-aid kit would not be adequate for either the ensuing pain or the probability of systemic infection. The victim can walk on a frozen foot and thus contribute to his or her own evacuation.

Mitten liners made from knitted wool or duffel cloth provide a nice, bulky, warm layer directly on the skin (see Appendix C for patterns). Moisture from your hands can transpire to the outside air if you have soft, breathable leather shells, or will at least frost up away from the skin level if you overpower the breathability of the shell material or if it is not breathable to begin with. In this way, your hands should stay warm even at rest after a change in activity level changes the amount of heat flowing to them or being generated by them. As with one's feet, there will be no moisture at skin level to conduct precious heat away.

Different individuals need different thicknesses in mitten liners depending on how hot- or cool-handed they are. Some people do fine with a thin, knitted liner, even in extreme cold. Others may opt for thick, fluffy, boiled-wool mittens, or Dachstein mittens, which are very thick and warm. Silk or synthetic liners are available for those with wool allergies or those who use a layered system.

Leather "chopper" mitt shells are the best. The leather is breathable, abrasion resistant and not slippery on tool handles such as axes and ice chisels. Moreover, leather will not melt if you need to adjust a hot stove or stovepipe.

For people with poor circulation, chronically cold hands or Raynaud's Syndrome, it is wise to have a pair of expedition down-filled mitts as backup for extremes.

Other hand-protection strategies can often improve life on the trail. Silk gloves are a necessary part of the serious photographer's outfit. These are close-fitting and allow the manipulation of lens rings as if you were barehanded. They will work by themselves for short periods to about minus ten degrees Fahrenheit; below that, you should have a pair of fingerless gloves over the silk liners to keep your hands hot enough to allow circulation to the relatively unprotected fingertips. The thin shield of silk will prevent you from freezing your fingertips upon contact with aluminum or plastic camera parts that are at ambient temperature.

Silk or fingerless gloves can also be worn under your mittens, or alone for brief periods, for load lashing and other jobs that would otherwise require the full baring of hands.

The head is even fussier than the hands and far more sensitive to subtle nuances in thermoregulation. In dead calm and deep cold, you might throw back your hood and take off your hat to keep cool. However, if even a slight breeze rises, you may need to put your hat back on. If a gale rises, you might need a hat or even two, your hood up, goggles to protect your eyes and a scarf to protect your lower face.

One of the best hats is the balaclava. This can be worn hat-fashion, covering head and ears only, or it can be rolled down so that the neck and chin are totally covered as if inside a helmet. Balaclavas are available in wool, wool/silk blends and all synthetics. Many people get a silk balaclava liner to wear under a wool hat or even to line a full, thicker balaclava. Those with beards are well advised to get a silk-liner balaclava, as the smooth finish and tight weave prevent beard hair from freezing into the coarser weave of wool hats and scarves that cover the throat and lower face.

The Inuit of the eastern Arctic have developed a crocheted hat generically called a Chimo hat after Fort Chimo (Kuujjuaq). It is a thick hat that covers the head and ears and has a large, bulky tassel. The tassel is more than decorative as it can be placed on the windward side of the hat inside a hood and hold the hood out against the wind, maintaining airspace between hat and hood. The tassel also takes enough space so that the hood will turn with your head, rather than your hood staying in place and giving you a close-up view of its interior when you turn your head.

In addition to knitted and synthetic hats, there are fur hats that are suitable for expedition use. Mad Bomber makes a series of hats with rabbit-fur interiors and tightly woven cloth exteriors to cut the wind. A model derived from the Chinese army even has ear holes to hear through with their own little button-down flaps for really extreme weather.

Proper head and hand care requires a bit of vigilance and discipline. As conditions change, you must make adjustments immediately, either venting or adding layers. At the extreme ends of the comfort scale, speed is of the essence. You may have to vent excess heat quickly to prevent anything getting wet with sweat, or you may have to cover up quickly as the leading edge of a crisp and windy cold-front strikes.

An anorak sash holds up a pair of mittens that are fastened together with a blanket pin. The hands are bared to radiate excess heat. Likewise, the hat and goggles are temporarily removed to vent heat through the head. Carry these items in a free hand, because heat is lost quickly through a bare head, and the cycle of donning and doffing head protection is more frequent.

It is far better for everyone if you eat and drink adequately and properly, thermoregulate intelligently and take special care of your head, hands and core. Prevention is simple, convenient and expedient. If you take care of immediate concerns regarding comfort, avoiding inconvenience and preventing getting chilled, you will have automatically taken care to avoid hypothermia and frostbite. Focus on prevention, but make sure you know how to respond in an emergency.

Understanding the clothing systems that keep head, hands and heart warm goes a long way toward realizing these goals.

EYE PROTECTION

Goggles with a UV coating are essential. Even in the weakened sun of winter, snow reflects a tremendous amount of light. As February arrives, the brightness is ever more intense. We go so far as to carry both UV-coated/polarizing sunglasses and dark goggles. More than once, we have worn both while heading into the light at the end of March and early April.

The second function of goggles is wind protection. Since it may be windy on cloudy days, it is nice to have a light or medium to dark lens so that too much light isn't cut. Also, a hint of darkness often lends a little contrast in near whiteout conditions and thus improves balance and the ability to see drifts and depressions.

Even if you do not need corrective lenses, you should get goggles that are made to be worn over eyeglasses. Such large goggles will also cover most of your nose and maxillary sinuses, thus protecting them from the wind.

Cheekbones (over the maxillary sinuses) and nose are extremely susceptible to frostbite. With these areas covered by goggles, you will feel quite impervious to both frosting and excessively watering eyes. Another trick is to learn to breathe by inhaling through the mouth and exhaling through the nose. In this way, air heated in your lungs keeps your nose warm. Because your mouth is larger than your nostrils, you will take one stride during the inhale and three during the exhale. The rhythmic synchronization of pace and breath is relaxing as well as efficient and comfortable.

A mix of wind strategies (left to right): A ruffed hood and scarf in combination with a wool hat; a synthetic-filled, snug hat with ear covers and scarf; a "Chimo" hat, hood with ruff and goggles large enough to cover maxillary sinuses; and a synthetic hat, neoprene face mask and hood.

People with eyeglasses have another reason to learn to exhale through the nose. If you exhale through your mouth and your mouth is covered by a scarf or the lower portion of a balaclava, your breath will be deflected upward and coat your lenses with a layer of frost that will have to be rubbed off. One false breath and you lose visibility. Fogged and frosted glasses are the bane of the winter trail and prompt more tantrums than any other single inconvenience. Glasses wearers get extremely good at exhaling strictly through the nose. They learn to prevent fogging and frosting by having their scarf or balaclava cover the chin but not the mouth.

Traditional eye protection, made historically by natives, were "goggles" of wood, birchbark or ivory, with thin slits to look through, which cut glare. Many were blackened on the inside to further reduce light. In an emergency, these same types can be made to replace lost or broken sunglasses or goggles.

PARKAS

Each person carries a parka filled with goosedown or synthetic insulation in a stuff sack that rides on top of the load and is always accessible. During the inactivity of lunchtime, unless the weather is above zero, everyone wears a parka. Likewise, in an emergency that requires a stop, parkas will probably be brought out and used until further movement generates mechanical heat.

A secondary use of parkas is in camp at night. Sleeping bags can be pushed to colder extremes by spreading a parka over the top as a quilt. Parkas are light enough not to reduce the loft of the sleeping bag underneath, yet they add significantly to the bag's insulation.

In keeping with the preference for multifunctional gear, you should select a parka that has a detachable hood. This way you can use the hood at times when you don't need the entire parka. If possible, select a parka with a heat-trapping fur ruff on the hood.

Rain Gear

Rain in winter is not a usual event, but it occurs

During a lunch break, travelers use their snowshoes as seats while their feet are further insulated within deep power. Whenever it is below zero during lunch, most people will don their goosedown parkas.

several times each winter in northern New England and can occur even in the farther reaches of the North.

Nothing is more miserable and uncomfortable than a winter rain. Usually, it is simplest just to stay put and wait the weather out. However, you will still need to get firewood, fetch water and do other chores in the rain. With luck your rain gear will ride in the bottom of your duffel and never see the light of day, but if you need it, you'll really need it.

Winter rains can develop suddenly. You may be in the midst of clear, brittle cold and look up to see dense blue air approaching. That is the time to camp. Try to get set up before the warm front hits and before any thing can get wet. In many cases, the temperature will rise from below zero to 40 above in a matter of hours. Drizzle and even a steady downpour are possible. Often you can't see the pattern coming because it is trailing a snowstorm that hides its presence. Slowly you sense denser air in your nose, the pressure in your ears changes, then the rain starts. Set up and dig in.

The departure of a warm front, or Chinook as northwesterners call it, is usually as dramatic as its arrival. The temperature will plunge to extreme lows in a matter of hours, and the following day is usually suitable for travel. In all the rain flashes we have endured, none has required more than a two-day layover, and most require only one day of sitting tight.

SLEEPING BAGS

Sleeping bags are essentially clothing one wears for the night. Of all the insulating and heat-retaining items on a winter trip, the sleeping bag is the most specific in design and function. A good mummy bag will cover the entire body with only a small breathing hole left open. The loft will be extra thick as the warmth of an adequately fed and hydrated body must be maintained for a long time with virtually no heat mechanically generated. Only metabolic heat warms a person asleep, and during sleep your metabolism drops to its lowest level. A lot is demanded of sleeping bags, and the best tend to be very expensive, reflecting a lot of attention to tailoring, design and quality of materials.

In addition to the quality of the bag itself, the insulation of the sleeping platform is of great importance. The best insulation to put down on the groundsheets that cover the sleeping platform is either closed-cell foam pads or the type (such as Therm-a-Rest pads) that are a combination of open-cell foam, introduced air pressure and an impermeable cover with a valve for air. Therm-a-Rest-type pads are the best. They are extremely comfortable and offer the best insulation. They roll up small, are basically unaffected by cold and are easy to repair with a simple glue-and-patch kit if punctured. If an unrepairable disaster should befall a Therm-a-Rest-type pad, it will not be thick enough in its deflated state to function well, and you will need to sleep on your extra clothes for adequate (but not great) insulation. In an emergency, you could rely on a bough bed, but the main benefits of carrying sleeping pads are to save time during camp pitching and to reduce impact in areas where collecting boughs is inappropriate.

Air-and-foam inflatable pads abound, and it is worth favoring the single flat type with one valve that inflates and deflates the whole thing. Simplicity is a prime virtue in the field, so avoid pads with multiple contoured compartments, each with its own separate valve, unless you are amused by endless fussing and fidgeting for precious little gain.

Closed-cell foam pads are not as comfortable, but they do provide adequate insulation, although a small amount of heat is lost through them. Most winter campers use two closed-cell pads, one on top of the other. This means carrying more stuff, but the additional insulation is worth the effort. Closed-cell pads must be warmed up in the tent before they can be unrolled easily, but not much can go wrong with them as there is no puncture potential. This point alone makes many people prefer them to pads that rely on air and can thus leak.

Getting a good winter sleeping bag is a serious investment, and the selection is limited. If you're committed to winter travel, get a good bag and don't worry about the price. But if winter travel does not occupy a large portion of your camping life, you would be better off doubling regular sleeping bags and living with the increased bulk and weight in the winter. This will save you from spending a lot of money on a specialized item that you'll use occasionally in only one season. For the best double-bag system, purchase a lightweight bag and a good three-season bag rated to minus ten or so. The light bag will work by itself in the heat of midsummer in a temperate zone; it will also winterize a three-season bag to a level appropriate to subarctic winter conditions. If it is small enough, use it inside the three-season bag. If not, it works just as effectively opened and spread on top of the heavier bag like a quilt.

For those who require a winter bag, there are currently three very good ones. The ultimate bag is made by Feathered Friends of Seattle and is appropriately called the Snowy Owl. Rated to minus 50 degrees Fahrenheit, it has nearly a foot of loft provided by 700 fill-power goose down. It is tailored so perfectly that the breathing hole is actually directly over the face. In fact, we have never snugged up the closure toggle, even at minus 58 degrees Fahrenheit. The cost of the Snowy Owl—currently more than $750—is commensurate with its perfection, but, for those who make the commitment, the bag is virtually beyond reproach.

Feathered Friends also makes the next best winter bag, called the Snow Goose (minus 35). The Snow Goose offers most of the features of the Snowy Owl, but weight and finer details have been scaled back in an effort to shave a pound off the bag for mountaineers. The third and fourth best bags are also in the Feathered Friends line. The Eider and Ptarmigan are fantastic minus-25-degree bags.

There are plenty of winter bags with synthetic fill on the market, but none match the quality of a good down bag. The main advantages of the synthetics are that they are inexpensive compared to down, and they are machine washable. Synthetic-filled bags also have another advantage that applies only to the careless traveler who allows his or her bag to get wet: compared to down, they dry quickly.

Synthetic fill's disadvantages, in comparison to goose down, are that it is not as resilient or long lasting in retaining full loft in the face of continuous, hard usage, and it doesn't breathe as well. To equal down for warmth, synthetic-fill bags must be made heavier and bulkier, and thus there are few such bags rated to less than minus 20. Recent generations of fill have attempted to solve the weight and bulk problems, thus far with minimal success.

Whether you choose to invest in a superb, serious winter bag or double other bags, you will want to achieve the equivalent of a minus-20- or minus-30-degree rating or lower. Those are ballpark figures because there is too much variation in individuals' sleep metabolism and in the type and quality of evening meals, the real heat source that each type of bag or bag system helps to retain.

The advantage of a well-tailored bag that keeps the face hole actually over the face is that it allows the sleeper's breath to pass directly into the air. A little frost builds up on the edges, but, for the most part, moisture in the breath goes directly into the air. In most mummy bags, a tightly drawn hood puts the breathing hole in some other location, leaving the breath to transpire through the bag and fill. This, of course, results in dampness in the bag, which makes you sleep cold, and which must be dried out in the morning. The drying chore is no problem in a stove-heated tent, but for bivouac campers, condensation within the fill is a serious problem that many have attempted to solve with vapor barriers and synthetic fill. Because breathing into the bag is moist and therefore cold, it is imperative that breath be vented to the air.

Most sleeping bags can be zipped together, which many couples prefer. Unfortunately, in winter, joined bags are not warm enough because the airspace inside is too large to heat adequately. To function well, a bag for two would have to be sized down to the equivalent of a bag and a half, and thus when not zipped together, the halves would be too small to be used singly. Fortunately, with a tent-and-stove combination, a tent can be maintained at such a high temperature that cuddling is not in the least bit dependent on the microclimate provided by sleeping bags.

Another way to avoid the sleeping bag issue altogether is to keep the fire going all night, which prevents frosting around the face hole and eliminates the need to carefully vent breath, as you can sleep comfortably with your head exposed. An added benefit is that water can be kept overnight without freezing. You will need two to three times more firewood than those who let the fire go out, but after a day or two on the trail, whoever stokes the stove every few hours or so will not even remember doing so in the morning. The chore becomes so second nature that the doer probably is not even fully awake during the process.

When a group occupies a wall tent in which the fire is not kept overnight, it is better if the people with the warmest bags sleep along the outside walls. The people in the middle then benefit from the warmth of adjacent sleepers.

Moreover, individuals can push their bags' ratings during extremes by several methods. A flannel liner sewn to the shape and taper of the sleeping bag not only adds a little extra warmth, but also keeps the bag clean, reducing the need to subject the bag to periodic laundering. In addition, you may choose to wear a set of longjohns, which also pushes the temperature rating a bit lower. Do not wear more than a single layer of longjohns, however, or you will actually sleep colder. The bag functions by holding your heat close and reradiating the heat as it is produced and maintained. If you are wearing too much insulation, you will prevent reradiated heat from reaching you.

A pair of dry socks significantly improves heat retention; in extreme situations, some people also wear a wool hat. Many choose to wear a silk balaclava or bandanna to prevent hair oils from soiling the interior of the bag. Liners and clothing items are much easier to launder than sleeping bags, so you will be rewarded for any pains you take to keep your bag clean.

Generally, you will want to wear as little as possible inside your bag, but whatever you choose to wear to bed, make sure it is completely dry before going to sleep. You will be robbed of heat if there is any moisture in your socks, or if, in the heat of the tent, you sweated in your longjohn top. Most people wear a spare set of socks to ensure dryness and then pack them away in the morning and change back into their trail socks. Likewise, a little time spent sitting quietly in the heat to dry your longjohn top thoroughly just before bed is a small detail worth attending to.

As soon as the stove is lit in the morning and cooking gets underway, the first chore is to dry and fluff up the sleeping bags. As soon as each bag is dry, it should be stuffed and passed out of the tent to create more room for breakfast and other preparations for the day. In the case of doubled bags, only the outer one will need serious attention. The inner bag will have passed most of the moisture to the outer as a gas, and only the outermost portions of the outer bag will have been cool enough for moisture to condense as frost upon or within it.

A sleep-related fear that seems pervasive is the one promoted by inexperienced and unknowledgeable fiction writers. It seems some folks can't get enough of that notion about people drifting off into some deep, hyperborean sleep from which they never awaken. This is physiologically impossible. The cold will always wake a person, unless that person is stupefied by alcohol or drugs. Often, just the increased metabolism of the wakeful state is enough to warm a person back up, and if it is not, the individual is awake and can eat a bit or build up the fire.

Actually, in some emergencies sleep is exactly what you need, for a well-rested person has better judgment and physical output. Arctic dweller Peter Freuchen tells of some Inuit hunters who were adrift on a broken-up ice floe, without food and equipment, and drifting out to sea. The men knew that they would die if the drift continued, and live if the wind changed and brought them back to their dogs, equipment and sleds. Such was the hunters' stoic acceptance of death that they did the smartest thing: they slept. In doing so, they lowered their metabolisms to preserve food and strength, knowing they would need both if things improved. When the winds brought them back to the ice edge, the men sang a song of joy and set off to find their gear.

Had the same predicament befallen someone from a culture not at home in that land, the outcome could easily have been different. Consumed with worry and therefore unable to sleep, they might have squandered their energy until they could no longer recognize an opportunity to save themselves.

A little experimentation on your first few trips will build your confidence and skill at managing sleep, and soon you won't give the process a second thought. Deep, sound sleep on the trail will leave you refreshed and eager for the gifts of the day.

USEFUL ADDRESSES

Wool Clothing

IBEX has an extremely informative woolen-wear catalog and a huge selection of gear, much of which is appropriate for snow walkers. Not only is it well tailored, but many pieces come in a wide selection of colors. Most remarkable of all is that they offer a full line of women's clothes with thoughtful care in sizing and design details.

IBEX
2800 Westerdale Cut-off Road
Woodstock, VT 05091
800-773-9647
www.ibexwear.com

C. C. Filson Company
P.O. Box 34020
Seattle, WA 98124
800-297-1897
www.filson.com

Bemidji Woolen Mills
301 Irvine Avenue NW
Bemidji, MN 56601-0279
888-751-5166
www.bemidjiwoolenmills.com

Wool Clothing (cont.)

Johnson Woolen Mills
P.O. Box 612, Main Street
Johnson, VT 05656-0612
802-635-2271
877-635-WOOL
www.johnsonwoolenmills.com

Silk and Silk/Wool blends, Gloves, Balaclavas, etc.

Wintersilks
11711 Marcdo Beach Drive
Jacksonville, FL 32224-7615
888-782-2224
www.wintersilks.com

Purveyors of North Woods Clothing, Tools, Books & More

Piragis Northwoods Company
105 North Central Avenue
Ely, MN 55731
800-223-6565
www.piragis.com

Miscellaneous Winter Camping Clothing

Duane and Margot Lottig of Empire Canvas make fine Arctic-style gauntlet mittens in canvas and leather with blanket-wool liners and fantastic cotton anoraks. They also sell Stanfield's wool long underwear and fine Icelandic wool socks:

Empire Canvas Works
P.O. Box 17
Solon Springs, WI 54873
715-378-4216
www.empirecanvasworks.com

Breathable Ventile Cotton Expedition Clothing

Snowsled Ltd.
Marketplace Mews, Tetbury
Gloucestershire GL8 8DN
United Kingdom
44 666 500852
www.snowsled.com

The Vermont Country Store catalog carries men's and women's wool longjohns by Stanfield's as well as the same Australian wool longjohns for women that are carried by L.L. Bean.

The Vermont Country Store Catalog
P.O. Box 6999
Rutland, VT 05702-6999
802-362-8460
www.vermontcountrystore.com

Moosehide Chopper Mitts

Piragis Northwoods Company
105 North Central Avenue
Ely, MN 55731
800-223-6565
www.piragis.com

Wool Longjohns
(lightweight and heavyweight)

Ullfrotte Original of Sweden makes fine merino wool underclothing and jackets. The U.S. distributor in South Carolina is also the source for Gransfors Bruks axes in North America.

Ullfrotte Original
821 West 5th North Street, P.O. Box 818
Summerville, SC 29484
843-875-0240
www.gransfors.com

Stanfield's Limited
P.O. Box 190
Truro, Nova Scotia
Canada B2N 5C2
902-895-5406
www.stanfields.com

Windsor Wear
Nova Scotia Textiles, Ltd.
1995 Weston Road
York, Ontario M9N 3W9
Canada
416-249-0822

IBEX
(See address on previous page)

Anoraks and Wind Pants

Four-ounce Egyptian cotton when available.

Sally Robbins
866 Middle Road
North Haven, ME 04853
207-867-2227

Wintergreen
205 East Sheridan
Ely, MN 55731
800-584-9425 (218-365-6602)
www.wintergreendesigns.com

Cotton Anoraks & Wind Pants

Craig MacDonald RR 1
Dwight, Ontario
Canada P0A 1H0
705-635-3416 (evenings)

Empire Canvas Works
P.O. Box 17
Solon Springs, WI 54873
715-378-4216
www.empirecanvasworks.com

High-Quality Goosedown-filled Sleeping Bags

Feathered Friends
1119 Mercer Street
Seattle, WA 98109
206-292-6292
www.featheredfriends.com

Synthetic-filled Sleeping Bags for Deep Cold

Wiggy's
2482 Industrial Blvd, P.O. Box 2124
Grand Junction, CO 81502
800-748-1827
www.wiggys.com

Winter Hats

Mad Bomber (fur hats)
130 Imboden Drive, Suite 7
Winchester, VA 22603
703-662-8840
www.madbomber.com

General Winter Camping Gear

L.L. Bean carries many good items including some wool clothing, sleeping bags, hats, mittens, sleeping pads, head-lamps, snowshoes, parkas and much more. The store carries more than what is shown in the catalog and is worth visiting. In addition, Bean's phone operators are exceptional. Via computer, they can locate any item in stock or on order, including items not listed in the catalog.

L.L. Bean, Inc.
Freeport, ME 04033
800-441-5713
www.llbean.com

North House Folk School

North House is modeled after the "folkehøjskoles" of Scandinavia where the traditional arts are taken much more seriously than they are in North America. North House offers a wide array of traditional skills, many taught by Finns, Swedes and Norwegians who have settled in northern Minnesota.

Some workshops of interest to winter travelers are Making Cree Mukluks, Traditional Anoraks, Felted Hats and Mittens, Making a Toboggan, Sled Dog Primer, Skijoring and Winter Treks (5-6 days).

North House Folk School
P.O. Box 759
Grand Marais, MN 55604
218-387-9762 (888-387-9762)
www.northhouse.org

Chapter 5
Tools for the Trail

TOOLS OF THE TRAIL

"Give me a tent and kittle
Snowshoes and axe and gun.
Send me up in Grand River
Steering by star and sun."

—Labrador trapper's song, sung by John Michelin to Elliott Merrick, 1930

PARADIGMS

Mark and Judy are hypothetical characters who, in the estimation of their peers, are skilled outdoors people. They are young adults in their final years at a small college located near some wilderness areas. Whenever possible, their vacation time is spent canoeing or backpacking. Judy has been a student in the Audubon Expedition Institute, has taken courses through the National Outdoor Leadership School (NOLS) and has taught Outward Bound canoe programs over the past two summers, one in Maine and one in Minnesota.

Mark has canoed with the Keewaydin Camps and has even traveled to James Bay in the company of Cree guides. As a child in Vermont, he developed ties with the natural world, which he has expanded upon as a young adult. He has been a NOLS instructor in Wyoming and worked a summer in the woods for a family-run logging company that practices sustained-yield and selective-cutting forestry in upstate New York.

Both are personable, good educators and are becoming quite skilled at leadership. With the exception of Mark's northern trips with Keewaydin, their travels have largely been conducted in the lower 48 states. Although their experiences in the Wind River Range of Wyoming and a foray to the Bob Marshall Wilderness of Montana included truly wild country of some scale, their outings have been within the confines of preserved habitat surrounded by land used for logging, grazing, ranching, farming, mining and other developments. They dream of Alaska.

Judy grew up in Cambridge, Massachusetts and as a child attended wilderness-oriented camps in Vermont. It was not until late in high school that she saw the trail as a serious opportunity and became enthralled with the natural world. Mark had some contacts with the woods and even got to know a few woodsmen when he was young, but from his home in South Burlington he had to go some distance to get to woods and waters.

By the time Judy and Mark's trail careers began to unfold, they were indoctrinated with a hands-off approach to wilderness. They were born into a world in which true, large-scale wilderness no longer existed. Small remnants had to be managed carefully lest they be loved to death. They knew all about overuse of pristine areas and that the only pristine areas left tended to be at high elevations, hidden in the desert or—through an earlier generation's foresight—protected by law.

Mark and Judy grew up with a tool tradition based on what became known as low-impact camping, an ethic with the rallying cry, "Take only pictures, leave only footprints." In time, the footprints began to erode some of the more fragile areas and more and more human management became necessary. Practitioners learned to walk softly and camp only in certain spots where they would leave few traces so that others could enjoy the illusion of wilderness. The campfire had to be abandoned, and small camping stoves took its place. Equipment became sophisticated, complex and increasingly high-tech. Little of it was made of natural materials, and nearly all of it had to be purchased, as little of it was simple enough to be homemade.

Mark and Judy knew no other way of being in the outdoors. The camps and outdoor learning centers they attended presented no other perspective. In fact, they taught the same gospel themselves.

Their education had given them a solid understanding of global economics and a good grasp of environmental problems, processes, politics and the need for ethics. They had no idea that their skills in the wilderness were the skills of an estranged visitor capable only of manipulating equipment, or that the tool tradition they espoused was based on nonengagement with the processes of living within an environment. It would never occur to them that their visits to wild areas were much like the visits of astronauts to space, totally dependent on an industrial complex that provided the equipment and even some of the food they brought with them.

Now jump several hundred miles north and meet a young Montagnais named Tekuanan McKenzie. He is not hypothetical, although he may as well be. He is one in a million among his peers, and his only counterparts are a full generation older, from a time when nearly everyone spent a major part of the year on the land. We were lucky to meet and become friends with him. At the time, he was the first mentor we had had who was younger than ourselves rather than two or three times our own ages.

Tekuanan hunts his immediate family's ancestral territory of the central Quebec/Labrador plateau—an area the size of Massachusetts, Connecticut and Rhode Island combined. Of eleven children, he is the only one to become an active heir to the territory of his clan. His knowledge of traditional bush skills is phenomenal. He knows less than his parents of life in the bush, and much less than his grandparents, but for this he compensates by knowing the skills of his own time.

With axe and gun, snowshoes and canoe, he could go anywhere on the Ungava peninsula. Everything else he needed would be carried in his head, and in this regard he is much like his forebears. As a man of his own times, he also has a chainsaw, outboard motor, snowmobile and two-way radio in his tool kit. Tekuanan grew up with these tools—he has mastered their potential, yet he is not mastered by them. If they fail, he still has the skills of his parents' time, and they serve him well.

Once when we were in the Quebec/Labrador interior with Tekuanan, his snowmobile stopped working, dealing a blow to our firewood-hauling operation. The fact that it was well below zero and terrible winds had been screaming down the lake for days did not seem to upset Tekuanan. He took the motor off its mounts and carried it in next to the stove until it was warm enough to work on. He got out an exploded diagram from a mechanics manual and took the whole thing apart. In the process, he discovered a mangled bearing in the bowels of the engine and removed it. Then he continued to explore for more damage.

That evening, Tekuanan clipped his radio into the antenna wire that was strung between two trees and radioed to another family in the bush within radio range of his mother's home on the reserve. When he raised a voice on the air, we heard him chatting in Montagnais, shifting to French for the parts coding and names. We were trackside the following Thursday when the once-weekly run of the Quebec North Shore and Labrador Railway snaked its way into the bush, delivering the replacement parts we needed. Until then, without a snowmobile, we were pedestrians, and the daily chores of fetching wood and water and ptarmigan hunting took more time to accomplish.

Tekuanan McKenzie at home on the trail. Warm in his late father's coat, secure within his skills and content upon his ancestral territory.

But Tekuanan is as comfortable traveling on foot as by machine. He goes nowhere without an axe and gun, and if reduced to one or the other of these, he would choose the axe. If Tekuanan were to become lost, it would be in his own living room. In the natural world, nothing is strange to him. His knowledge of everything around him is consummate, and there is little he cannot make or do. His understanding is not limited to skills and resources but contains the stories, history and spirit of his people. These elements define his sense of belonging and balance. If someone were to suggest that his use of an axe or gun or internal-combustion engines constituted unacceptably high impact on the environment, he would think that person daft.

Judy and Mark and Tekuanan share a love of wilderness, but their ideals are widely divergent. Neither view is intrinsically right or wrong. If anything, they are both right within the appropriate context. Both philosophies merit examination, for they illuminate and inform each other, and the space between them provides a continuum of ways of thinking, doing and being in the wilds. Along that scale, taking care to achieve balance, each of us can find a well-reasoned place to settle.

To remove Tekuanan from the McKenzie hunting territory and transpose his tool tradition to a confined, overused area that is extra fragile due to elevation would be folly. Although he would survive comfortably in the short term, the area could not sustain extended occupation, and the level of impact would shock other users as well as management agencies involved in protecting the area. Tekuanan's way, though benign when compared to the clearcutting, grazing and other activities on the land all around such an area, would be inappropriate.

Similarly, if Mark and Judy were transposed to the subarctic forest with their tool culture, they would be able to stay only a short time. They would not be comfortable, nor could they sustain any long-term emergencies or survival situations. Sure, they would enjoy a six-week boreal canoe trip if they were flown in and out, but they would be well advised to keep their winter travels to a minimum. If anything went wrong with their equipment or supply systems, they would be helpless. Much of that equipment is neither adaptable nor repairable in the field, and even if it were, high-tech campers such as Mark and Judy would not know how. Adopting high-tech gear means subordinating oneself to it. Without woodcraft skills as a backup—skills that require a lot of technique and finesse—one is in great danger of being unable to take care of things in an emergency or even create comfort in a situation that is merely inconvenient.

Furthermore, high-tech campers are insulated from direct engagement with the environment by the nature of their equipment, by management and cultural conditions that favor a look-but-don't-touch approach and by essentially being visitors and privileged aliens in the wilds. On the other hand, a camper who relies on a little technology and a lot of technique has a deeper understanding of the wilderness and real living skills. Unfortunately, the only wild areas large enough for people truly to live within are the subarctic forests and the interior tropics. And unless humans suffer a major catastrophic reduction in population, both these areas are doomed. The exploitation of the North for power and an exportable fresh water supply is already advanced. The cutting of the jungles for lumber, fuel and grazing land proceeds at a horrifying rate. Both biomes feel the bludgeoning from the mining and wood industries trying to satisfy market demand.

Perhaps the most cited symbol of the low-impact school of campcraft is its insistence on the use of a camping stove rather than an axe to build open fires for cooking. Ostensibly, use of gas stoves for cooking eliminates the need for fire building and using up dead wood for fuel. In heavily used areas, firewood becomes scarce, and in many areas such as high elevations, deserts or north of the treeline, dead wood for fires is extremely limited and best reserved for those in true emergencies. Most heavily used areas also require that campers stay in established campsites (a management tool to control and centralize erosive use), and even in a firewood-rich area, such sites have little remaining wood. In these situations, using a stove is a way to reduce immediate impact.

The irony embodied in considering gas stoves as low-impact tools requires a more encompassing view. A stove user unwittingly enlists a global army of extractors, smelters, refiners, machinists, manufacturers and distributors, all of whom consume nonrenewable resources, contribute to toxic waste through manufacturing and transportation and create a product that demands still more finite fuels once in use. Stoves have their place, but they are anything but low-impact.

For the conservation of limited, artificially bounded preserves, a stoves-only policy is a necessary and useful management tool. Stoves also have a place in fragile environments that have little wood to begin with, and in all woodless areas such as the high Arctic, the Antarctic, extreme elevations and upon the seas. However, the stove might be best regarded as a displaced-impact item, and not held aloft as the shining symbol of a camper's light and caring touch in the world.

In the view of many in the low-impact school of thought, the axe is an outmoded tool of the pioneer era that is dangerous, as well as destructive. Unskilled use of an axe can indeed be dangerous. An uninformed, uncaring person may well be destructive, but the problem lies not in the axe, but in the person who wields it. Just consider what an axe can do in the hands of a skilled person in an appropriate environment.

The axe's primary use is in fire building. In any weather, under any conditions, a fire can be made simply and quickly with the aid of an axe. Wood gathering is efficient, and a few select billets of wood with good grain can be split into kindling and tinder. A good fire expands cooking options and adds psychological pleasures that are an important aspect of camp life.

In addition to its use in fire building, the axe has a role in repair and first-aid kits. With an awl, a crooked knife and an axe the traveler has a portable workshop that weighs only a few pounds. Using only an axe, one could manufacture the tools to make a friction fire, make deadfalls for acquiring food and build the simplest of emergency shelters or the most elaborate of log homes. Snowshoe frames, toboggans, canoe parts and hundreds of other tools could likewise be produced.

As a component of a first-aid kit, an axe lets you manufacture all manner of splints, traction devices and backboards. And in a serious emergency, the fire and shelter an axe facilitates are as much a part of first and secondary aid as a knowledge of backcountry medicine.

With an axe, you can build a life. With a stove, you can heat water—that is, if you don't run out of fuel and nothing malfunctions.

In much of the vast reaches of the boreal forests, use of an axe is entirely appropriate. The few parties of travelers and the ever fewer native families truly living on the land will surely burn a few standing dead spruce and larch for firewood and build the odd cabin here or there. The impact thus created is extremely localized and scarcely leaves a scar. In such an area, it's hard to view an axe user as an abuser.

To become skillful with a stove, one merely needs to purchase one, keep it supplied with fuel and observe some easily learned precautions related to cold-weather use (use at high elevations and use within small synthetic tents or tent vestibules).

To become skillful with an axe, one must become familiar with all sorts of surroundings and possibilities. The skills of handle making, sharpening, use and maintenance are lifelong processes that can be refined to exquisite expertise. For wood selection you must learn about trees, their properties and characteristics. You begin to connect habitats, species and interactions. Basic knowledge may evolve into craftsmanship, and craftsmanship into art and artistry into something symbolic of place and being. The axe is liberating, a tool of self-reliance, engagement and growth.

Most habitat suitable to travel by toboggan and snowshoe is also suitable to traditional tools and methods. A few provincial, state and national parks in the North have special rules that might exclude tobogganers or require them to modify their approach. But these are clearly defined areas, and they make up an exceedingly small portion of the snow walker's habitat.

TOOLS

One of the many advantages provided by toboggan travel is the ability to make use of full-size tools. Where backpackers and climbers must often do without, or use ultralight, down-sized items, the tobogganer can realize the efficiency of items built to do the job. Undersized items usually are adopted to save weight, but you pay for such lightness in inconvenience or, in the worst cases, nonfunction. For each tent group on our trips, there will be a full-scale shovel, a full-size trail axe with a 2$1/4$-pound head and a 30-inch folding saw or bucksaw. The entire party, regardless of the number of tents, will be outfitted with a repair kit, slush scoop and ice chisel. And, on longer northern expeditions, an Emergency Position Indicating Radio Beacon, or EPIRB (also known as Emergency Location Transmitter or ELT), a satellite phone and perhaps a combination rifle/shotgun will be along.

Trail Axes and Saws

Trail axes should be large enough to do full-scale two-handed axe work as well as light enough to do one-handed refined work. As such, they tend to be fairly short handled (about 24 to 28 inches) with a 1$3/4$-pound head, as is typical of the Hudson Bay cruising axe type. Two-pound and even 2$1/2$-pound heads are not unseemly, but anything bigger is unnecessary. Naturally, axes should be razor-sharp and fitted with a balanced handle. Neither of these last two properties are possible without your own customizing attention.

Avoid hatchets entirely. They are too small to accomplish much and are nearly as heavy as a full-size trail axe.

It is extremely easy to hurt yourself with an axe and easier still to break handles, nick the blade or accidentally hit your snowshoes. Even experienced axe users, when fatigued, are at risk. On our trips, in consideration of the safety of people and of the tools, only the guides or apprentices use axes. This pleases our liability carrier and saves worry about broken handles, nicked blades, damaged snowshoes or injured guests. On a trip with peers, you can decide who brings what and abide by the personal rules of the owner. Most people who keep a well-honed axe will not lend it. And anyone who understands the time, care and expertise involved in maintaining such an axe will not ask to borrow one. Reflective of this point is the apocryphal northern yarn of woodspeople willing to share their spouses but not their axes.

If you are new to axe use and still developing your expertise, you will want to do all your chopping and splitting while on snowshoes from a kneeling position. This reduces your effectiveness biomechanically but will preserve your snowshoes, moccasins, feet and shins. This kneeling stance is used by even the most seasoned experts in times of icy mittens, darkness or fatigue.

In the firewood department, a good bowsaw or folding bucksaw complements the axe, and all participants on our trips are encouraged to take part in bucking up firewood. A minimum blade length of 24 inches is good, but for portability and lightness, anything more than 30 inches is unlikely to be useful on a nomadic trip.

Edged tools such as ice chisels and axes are best kept razor-sharp by being lightly sharpened frequently, with major regrinding to maintain the bevel being done only as necessary. A good leather sheath for each will likewise maintain a keen edge.

The small, aluminum-framed folding saws for backpackers are useless. The blade is short to begin with, and because the saw frame is triangular, you cannot cut anything of much diameter without seriously reducing the length of the draw of each saw stroke. The wood-framed folding bucksaws available through some catalogs are very good. Most have a 24-inch or longer blade and can handle up to a six-inch log before inconvenience sets in. Because the frame is nearly vertical at each end of the blade, the full length of the saw is engaged with each draw.

Folding saws can easily be stashed inside the stove or in a duffel bag for transport, and the wood frame covers the cutting edge of the blade.

Metal-framed nonfolding bowsaws are also usable, but they need a sheath of some sort for the blade and are not as compact.

Ice Chisel & Slush Scoop

The advent of ice augers, and now power augers, has had a bad effect on the companies that formerly made ice-chisel blades. Blades are now almost impossible to find, and the few that some northern hardware stores carry are ill-designed and nearly functionless. It is worthwhile to keep an eye out for older ice chisels in antique shops, or in a pinch, retrofit a woodworker's slick into an ice chisel. Recently, Empire Canvas Works has started selling a fine five-foot long ice chisel that weighs four-and-a-half pounds.

The best chisels are perhaps a couple of pounds or more, with a good spruce pole handle that brings the overall length up to five-and-a-half or six feet. This is long enough to get through most ice thicknesses.

Chisel blades are beveled on one side only, and sharp ones will cut and explode ice out of a hole with remarkable speed. The steel need not be tempered hard, as you will want to be able to touch up the blade with a file and axe stone to keep it razor-sharp. You will hit rocks sooner or later so that sometimes you will need to do serious regrinding and shaping of the cutting edge. Steel of woodworking hardness is difficult to file quickly, and chips rather than folds when nicked or driven into a rock. Should you be using a retrofitted woodworker's slick, be sure to test whether or not it can be filed easily. If the file cuts well, you can use it as is, but if the file slips and skids without cutting, you will need to soften the temper. The simplest way to do this is to heat the blade with a torch or by putting it in a fire until it glows, then remove the blade and let it air cool.

As with an axe, the weight of the chisel's head and the explosive nature of chip production are the keys to cutting. Never pry with the chisel, as this could break the handle. Take care when using force with a sharp-edged tool, especially when you're wearing snowshoes and moccasins. An errant blow could easily damage the snowshoes, or injure your foot. As you get closer to breaking through to water, the sound will change; then it is wise to put your top hand through a loop of line that has been fashioned into the handle end. In this way, you can't lose the chisel to the bottom of deep water.

On a deep-water section of river with no open leads, you can expect 18 inches of ice or more. On lakes, two to four feet of ice is not uncommon. Ice chiseling is a strenuous

The explosive force of a sharp and skillfully used ice chisel can make a 15-inch-diameter hole in two or three feet of ice in ten minutes.

enough activity to be warming and tiring, and often two people can be sent out on the job so that they can relieve each other. In average ice conditions, the creation of a water hole is about a ten-minute job.

The water will rise to the top of the ice under normal conditions. Thus, you should make a big and deep enough hole in which to insert the largest camp kettle. This portion might be two hand-spreads wide and perhaps a foot deep. Beyond this point, you can make a hole of smaller diameter to reach the water below. The narrower diameter will speed the chipping process, and an eight-inch width here will still allow easy chip cleaning with the slush scoop until you reach the water. Then the upward rush floats all the chips to the surface, where they can be skimmed off. Slush scoops are available at any store that caters to ice fishermen, and since even users of power augers still need them, they will presumably remain available.

The ice chisel can usually be left upright in the snow next to the hole and the slush scoop hung from the wrist-loop at the top of the handle. Our habit is to place the chisel in the nine o'clock position to the left of the hole and one foot back from the edge. If the hole fills in with snow overnight, you will know exactly where to find it. Only an inch or two of new ice will form overnight, no matter how extreme the nighttime cold. This is easily cut through in seconds in the morning. If snow blows or falls into the hole, you may have only a thin layer of slush to clear, as the snow will insulate the surface and may prevent refreezing.

There are some tricks to know about fetching water on a winter trip. You can put empty buckets down in the snow, and none will stick because the buckets are as cold as the snow. Once they are full of water, they are relatively warm as the water is at least 32 degrees Fahrenheit. Put a full bucket into powder snow, and it will be instantly coated with thick slush. A slush-coated bucket on a hot stove creates a horrendous steam problem and is not good for the stove. Therefore, before you go to the water hole, establish a few firewood platforms in the tent or just outside to set the full buckets on. Once you fill them, you simply can't put the buckets down except on snow-free surfaces.

Often at the water hole you will have shoveled the snow off the surface of the ice in an area much bigger than the hole itself. If there is glare ice, you can put a full bucket down on that. The other trick, if you must put it down, is to put your full bucket down on the toe section of your snowshoes. Once you leave the waterhole, go directly to the tent and either pass the bucket to someone inside or temporarily place it on a firewood platform outside.

Recalling our earlier comments on the inadvisability of using ski poles as snow-shoeing equipment (see Chapter 1), you can now appreciate your greater balance and expertise as you approach the tent with a full bucket of water in each hand and not a drop spilled, nor a hint of slush on the outside of either pail.

Shovel

There should be one shovel for each tent on the trip. The best we have seen are made by True Temper and have a rectangular aluminum blade and a good white ash handle that is a full 48 inches long. These are lightweight but strong enough for all uses except prying up extremely hard wind-pack. Most uses will be related to tent pitching and putting snow on the snowcloths, leveling sleeping platforms and making kitchen pits. As mentioned earlier, it is useful to clear the ice of snow with a shovel before chipping access to water. In extreme wind in the open, you might end up cutting snow blocks to make a windbreak upwind of the tents. All in all, there is enough work for shovels to merit having them along.

Whisk Broom

The absence of a good whisk broom would be a major calamity on a trip. Although a broom is not something you might anticipate needing, the clamor for the whisk during the first hour of camp pitching makes each tent group sound like a nest of hungry baby ravens. The number of times when items and people need snow brushed off is remarkable. By removing the snow and frost before entering a heated tent, you prevent it from turning to water. The groundsheets in the tent will need periodic sweepings too, until things are stabilized, and as people move in for the evening there is a thorough brushing off of moccasins and felts. Crumbs after meals and other little things too numerous to mention mean one whisk per tent, never to be misplaced without a "Where's the whisk?" chorus.

Ice-Fishing Equipment

On all northern trips, we carry a couple of heavy ice-fishing jigs (the Swedish Pimple is a good one, readily available). These are slightly curved lures, triangular in cross section, and can either be jigged vertically through a hole in the ice or in summer fished by trolling or cast-and-retrieve methods. They come in a variety of sizes ranging from tiny inch-long versions that weigh less than an ounce, up to four ounces. For Canadian trips, we favor the three-inch variety and carry one each in silver and gold. Thus far, the fish have not shown a preference.

The other equipment we have learned to carry after fishing with the Naskapi and Montagnais is a few outsized (to our eyes) hooks. In lake trout and pike country, which is just about every body of water in Ungava, a 3 3/4-inch single hook with a 1 1/4-inch gap between the tip of the point and the shank is the tool of choice. The Indians use cut red suckers for bait, or, in a pinch, pieces of newly caught lake trout or pike. Ptarmigan gizzards are also good, as they are tough and stay on the hook indefinitely when used as set baits. All baiting is done carefully. The hook tip hides just below the surface of the bait, which lies in a strip along the length and curve of the shank.

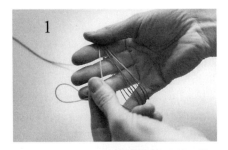

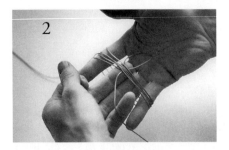

How to tie a pull-release bow to hold loops of slack in the line of a set bait.

(1) Wrap three or four loops of line around your fingers, and make an elognateed loop in the strand coming from the final wrap.

(2) Tuck this under the wrapped loops.

(3) With the strand that comes from the elongated loop create a second loop that passes over the bundle of wraps and behind the elongated loop.

(4) Pass a third loop (from the same strand) through the second loop.

(5) Tighten this third loop; this will create a snug bow, all tied from the single strand. A fish moving off with the bait will untie the loop of the bow that runs to the hook, and resistance from the line tied to a spruce stick above the ice will untie the loop of the bow that runs to the stick.

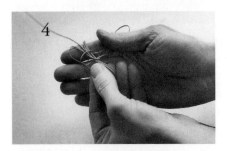

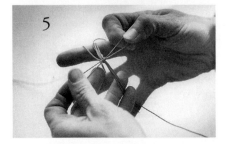

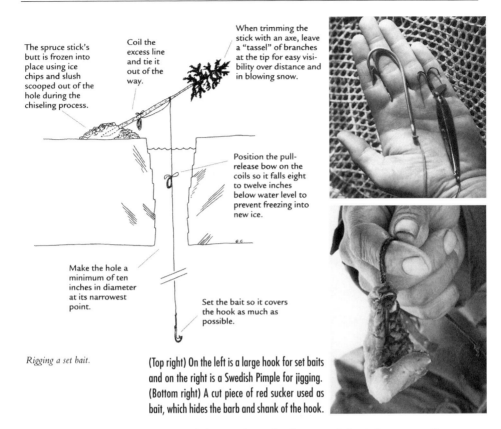

The spruce stick's butt is frozen into place using ice chips and slush scooped out of the hole during the chiseling process.

Coil the excess line and tie it out of the way.

When trimming the stick with an axe, leave a "tassel" of branches at the tip for easy visibility over distance and in blowing snow.

Position the pull-release bow on the coils so it falls eight to twelve inches below water level to prevent freezing into new ice.

Make the hole a minimum of ten inches in diameter at its narrowest point.

Set the bait so it covers the hook as much as possible.

Rigging a set bait.

(Top right) On the left is a large hook for set baits and on the right is a Swedish Pimple for jigging. (Bottom right) A cut piece of red sucker used as bait, which hides the barb and shank of the hook.

Baited hooks are often jigged, but ordinarily they are left tied to a small spruce stick angled over the hole. For set baits, there is an ingenious loop system with a pull-release knot tied in at a position along the line that will hang about eight or ten inches below the water surface where it will not freeze into the ice between checkings (see photos on opposite page). The loops are made by taking four or five wraps around the three middle fingers of one hand and creating a simple bow out of the strand that continues up to the stick. This bundle of loops yields about three feet of additional slack, and the slack is loosely held by the bow, which is just strong enough to hold the weight of the hook and bait. As a fish moves off with the bait, increased tension on the line unties the bow, and by the time the end of the slack is reached and the line jerks taut, the hook is in perfect position to be set by the momentum of the fish.

While jigging, you lip-hook the fish with a lure or drive the big, baited hook through the upper jaw. A set line will hook the fish through one of the gill slits several inches down the throat. To disengage the hook from jigging, you merely back out the barb. For a fish caught with set bait, gain access through the gill cover, turn the hook around so it can't catch and pull it out of the mouth in reverse. You will learn to do this quickly, as handling wet fish in subzero cold with a breeze or wind blowing inspires great concentration.

The same holds true for the loop in the set lines. Practice this in the warmth of home or camp until you can do it quickly and accurately every time. Fiddling around with wet line must be done quickly so you can get your hands back inside your mittens.

David Swappie holds a lake trout, or kokomesh to the Naskapi, a staple of both the winter and summer diet.

Use a minimum of 40-pound-test braided fishing line; with set lines, heavier braided nylon twine is often used. In jigging, you will jerk the lure vertically through 12 to 18 inches of water. This can be done by hand, or you can cut a short stick to which you tie the line and then jig with more economical wrist action. The curve of the lure will give it an erratic action that attracts fish. With baited hooks, go for more subtle twitches. You will also want to carry a short stick with which to give the fish a sharp blow to the back of the head. This kills them quickly and eliminates suffering.

When traveling through country that you don't know or haven't seen in open-water seasons, you will have a hard time knowing where to fish if you should need to. In rivers, favor the deep pools, where the ice is thickest. In large, sprawling lakes, which often have narrows with a little current, you will often find open leads or much thinner ice. On a five-week trip with an older Naskapi couple, we fished exclusively at two different sets of narrows in only three to four feet of water. The ice was only a few inches thick, so chiseling holes was very easy, and because the ice was so thin, a lot of light passed through it. You could watch your bait while you jigged and see the great torpedo shapes of five- and ten-pound kokomesh (lake trout) cautiously circle the bait, then dash in to strike.

In shallow-water fishing, you will want your bait or jigging activity to take place a few inches above the bottom. In deeper water or uncertain conditions, you might try various depths, as you won't know where the fish are.

Whether or not you plan on fishing, be prepared to, and carry a small packet of gear in the repair kit. On our walk to Kuujjuaq during our flirtation with serious hunger (see Chapter 6 and Journal insert), we were happy to have the jigs along.

Firearms

On Canadian winter trips, we carry a combination rifle/shotgun as emergency backup. A blizzard that dumps two feet of snow suddenly and at just the wrong time in Labrador could cause a party to miss a once-weekly train. A long siege of bad weather could prevent a planned rendezvous with a ski-plane for days on end. Or recovery time following an accident could precipitate a delay lasting longer than emergency rations could be stretched. If you are a group leader in the vastness of the subarctic, it would be irresponsible not to be prepared to hunt under such conditions. Furthermore, if you guide commercially, your liability carrier may require such equipment.

Many people are not interested in hunting, and many are ethically opposed to it. Long before a trip begins, leaders must make it known whether firearms will be present or not. Group members will then either accept the policy or withdraw, depending on their comfort with the leader's choice.

Of course, preparation does not guarantee comfort or survival. Although the North is famous for great concentrations of wildlife, it is even more famous for vast areas that are, in some seasons, devoid of wildlife. General migration patterns are known, but the specifics of location generally are not. In addition, there are annual and longer fluctuations in population. Memories of starvation winters are ever-present, and legendary human deaths sprinkle the folklore of the North like snow.

Imagine a missed connection, reduced rations, continued bad weather that keeps supply planes from landing and people growing crankier by the minute as their hunger and fatigue grow. Back in the warmth of homes, it seemed reasonable not to bring firearms. Now, on the fourth day of reduced rations with no drone of an airplane heard above the screeching wind and snow, things look different. For two days, thousands of caribou have streamed down the lake in front of the tents, and everyone has watched them helplessly, knowing that a yearling would last the eight-person party only a day, an adult only four or five.

Should you choose to cover the options by acquiring a firearm, you will not only want to get the best, most versatile piece of equipment possible, but you will need to get proficient at its safe use and maintenance. Get the firearm well before the trip—you may need specific training in the gun's use from a professional instructor or a trusted friend who knows firearms.

Combination guns are not popular in North America, so we ended up getting a fine one made by Valmet Firearms in Finland. The top barrel is a 12-gauge shotgun, the lower a .308 rifle. This allows the taking of small game such as ptarmigan with the shotgun as well as big game such as caribou or moose with the .308. By offering both options in one gun, the combination firearm saves weight, even though the resulting piece is heavier than either a shotgun or a rifle by itself.

In North America, the Savage Arms Company makes combination guns in several formats. The type that is of interest to the northern traveler is a 30-30 rifle over a 20-gauge shotgun. Savage's quality is not high compared to some of the European possibilities, but the guns are inexpensive, and this is important if the gun is to be an emergency item only and rarely used. Nearly every bush pilot north of the 45th parallel carries one of these in the plane's crash kit.

People who live on the land are seldom not hunting. No one goes anywhere without a gun because you never know when or where game will show up. If ptarmigan or caribou come while you are off in the spruces going to the bathroom or across a bay cutting firewood, you need to be prepared. It doesn't do to head off to check the fish sets with only an ice chisel. There just might be 40 caribou around the first point along the way or the lake-edge willows might be full of ptarmigan.

When we walked to Kuujjuaq, we planned to add 30 ptarmigan to our carried food in the course of the trip. Over the two-month journey, many factors conspired to reduce our larder faster than we anticipated. We ate 84 ptarmigan in all and finished the trip just on the edge of serious depletion. One of us had no more ammunition, the other had five shells left. As has happened to so many people who have wintered on the land, the caribou migration missed us (see Journal insert).

Should you undertake serious private journeys or participate in commercial outings where your responsibilities will require a firearm, you will want to learn enough about ballistics and marksmanship to sight in the rifle element for 100 yards. In the process, you will do enough shooting to become thoroughly familiar with both the gun and yourself. By the time you have fired enough rounds to have adjusted the sights so you can put a group of shots in a tight cluster in or near the center of the target, you will have gained tremendous confidence. Should you ever need to deliver a well-placed, lethal shot to the vital part of an animal, you can make the attempt responsibly. The animal will not suffer, and you will not lose or waste ammunition through sloppy shooting.

To understand the shotgun element of a combination gun, shoot at big sheets of cardboard at various ranges to observe the diameter of the shot pattern. Shotguns are a close-range firearm, and, fortunately, ptarmigan often let you get very close. With luck, you will never have to shoot at anything past the range at which the shot pattern flares beyond a three-foot diameter. To observe how quickly the pattern spreads with increased distance, take a shot at the cardboard at 25, 50, 75 and 100 feet.

Gun dealers have all sorts of literature regarding safety, ballistics, sighting-in and everything else you need to know regarding responsible ownership and use of a firearm. Study the literature well, practice and take a hunter-safety course through your local Fisheries and Wildlife Department. You will go to considerable expense to prepare for something you may never need to do, but it would be irresponsible to do anything less. Emergencies require your best care and skill.

As with axe use, make rules regarding the firearm before you embark on a trip, and make sure everyone is aware of them. In our case, only the guides use a firearm unless the guides are incapacitated through injury or must respond to a more pressing part of a compound emergency. Write out the chain of command and carry it in the first-aid kit, or at least have it in mind to write out in the moment of need.

Among peers, it is still wise to delegate gun use to the owner or leader only. If the trip has only one leader rather than co-leaders, you may want to train at least one other person before departure.

Should you decide to purchase firearm-related equipment, any sporting goods dealer who carries hunting supplies will be able to order what you need, give advice, or locate distributors if you need something he or she does not carry.

One subject that you will not encounter in advice from sporting organizations or sportspeople has to do with bird hunting. Although responsible hunters go for quick, clean kills and zealously avoid sloppy shooting and wounding of animals, they often harbor one major inconsistency: it is considered ethical to allow game birds to flush and take wing before shooting. Ostensibly, this is to give birds "a sporting chance" at escape. Unfortunately, it means that birds do escape, carrying stray shot and wounds from being poorly or incompletely hit, or hit at such range that the pellets have lost their knockdown power.

You will not find true survival hunters wasting ammunition, reducing their success rate and wounding birds they do not recover for the ideals of sportsmanship. A true predator/prey relationship is far too serious for that. Be quick, clean, close and certain. Birds on the ground and in the willows offer the best opportunity. If sportsmen call you vile names and hang you in effigy, let them. This is not a game. Taking the lives of animals is no less serious than falling through the ice or slipping into hypothermia.

EPIRBs & Satellite Phones

Technology has provided several items for the emergency kits of travelers in remote regions. A battery-powered EPIRB beams distress signals to satellites that do nothing but monitor the emergency frequency. With monitoring stations in motion and the transmitter in a fixed position, monitors are able to fix the position by triangulation. EPIRBs allow no communication other than a signal that expresses life-threatening danger requiring rescue. A beacon beeping in the snow tells nothing of the scale of the disaster, only that a disaster has occurred at a specific location.

Activating the signal by inserting the antenna and flipping a switch initiates an extremely expensive rescue operation. The more remote you are and the more logistically complicated and equipment-intensive the operation, the more costly it will be. The issue is never simple. Suddenly, you must simultaneously consider economics, liability, a maze of moral obligations and a host of serious decisions. The more you can think about in advance, rather than in the frantic emotional heat of a frightening emergency, the better.

Commercial trip leaders may be required to carry an EPIRB; a group of peers might choose to bring one or not. In either event the presence or absence of an EPIRB on a trip must be agreed upon in advance and put in writing by each member. Willingness to accept hypothetical consequences in a warm living room is one thing. A person might change his or her mind while writhing in the pain of an acute appendicitis attack three weeks into a snowshoe trip.

In theory, you should use an EPIRB only in potentially survivable but life-threatening situations. You would set it off in the event of starvation, suspected appendicitis, a thus-far-survived cardiac problem, injury to the spine or head or anything where treatment in the field would fail or probably fail but where immediate evacuation might allow survival.

In less dramatic situations where care, control and self-evacuation are possible, the decision to call for help becomes murkier. What if infection develops? What if you don't recognize the full dimensions of the problem? What if a million other puzzles complicate the scene? The best one can do in such a situation is to have a checklist or protocol to follow, and err on the side of caution if errors are to be made. No matter what happens, keep a complete narrative of the event, all decisions, measures taken and plans for care and progress. Keep the group aware of and in agreement with the narrative as it progresses, and have it signed by each member periodically throughout the emergency as proof of accuracy. This will vastly simplify the full investigation that will unfold after the event. Under duress, people's interpretations, memories and objectivity can vary and fluctuate wildly.

Satellite phones are small, light and affordable. Unlike EPIRB/ELT technology, "sat" phones allow two way communication anywhere in the world. The ability to have conversations vastly improves all aspects of an unfolding emergency and allows the most effective solutions to emerge. Not only can you call out, but you can leave the phone on at specified times for people to call in.

Get good batteries, and in winter keep them warm by wearing them next to your body and sleeping with them. If possible, use the phone only in the heated tent to prolong battery life. Insert batteries only for phone use, then remove for keeping them warm. Assume that battery life will be cut in half in the cold. This still leaves a significant buffer if you keep them warm and you may even realize the full four to six hours of life for each battery.

Make rules. We prefer that our guests are not even aware of the presence of satellite phones, for if they are, they unknowingly seem to behave more carelessly. And, they want to use it. As with cell phones, e-mail and land-line phones, it is probably safe to regard most messages as non-essential. So make it clear to your group that this is emergency equipment.

Finally, manage the trip as if no outside help is a possibility because it may not be. Don't be seduced into feeling secure because of such great technology. Use of a sat phone or an EPIRB does not guarantee rescue. But with vigilance, great care and clear rules, you can then be witlessly pleased when they work. If you're really lucky, you'll never need to use such fabulous back-up systems.

First Aid Kit

In decades of guiding, we have made one psychological evacuation and one injury evacuation. The five or ten incidents that required first aid were all minor—small cuts, a burn or two, dehydration, sunburn and the like. These have not been enough to keep us fluent in first and secondary aid, nor up to date on evolving methods and strategy. The best advice is to take hands-on courses, read the best of the literature and keep your skills current with refresher courses. Try one of the courses offered by organizations whose instructors are active in search and rescue. In this way, you gain real-world know-how through exposure to hundreds of actual case studies. Avoid standard first-aid courses as offered by adult education programs and well-meaning extension programs; these are predicated on the availability of ambulances and paramedics and teach you little of practical value except how to dial a phone. The best option is to enroll in a W-EMT course, the "W" signifying wilderness. At least take some shorter courses or workshops in what might be called backcountry medicine or wilderness first aid.

Some additional points of advice: Keep your first-aid kit simple. Don't bring anything you are not qualified to administer or use. If you want prescription drugs such as a more powerful painkiller than is available over the counter, consult a physician and describe your backcountry needs. You may find a doctor willing to write a prescription for your first-aid kit. Keep your medicines updated for full effectiveness. And apply common sense at all times.

In the age of HIV and AIDS, you will want latex gloves on the very top of your kit. Don't take chances with anyone, even if you think you know them. In addition, keep each person's medical form and questionnaire in the kit, as well as forms for yourselves, should you be the ones to get hurt. An outline to guide people in the basics if they get frantic, SOAP notes*, pencils, paper, small flares and a card with international ground-to-air symbols that can be stomped into the snow for aircraft, are just some of the nonmedical first-aid items to keep in the kit. (Another nonmedical item you can carry in the kit is several pairs of soft earplugs to issue if chronic, loud snorers share your tent.)

If you evacuate someone not accompanied by a member of the party, be sure to

---

*SOAP is an acronym for:
S for Subjective (age, sex, chief complaint, type of injury, description of event)
O for Objective (vital signs, patient exam)
A for Assessment (problem list)
P for Plan (treatment of each problem)
(Written SOAP notes should accompany the victim along with any narratives, medical forms and other information.)

put any notes, forms, instructions or incident narratives into the victim's shirt pocket and safety-pin it shut. This way, if rescue personnel forget to give these papers to the physician or other authorities, they will still be with the victim.

If you don't create your own kit, there are some excellent ready-made first-aid kits available through organizations and companies that deal specifically in backcountry items (see the addresses at the end of this chapter).

Repair Kit

Repair kits see a lot of use on almost any trip. Since they are designed to cover a diversity of possibilities, they are almost always complex, but this does not mean they have to be overly burdensome or heavy. We carry ours in a cotton sack, and inside there are smaller bags containing related items.

The glue kit contains the Therm-a-Rest repair kit just as it comes from the company. We also carry Five-Minute epoxy and Ambroid cement.

In little film canisters, we carry small bronze ring-nails, copper rivets and burrs, a few self-tapping sheet metal screws of various sizes for stove repair and several sizes of flathead wood screws for toboggan repair.

The sharpening kit contains an axe stone; a finer Arkansas stone for putting a razor edge on knives, axes and the ice chisel; and a fine tapered round stone for the inside curve of crooked knife blades. Related to sharpening is a six-inch medium file for regrinding the chisel or axe should either tool get a nick in its blade.

The sewing kit contains a Speedy-Stitch awl with accompanying needles and a bobbin of waxed thread; assorted regular needles; heavy and light thread; heavy waxed thread; a darning needle and several yards of yarn for sock and mitten repair; patching material in Egyptian cotton (four-ounce weight as used for tents and wind gear); patching material in marine-grade canvas for duffels, toboggan tarps and clothing; a small swatch of soft leather for patching; and at least a few triangular "glover's" needles for leather sewing.

One small bag contains a tiny pair of Vise-Grips; a finger plane (a great gift for native people); a spool of 23-gauge wire for repairs and for building good snares for snowshoe hare; a few feet of very heavy wire of the type found in the woodstove section of a hardware store; and a screwdriver with a Phillips head on one end, slot head on the other.

Odd items include a portion of a roll of duct tape, spare lampwicking for snowshoe bindings, a roll of babiche for snowshoe repair, a Swiss Army knife, a spare container of matches, a block of paraffin for waxing toboggans, the aforementioned fishing gear and several feet of tanned leather thong for a variety of fastening needs.

This all fits in a small cotton sack and resides in the duffel that contains communal gear.

There are other items that properly belong under the repair-kit heading but are

Winter Walk to Kuujjuaq

A Two-month 350 Mile Journey across Labrador

For 58 days, through February and March of 1991, we embarked on our first big unsupported snowshoe and toboggan trip. Here are some excerpts from our trip journals.

[Garrett:] In most cases journals exist to serve as a trigger for the memory of the writer who will then fill in with the fuller picture of the experience and accompanying emotions. They tell with details rather than show with imagery part of a much more complex picture. As my friend Rob Perkins observes, "Life is what happens between the facts."

On the other hand, I am among those who compulsively read as many trip reports and journals as I can...and get great joy in comparing notes and learning whatever each of our various explorations has to teach.

[Alexandra:] My journal is an utterly candid and unedited account of what I saw, felt and dreamed during our journey. I didn't have an audience in mind when I wrote in my journal; rather, it was a time to have a friendly chat with myself; an end of the day gathering of vignettes and thoughts. Many of the most poignant moments never made it to my journal because of fatigue. But one sentence can bring back all the stories to me for further reflection, which is the intent of this journal.

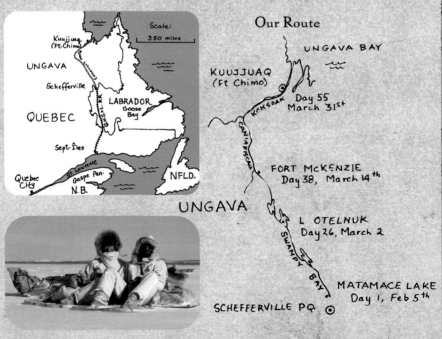

Our Route

WINTER WALK TO KUUJJUAQ

Select entries from Garrett & Alexandra's Trip Journal

ALEXANDRA

February 5, Matamace Lake

Day 1

6 1/2 miles traveled (6 1/2 miles traveled, 343 1/2 to go.)

I lit the fire around six and we had leftover caribou and bannock. Made a bannock for lunch. Four degrees Fahrenheit and the wind rising in the northwest. Fairly strong all day, so you had to lean into it. And of course, the loads were heavy so we stopped often for short spells. Surprisingly able to move, and we actually camped next to the spot we camped in three years ago. Used our old tent poles for firewood. We went nearly seven miles today! I thought we would go half that and be exhausted. It was tiring but not impossible. My toboggan carries the tent, my axe, stove, my gun, group gear duffel, my sleeping bag, daypack, my duffel, a 71-pound food duffel and the thermos. It weighs 170 pounds. On Garrett's toboggan is the ice chisel, tent pole, shovel, his axe and gun, the kitchen bag, his sleeping bag, daypack and duffel, the maps and three duffels of food. It weighs 244 pounds.

GARRETT

February 6

Day 2

Minus 5 degrees Fahrenheit at dawn, 11 degrees at lunch, 22 degrees at dark.

Made good time on the wind-pack of several lakes, which was hard enough so we didn't need snowshoes part of the time. On these stretches the going was easy enough so my mind had time to wander, and I found myself thinking about the visit by [our Naskapi friends] the Swappie's. David had been particularly interested in our equipment and looked at everything quite carefully, and really appreciated the light Egyptian cotton of the tent. At one point after sweeping his eyes across the food duffels he said, "Long way, not much food. Maybe get hungry, maybe die." This he said matter-of-factly and with the stoicism and acknowledgement of the "maybe" factor that is such a part of the native thought pattern, but he looked directly at us as he said it, and perhaps he was testing our readiness.

Alexandra and I responded simultaneously, and with essentially the same answer, "Well, if we die you can have our stuff." He heard our respective answers and broke into a grand grin. In Naskapi he translated to Susan and they both laughed hard and long and smiled broadly. It seemed that perhaps we had given a satisfactory response.

The recollection of the statement seemed to strike Alexandra also, for when we rose from a brief rest and looked down several miles of lake toward the

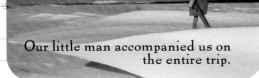

Our little man accompanied us on the entire trip.

Naskapi friend, David Swappie.

Michel, a Swiss man we met along the trail.

RIVIÈRE

outlet she said, "Long way, maybe never get there." And we knew we had a joke that would last the length of the trip.

ALEXANDRA

February 20, Swampy Bay River

Day 16

9 1/2 miles traveled (80 miles traveled, 270 1/2 to go.)

Having a lovely Sobranie (a fancy Turkish tobacco) while Garrett prepares super. It's so calming, puffing away. Three things come to mind once my pipe gets going. Tonight I thought of that which has been, that which is happening and that which has yet to come.

I played a joke on Garrett today. He was up ahead and had passed a ptarmigan sunning in the woods, not noticing it. I shot it and I smiled because I could just see Garrett jump. I know what that's like, because as I was walking along up in the lead one day, he did the same thing. It startles the living daylights out of you. Anyway, I plucked and cleaned the bird on the spot while it was still warm, cleaned my hands with snow and heated them back up again holding the still warm body of the bird.

Beautiful, bigger moon tonight lingering over our campsite. Garrett got up at 5 a.m. and we were walking around 8:30, earliest yet. As the sun was setting there was very fine snow in the air and the air in the sun's direction was hazy pink and purple and gold, all mixed up.

Saw a marten scamper across the river not too far from this campsite. Earlier, in the open water at the outlet, we watched an otter in and out of the water, going about his business. While Garrett was cutting wood he looked up as a gyrfalcon swooped low through the woods, scaring a whiskey jack [gray jay] even.

ALEXANDRA

February 27, Narrows Moonrise

Day 23

5 miles traveled (114 miles traveled, 236 to go.)

Beautiful golden sunrise bathes the tent in color and seeming warmth. It was so hot in the tent I finally took off all my shirts. Usually it's barely cold enough to keep ones long john top on. Once again I cheerily announced how much warmer today was—only to find out it was significantly colder than yesterday.

As I hauled water up from the hole tonight, the air stinging my lungs and nostrils, I was struck with the golden, glowing tent and the smoke rising straight up. Moonlight. Black and white mountains looming. I thought how fragile and tentative our existence is. If the tent were to burn down, if one of us got hurt...Hard not to think about ones existence. I feel much closer to spiritual matters here, and more connected because I feel so fragile.

Down home everything goes along at a pace too busy to feel like one's NOT in

charge. Up here you know you could be snuffed out just like the ptarmigan sunning themselves and never knowing what hit them.

GARRETT
March 2

Day 26

Alexandra: 3 ptarmigan, 2 shells. Garrett: 2 ptarmigan, 3 shells (one miss).

Saw another gyrfalcon and perhaps a total of 100 ptarmigan in various smaller groups among the thick willow islands where the river braids into Lac Otelnuk.

Fine hauling conditions with the exception of our balance and perception being thrown off during white-out conditions. Spent a fair amount of time falling forward when encountering invisible drifts, and occasionally leaning off them on one side or the other.

Entered Lac Otelnuk in a full blowing storm so couldn't see much. Kept an indistinct shore on our southwest side and a blank white void on our northeast. Even with the ferocious headwind the temperature was fairly mild. We were overheating about every half hour or so and would rest on the ice to cool off. On one of these pauses the snow was falling very thick and blowing hard. We sat on the ice facing away from the blast of wind and looking into the oblivion of down-wind whiteout. Alexandra and I got to laughing about how horrible a picture of the situation would look out of context. She said, "Anywhere else they would be closing schools, shutting down roads, and letting people out of work. And here we are walking along on a lake and reclining on the ice to cool off." This only made the image more lunatic—two blizzard buffs more than a hundred miles from anyone collapsed on the ice laughing uproariously.

ALEXANDRA
March 2, Lac Otelnuk

Day 26

8 1/2 miles (133 miles traveled. 217 to go.)

My right eyebrow ridge and lid is swollen from frosting it a few days ago when I was unaware. A few bumps on my cheeks have appeared from the cold or diet. Nothing to complain about, just observations. My heartbeat was so slow when I awoke, I was startled. I've noticed the veins in my arms are large and my right forearm bigger than my left from limbing pickets every night. Fun to see these changes.

ALEXANDRA
March 3, Les Haute Chutes

Day 27

3 miles traveled (136 miles traveled, 214 to go.)

Very cold today, and a wind. Garrett's nose kept turning white and all morning we both fought to keep face parts from freezing. The only way to solve it was to

remove our glasses (which keep fogging up with or without scarves) and cover our faces with scarves and goggles. But it's disconcerting to travel when one is so nearsighted. So our noses hurt ... and cheekbones ... and eye sockets.

We lunched at the beginning of the outlet just out of the wind so it was quite pleasant. When we rounded the corner, all sorts of mist was in the air, coating all the trees heavily with frost. It looked like fairyland. We packed a float on the wooded south shore mostly because we were on that side. The falls are stupendous—100 to 150 feet high and quite wide. Water thundering down and a mile-long canyon below. Deep caverns and huge icicles hanging off the cliffs everywhere. Mist rising hundreds of feet in the air and then the west wind would hurl and disperse it over the land upstream.

We packed a float until 3 p.m. and then dragged our toboggans partway over the trail. We set up camp just below an outlook of the falls that is perfect. We are in a protected hollow. Scarce dead wood. Five inch diameter white birch here and there. Clear as can be now. No moon yet, just brilliant stars and planets.

GARRETT

March 3

Day 27

This is our "half way" day and we are a little more than 30 miles shy of the half waypoint. We are as much as a week "behind" if one doesn't factor in conditions and expectations of good or bad going. Ahead of us are nearly 60 miles of lake travel, which we hope will provide wind-pack and improve our average. River sections between could contain serious hard going both through lack of wind-pack and the sections where we must get around canyons and rapids. We are counting on wind-pack, lengthening daylight, moderating temperatures, lightening loads and increasing strength to make up the difference. We have suspected for more than a week now that as we get closer to the threshold of extremely difficult, or even no return, that we will be continuing on; and for the moment so we are.

We have moved 19 days in a row with no break and are looking forward to the layover with keen delight. In addition to figuring out a route and packing it, we are greatly looking forward to full baths, washed hair, laundry and a hot lunch in camp. If there is time, a number of small repairs need to be made and the sharpening of edged tools to be done.

ALEXANDRA

March 5

Day 29

7 1/2 mile traveled (143 1/2 traveled. 206 miles to go.)

Burn site. I arose at 5 a.m. and lit a fire, noticing it was a tolerable temperature. It was the perfect temperature all day—warm enough, but not enough to melt anything. We warped each toboggan down the canyon side. We used a

Les Hautes
Chutes

Les Hautes Chutes,
the stupendous 150-foot falls
at the outlet of Lake Otelnuk.

B

stern line wrapped around a tree and then around the person. The front person warped short stints around trees too, with the haul line. Took one and a half hours to get them down onto the riverbed. I can't imagine going upriver.

The going was wonderfully good and away we went. Had an enjoyable lunch telling each other "Little Benjamin" stories. The stories feature Auntie 'Zandra and Uncle Garrett telling stories of their trip in Ungava in a quavery old person's voice (as we are now in our dotage), to a young fidgety boy who'd rather be playing.

"Now Benjamin, these are the very pair of snowshoes I wore on my trip to Kuujjuaq.... Did I ever tell you about our trip to Kuujjuaq? Up on the mantle there, that's a piece of bannock from our last night on the trip to Kuujjuaq..."

We get laughing hysterically sometimes over these vignettes.

I had a vignette tonight: "Now Doc, I just don't understand these abdominal pains I've been having. "Well dear, what have you been eating?" And then I start listing what I've been eating...

For breakfast, 8 eight-inch pancakes plus a half cup syrup, 1/8-pound bacon and 2 to 3 cups tea, ummm, then a hunk of bread eight-inches across by two inches and four inches thick, a half ptarmigan breast, 1/4 stick margarine, 4 tablespoons jam, 4 squares of chocolate, 1/2 round of fruitcake and 3 cups of tea...that's lunch. And for supper, usually one ptarmigan, 2 to 3 cups of broth, 1/2 cup of rice, half a bannock (like lunch) and one cup of cocoa with milk in it. What have I forgotten? Oh yes, a bit of boiled dried fruit for desert." The doctor's face tells all.

We went six miles after lunch. Came down the northeast side of the river and there was a perfect toboggan-width path the whole way, past the rapids and chute. The kind of open water that our friends and families are justifiably worried about.

Great northern lights tonight. I liked a particular swirl that lasted only a few minutes. Marten everywhere.

ALEXANDRA

March 7, The Birds of Castignon

Day 31

11 miles traveled (162 miles traveled, 186 to go.)

Warm day with a steady south wind. Pulling was fantastic. Must have been 26 degrees Fahrenheit or so because of the feel of the snow, the ease and glide of the sleds, the melt on our mukluks and gear etc. We fairly flew down the lakes with the wind at our backs helping us.

Lunch supplies are almost out (2 pounds of salami, 1/2 pound of pepperoni, no cheese, no peanut butter, a little jam and that's all). We make a 3-cup bannock and spread some butter on it (which we're low on too). It's hard to conserve everything, but we have to. We'll try for more ptarmigan and have them for lunch too.

GARRETT

March 8

Day 32

Alexandra: 2 ptarmigan, 2 shells. Garrett: 1 ptarmigan, 1 spruce grouse, 2 shells.

As I cooked breakfast, Alexandra is out to see if any ptarmigan were in the willows around camp. She returned with two birds.

Very warm and gray. We'll be quite wet today. Must have reached 35 degrees F, the kind of thaw that is the bane of the snow traveler's existence. Somewhat hard going in flat light. The lake was quite good with the exception of stumbling on unseen drifts. At the outlet we entered deeper softer snow while skirting leads. Between Castignon and Minowean was a very rocky section and a steep rapids. House size boulders tipped and leaned every which way where the river cut through, but there was still a narrow shelf among the rocks that let us slip through.

Tired and a bit grumpy about the thaw tonight, but the good part of it will come when the cold returns to harden up this layer of snow that got damp.

ALEXANDRA

March 9, Camp Picturesque

Day 33

4 miles traveled (173 miles traveled, 176 to go.)

We're camped by a rapid and steep drop in the river on the west bank. Axe marks on branches and trees nearby. Nice feeling to know others came by here too. The leads started early out of Minowean and the ice was thin with many places where the water came through. Blue black holes in the snowy river ice field. So we had to stay on shore for the most part. That means float packing because of deep, unpacked snow and up-and-down grade. But it was mild (15 degrees Fahrenheit) so the toboggans pulled wonderfully. Our moccasins stayed unthawed.

At lunch we merely sat by the toboggans again on the ice where we were crossing a small cove. Lunch was great—bannock and ptarmigan, jam, tea and chocolate. Afterwards Garrett jumped to his feet and instantly fell in the river. He hit a rock or he says he fell back in time to prevent going in deep. He spread his legs and arms and looked incredibly funny sitting by that hole twelve inches from the toboggan, lunch crumbs all about, and an unspilled cup of tea in his hands.

Snowed lightly all day making the woods really pretty. Water and rocks were pewter gray and dark blue. Lovely.

Funny to hear water rushing by ... makes me think it's spring. It was getting light at 5 a.m. when I arose. Early. And not dark at 6 p.m. when I was making supper. We have twenty days more food with us. It took us 35 days to reach the

A lone ptarmigan blending in.

An unwary spruce grouse.

Alexandra's bag decorated with a traditional "ptarmigan tracks" pattern.

halfway point, which was today. If it takes us 35 more days to go the next 170 miles, it will be April 11 and we will have to find our own food for roughly two weeks. None of this scares or bothers us. Just keeping it in mind.

GARRETT

March 10

Day 34

Garrett: 1 ptarmigan, 1 shell.

Packed a float at the falls and returned for lunch before hauling across. On the trip back over we had our closest encounter with disaster. All went well until a fairly steep section where we started to descend to the river. This point was exactly above the foot of a deep strong-water lead, and it was also the point where I stumbled after catching my snowshoe frame in the wind-pack. My toboggan jumped track and slid by me pulling the towline off as it went. The wind-pack held it aloft where in deep snow it would have plowed to a stop or perhaps tipped over, and of course the path of least resistance was straight down the hill. It gained speed, never hit anything to stop it or change its direction, and headed straight for the open water.

Alexandra saw the event begin to unfold, threw her line and attempted to lunge forward to grab my sled before it got away. Her towline caught on her shoulder, which jerked her toboggan forward, and it too jumped track and headed downhill. Fortunately hers began to carve a long turn and flipped over.

Mine crested a small rise, almost stopped in some willows, but then leapt onward again as momentum and speed increased on a steepening slope. We could see the ice and the edge of the lead just above where it closed in again to a river of solid ice, but not the steep section of slope the toboggan was rushing down. The wait for the toboggan to appear, as it must just before plunging into the lead, was one of sickened and horrific anticipation. Yet the sled never appeared. The seconds ticked by with that interminable slow motion and heightened perception peculiar to those participating in an emergency. Still nothing. My brain had already cataloged the load: axe, gun, sleeping bag, personal gear, ice chisel, two-thirds of remaining food and the kitchen kit. No sled appeared.

We dashed forward, beginning to grin with relief but not quite daring to hope the load was saved. But it was. Along the entire stretch of shore there was just one big rock and my sled had run smack into it and stopped. Somehow the sled had bent upwards and flexed, absorbing the shock, then slid back down the face of the rock to repose as if nothing had happened. Three long gouges in the bottom were the only hint of the dispersal of energy. Not a plank was smashed, not a bit of the load loosened or askew.

I hugged the rock, my sled, thanking them all in a flood of unabashed and unbelieving relief. Another 50 feet and all would have been irrecoverably lost. The only items on the sled not essential to convenience and survival were my camera lenses, film and the French-Naskapi-English dictionary.

Shadow of the "ptarmigan track" woven into our snowshoes.

ALEXANDRA

March 10, Camp Thankful

Day 34

7 miles traveled (179 miles traveled. 169 to go.)

Pure contentment. Pipe going, me resting against piled up sleeping bags...hot fire crackling, Garrett cooking supper quietly, my mind and heart calm. Thankful, because we came very close to disaster. I don't know what saved us.

Why did Garrett's toboggan successfully careen down a steep slope missing trees and willow patches and drifts and head for the only open water and be stopped by the only obstacle at the water's edge? We felt like Sebastien McKenzie (the mail carrier from Sept Iles to Fort Chimo I had heard about on my first trip to this region 18 years ago) and Susan Swappie were looking out for us. We really did feel that.

If Garrett's toboggan had gone in, there would have been no way to retrieve it. Gone would be his clothes and sleeping bag, gone the maps, gone the food except 25 pounds of flour I had, gone a gun and an axe, gone the cooking pots. If mine had been lost, we would have lost a stove and tent, most of the flour, my clothes and sleeping bag, the ELT (emergency location transmitter) and repair kit, first aid, candles, ammo, a gun and an axe. Everything we have we need very much. There is very little spare.

GARRETT

March 14

Day 38

Woke to a brittle cold day with the air full of ice crystals. Made 11 1/2 miles on the lake today and are camped at the site of old Fort McKenzie. Not much firewood here and a wide-ranging search yielded only a few spindly sticks. I was able to get just enough but was greatly vexed in the search and completely tired out from floundering in the deep snow.

Passed the 200-mile mark a few miles before reaching the site of the fort. Lac Canichico was making frequent and regular adjustments all morning in the cold. Great thunderous groans and grindings would rattle down the lake as if the impact of distant bombs were shaking through our feet and assaulting our ears.

We have a special cup of tea after supper to toast the old ones if their spirits are around. Alexandra thanked the ones who were born, or died, or spent time here and so inspired her to want to make this trip. To see this landscape, and imagine how things might have been. I hoped that they could hear us and know our thoughts and dreams were open and welcoming.

ALEXANDRA

March 14, Old Fort McKenzie

Day 38

I wonder what the sounds of the night would have been here in 1925? Dogs? Daytime children yelling and laughing? Axes chopping? People hauling water from the river? The cry of Susan Swappie as she was brought into this world? Sebastien MacKenzie was the manager of the Hudson Bay post here from 1916 to 1936. The post was abandoned in 1948. Susan Swappie was born here. How many people have been born or died here?

ALEXANDRA

March 18

Day 42

9 1/2 miles (239 traveled, 95 to go.)

Despite our regular food, I find I am getting hungry. I need more to keep me going. So we had a half ptarmigan breast a piece with two slices of bacon and a plate of hot cereal with a few fruits and eight small bunkers (fry biscuits). Just have to get more birds to eat, as they are the only replaceable item.

I am lean and hard and my veins are very pronounced; Even that one that goes from your ziphoid process down toward your belly. Legs look smaller in the thigh. Face has all sorts of frost patches that itch and hurt all at once. The bone of cheek and eye hurt a bit. But overall feel just wonderful and strong and steady in spirit.

GARRETT

March 18

Day 42

Alexandra: 1 ptarmigan, 2 shells. Garrett: 2 ptarmigan, 2 shells.

Cold morning after a clear night. Wind is gone. Ran out of dried banana chips this morning and whole wheat flour last night. Up until now, all bannocks, duffs, drop biscuits and flummies have been half unbleached and half whole wheat. Twenty pounds of white flour left. Ran out of jam at lunch today.

Clear sunny beautiful day that was warm, but still below 20 degrees Fahrenheit so everything stayed dry. After lunch we walked side-by-side in fine conditions and conversed our way through magnificent views. Saw a plane. Camped 99 1/2 miles from Kuujjuaq. I think because we have never been there, Kuujjuaq does not loom as the "end" of a fantastic trip. I have thought of it a few times over the past few days and always with excitement and wondering anticipation. I'm delighted it doesn't appear on the edge of thought as a final bracket.

Rewaxing using heated tin cups and paraffin.

GARRETT

March 19

Day 43

Alexandra: 1ptarmigan, 1 shell.

Not long after lunch we saw a wolf coming toward us with the wind in our favor. We hoped it would come close to check us out but it remained quite cautious and stayed about a half mile away. We tried to keep its curiosity up by flopping around on the ice like wounded caribou. It still retained a great sense of caution though we nearly drove it crazy with curiosity. It barked a one-syllable, frustrated bark three different times, and tried to illicit a response from us that might reveal what we were by prancing around in place and feinting this way and that. We finally got too cold to stay still any longer and got up and continued on our way. The wolf followed our progress but stayed about a mile off to our side, and finally went off through the deep snow in a burned patch of woods.

My Achilles tendon has been bothersome all day.

Alexandra's statement of the day: While peering into a blistering headwind through goggles, with face wrapped fully in scarves, she stated, "Well, we didn't come all this way to be molly-coddled."

ALEXANDRA

March 20, Garry's Cove

Day 44

9 miles traveled (257 miles traveled, 78 to go.)

Really cold in the night...and all day. Never really warmed up. The sun warmed the snow some because pulling wasn't too bad. Certainly not compared to the early days. But I'm not sure we have the surplus strength to haul what we did the first month. We are clearly burning all we eat plus our own cells.

I can feel all the bones of my pelvic girdle from the back and it's spooky. Haven't taken my longjohns all off at once to look myself over and now I'm not sure I want to. We talked about it at lunch and Garrett finally realized the seriousness of losing that much weight. He's lost a lot too but is not at the point where it's unusual looking. My facial sores aren't healing very fast either. So tonight I'm brewing up some larch [tamarack] inner bark for vitamin C.

After I eat, I have tremendous energy. But an hour or so before lunch it's amazing how far away a half-mile looks and is in terms of getting there. So, we can do two things. One, eat more of existing supplies and work hard at getting to Kuujjuaq as soon as possible. Or two, eat frugally and hunt ptarmigan hard (takes time and uses up miles and energy) and get along as best we can. In both cases we have to hope a winter storm or unforeseen event doesn't stall us. I'm sure we'll blend the two. Eat somewhat more, hunt persistently, and move steadily. No layovers unless they're necessary. Garrett's Achilles ache

Wolf tracks

Alexandra's back reveals the first stages of starvation.

cleared up overnight. Hard not to focus a bit on one's physical state. Spirits are high and we continue to joke a lot and have good fun.

Beautiful views. Large mountains on either side of today's four miles of narrows. I got one ptarmigan this morning. Later I was sneaking up behind a point to get some on the other side when I heard in the distance a bird cry. It was a gyrfalcon harassing an immature eagle. As the eagle came towards me and the gyr flew back to the mountains, I was thrilled at the sight. Then dismayed as every ptarmigan lifted off and flew out of range, scared by the eagle. So, everybody ruined everybody's meal. Pretty funny.

ALEXANDRA

March 21, Fruitcake Campsite

Day 45

7 1/2 miles traveled (264 miles traveled. 71 to go.)

First day of spring. Very, very cold last night and all day. And the damn wind blew, not hard, but steadily enough to make me have to fight to keep my face protected all day. Very tiring and exasperating.

I've decided food and one's metabolism are like a sand clock. You only have so much time to use the energy provided by the food. I feel like it's a bit of a race to get to Kuujjuaq while we still have food and energy. Ptarmigan are plentiful but hard to get more than one per flock. Then walk a half mile to where they landed and hope they won't be too wary and fly away again.

Saw "gold" in the pyrite rocks at the Chute, a steady two-pitch multiple lateral drop. Saw some amazing sharp pointed ice formations on the underside of a huge boulder so Garrett crawled inside and pretended he was being eaten. It looked real.

Had a nice big supper of one thermos capful of chili, one capful of peameal, one and a half cupful of dried meat, a few carrots and I put corn spoonbreads on top. Filled right up. Must have absorbed all I ate last time, no consequences. Excellent energy today...until we reached camp. Almost attacked my fruitcake. Two owls calling back and forth last night—great horned.

GARRETT

March 21

Day 45

Alexandra: 1 ptarmigan, 1 shell.

Very cold day with steady hard northwest wind. Not like spring at all.

Some interesting things are appearing as we enter our eighth week on the trail. Though food has held up well with easy voluntary rationing, we are getting very hungry and are losing weight rapidly. We have become much like our stove; We function best when full. For the last few weeks we have been less and less satiated after meals, and our intake has increased everywhere it can.

Pyrite, or
''fool's gold''

Minus 48

We have eaten double the ptarmigan that were planned into the menu, which means we have consumed a total of sixty birds thus far. Our helping size of such things as pancakes, hot cereal and pea meal has gone way up.

The past few days that have been cold have really pointed out how fuel related our work capacity is. Just before lunch stop we are really low and small efforts seem impossibly demanding. After lunch we can resume at normal speed and pace until an hour or so before camping time when we begin to flag again as our lunch is metabolized away. This is the first time we have ever experienced this level of hunger and have a very definite and visible end to our resources. The bird hunting is the one unpredictable wild card that keeps things interesting indeed. We have every expectation that the lack of any sign of caribou will continue.

ALEXANDRA

March 22, Camp Desperation, Forbes River

Day 46

8 miles traveled. (272 miles traveled, 63 miles to go.)

We traveled hard all day into a steady and infuriating wind. Very cold day too. Fought to keep my face from freezing as usual. The most frustrating part is I have discovered no solution. Even with glasses off and a scarf totally over everything (for I cannot breathe in air directly), in an hour the scarf is so wet it is useless. I rotate the scarves to keep dry as possible. Maybe I'll try a full balaclava someday and see if that works. Garrett seems to do fine exposed to the wind. My lips and mouth get too cold for it, unless it is just after lunch and I am good and warm.

I swore and swore at the wind and even privately burst into tears late in the day as it crept under every layer, laying its icy touch to blister cells. Infuriating.

Bit of a canyon, steep sided and narrow 1½ miles before Forbes River and we got caught there at camp set up time. Garrett went up the lowest bank he could find and scarcely had the energy to reach the top. I was waiting at the toboggan to preserve strength, saw him struggle and realized we had to find something else. Scouted down the west shore as fast as I could, came around a point and there was the mouth of the Forbes River, a half mile closer than anticipated! Shelter from that wind. We got here around 5:00 p.m. and were tucked in by dark. Tough camp but everything's fine now. Even washed up and admired my new bony body. Have to put padding all around my coccyx bone it protrudes so.

While Garrett was preparing our breakfast, I went out to the water hole and jigged. In ten minutes a 16-inch Brook Trout hit the lure and out onto the ice he came, flopping and flipping and turning hoary white fast. The sun was just rising, its rays just reaching the water hole. Oh, I was thankful for that. Garrett's cooking the whole fish up tonight—boiling it so we get all the goodness.

Tried to sneak up on ptarmigan twice but they were too wild. Hope this wind drops so we can get some birds. Or maybe see and get a caribou. Wouldn't that be great? Found a freshly shed antler yesterday (month old maybe) and a few yards away, a shed one from a long time ago as lichens were growing on it.

ALEXANDRA

March 25, Camp Twenty-five Ptarmigan

Day 49

4 1/2 miles traveled (286 miles traveled, 55 miles to go.)

Ptarmigan were tame today. We got 25 birds! We only need 24 so we can have three per day for eight more days. One each for supper and one divided up for breakfast (parts) and lunch (breasts). What an incredible relief to have so much meat now. Everything else is so pitifully low. Just a half-cup of lots of things. We keep halving and dividing again until it's almost ludicrous. Our "cocoa" is one spoon of cocoa and one of milk. Watery and bland but we think it is sweet and creamy!

Ring around the moon. Mars glowing brightly in the south, setting. Brightest I've ever seen it. Northern Lights through the hazy night sky. Tonight we celebrated reaching the junction of Riviere Melezes and the Koksoak by bringing out a package of condensed mincemeat. I always keep it in the bottom of a pack pocket for emergencies and had forgotten it was there. We used a little of it in a bannock and it was so sweet I thought I'd gone to heaven.

Today, looking at the white mountains that turn this big river north west, I was filled with a joy. And I thought "You know you are in love with a place when you feel homesick and you haven't even left." I'd do this trip over at the drop of a hat. I don't do trips for the adventure, rather the romance. Adventure suggests not enough forethought to keep you from them. Romance, however, engages one's mind, heart and the landscape.

ALEXANDRA

March 27

Day 51

9 miles traveled. (303 miles traveled, 39 miles to go.)

We met two Inuit on snowmobiles; a father Bob and son John, heading upriver. They had a big komatik and supplies. Just for an overnight. They came tooling around the corner and were no doubt as startled and surprised to see us as we them. VERY nice people. Simple conversation. They introduced themselves right away. Unusual. Poised. Had Chimo hat on (we did too). No caribou. Not trapping. Just hunting. Has camp up Riviere Melezes. He simply said, "the river to the west." We had not seen anyone for 46 days.

In the night I awoke twice feeling uneasy. The third time I awoke just as our aluminum center pole folded. The tent came collapsing down with a load of

snow on it. We dressed under the confusing folds of cloth, found our way to the door. Garrett cut an eight-foot picket center pole. I carefully removed all snow from the tent. When Garrett went inside with the pole and raised it, it was a perfect fit—everything tight, snug and sturdy. During the night I remembered a sensation of a Presence [and it] didn't feel like a good Presence. Before sleep, my eye suddenly was drawn to high above the door flaps. I looked there hard, wondering why I was, and then tucked in and went to sleep. Where I had been looking was in direct line with where the break in the aluminum pole was.

ALEXANDRA

March 30, Camp Convenient Cove

Day 54

15 miles traveled. (324 miles traveled. 18 miles to go.)

We awoke to perfect temperature. The soggy snow has frozen to a hard glitter. Garrett got the fire going at 4:30 a.m. and after our usual three-course meal of ptarmigan parts, cereal and pea meal (no bunkers, flour's too low), we were on our way by 7:30 a.m.

The river gets wide and the banks are low. Lovely white mountains, single, rise here and there a mile or two from shore. I can hardly believe I'm sitting here so close to Kuujjuaq at last. Now our food supply seems ample. Yesterday it seemed so meager. Up and down, everything changes each day, each moment it seems. You can count on change.

If the going is as good as today, we could be in Kuujjuaq tomorrow night ... with four cups of flour to our name. Or, it could snow and take us two or three more days and we'd have a pitiful amount just for lunch. So, we're guarded with eating everything just because we're still 17 miles from town.

I was thinking today about this trip. I'd call it a "romantic adventure." Romance is something that is cherished and seldom occurs. Adventure is something that happens that you didn't plan on. This trip was a mix of rare occurrences, all memorable. Why did I want to do this trip? Simple. I wanted to see the country.

ALEXANDRA

March 31, Camp Kuujjuaq

Day 55

18 miles traveled. (342 miles traveled, 0 to go.)

I'm writing this in the morning, as I was so sleepy last night my eyelids kept drooping during supper. We arose at 4:00 a.m. and had a good breakfast and were on our way at 8:00 a.m.

Had our last tea and snack on the ice two miles from town. Hesitatingly we wandered toward town. Trying to take in the BIG CHANGE. As our luck

Kuujjuaq at last.

would have it, we found a place to set up camp on the outskirts of a tank farm, a half-mile out of town. The stove was lit at 7:00 p.m. and by 9:00 p.m. we were dining on ptarmigan and curry rice with apples and a two-cup bannock topped off with Koksoak cake. Then FELL into bed. I dreamt of two or three figures dancing in a close formation to imitate a ptarmigan. The Willow Ptarmigan—a small white bird. It saved our lives.

GARRETT

April 1, Kuujjuaq

Day 56

April Fool's Day. To celebrate, my Achilles tendon is stiff enough to make me hobble and be humble. My ability to stride makes the half-mile walk to town loom as a daunting obstacle.

There was another April Fool's joke in store for us. Town was closed. We had eaten the last four dried dates and last sixteen raisins we had to our names with the last of our breakfast cereal and had intentions of finding a store. Nothing was open, and town itself seemed amazingly deserted. We had two names of people we had never met, one was Sally Chislett who had worked for the Quebec/Labrador Foundation.

We were getting faint with hunger by this time as our usual re-fueling "lunch" had crept up to 10:30 a.m. during the last week on the trail. No one was home at Sally's ... just then a truck pulled up, we flagged it down and met the surprised driver—Sally Chislett.

The town was taking a holiday. Everyone was gone to a picnic at a lake 20 miles outside of town. Our bellies growled. I think hunger played tricks with my vision all the way out. I was glad to be a passenger and all I had to do was hang on and absorb the bumps.

The whole community with only a few exceptions was gathered on the lake, and there were Ski-Doos and komatiks everywhere. Races were in progress, many people had fires going along the shore and were having lunch and boiling kettles. My concentration began to waver as lunchtime came and went. I was aware the news of who we were spreading in little ripples, like northern lights pulsing through the crowd.

Suddenly Sally appeared moving quickly and purposefully, "Are you hungry?" We allowed we were with vast ridiculous politeness. She herded her small group of friends to a recently vacated picnic fire and we began to eat. Everyone gave us food and our graces lasted only so long. We gulped stuff down like puppies who knew the rules of etiquette but couldn't quite muster the discipline to follow them.

Later, as we said good night and were ready to return to the tent, Sally told us of the old Inuit ladies who had saved us at our mid-afternoon lunch. "I'm sorry. I didn't think of hunger. I was telling the old ladies of your trip and they looked right at me, interrupted, and said, "Did you feed them?"

"Well, no not yet. We're going..."

"Feed them. Now. People always hungry from the bush. Go!"

The last supper—ptarmigan and curry rice with apples and a two-cup bannock topped off with Koksoak cake.

Carrière

Anse 57, 58, 59,
(NEXT TO
FUEL TANKS)

Our last campsite.

Friends. David, Su___ _nd Noah Swappie.

Hard to believe we can fly in several hours what it took us two months to walk and snowshoe!

GARRETT

April 4

Schefferville, Quebec

At about 3:00 p.m. we jumped into the plane and were off. Had a short flight due to a powerful tailwind. We reached Schefferville in just under two hours.

Had a fine supper with friends but excused ourselves at 8:00 p.m. to go see the Swappie's on the Naskapi Reserve.

David Swappie was waiting in the yard of his house. He waved us in, but didn't greet us at the vehicle. He brought us all the way to the kitchen where Susan was. She was all excitement. We hugged and kissed each other all around, and I felt witless and overcome. Somehow our reunion was that of a long lost family. Somehow the trip had brewed a kinship. Walking the heartland of our host's home had spoken for us all. The common love of land and place possessed no language barriers here. Over tea we exchanged the stories. David and Susan had prayed for us apparently as often as we had thought of them. And with each story and response and our mutual grins a bond grew inexplicable stronger and more profound.

What an irony. In the absence of any young native people with an interest in the bush, a couple of middle-aged white wanderers will make it possible for the older couple to throw off the confines of the artificial reserve town for a while. For us it is a dream come true. Since our first travels in this country, we have hoped to spend time in the bush with people old enough to be incredibly skilled and have clear memories of the time when the people were truly on the land.

As we leave, David presents us with a black fox pelt. "Don't sell. For you!" he says. Susan gave Alexandra a new Chimo hat she had crocheted. We part in another blizzard of warmth and love and giant smiles and crinkly eyes.

How could this bridge of friendship be so strong and present? We drive back to McGill in silence, each stunned and wrapped in an overwhelming blanket of joy.

carried elsewhere. In a daypack containing photographic gear is a small jeweler's screwdriver set. These small screwdrivers are great for working on glasses frames, camera parts or anything held together by tiny screws. Also in the daypack are personal items such as a crooked knife, spare batteries and a few spare safety pins. (Each person carries two or three big safety pins ("blanket pins") in his or her shirt pocket flap. They are used to pin together felt liners, mittens or anything that can be hung over opposite sides of the drying lines in the tent at night.) A sharp triangular awl is also along for boring wood or puncturing sheet metal to start a self-tapping screw.

Moccasins and liners dry in the heat of the tent's peak.

Of course, the largest item in the repair kit is the axe, and this is kept accessible on top of the load during travel in case it is needed en route. Each person should have a pocketknife, as well as a match case.

On trips with a firearm, the ammunition and gun-cleaning kit are generally carried by the person in charge of the firearm rather than with the group gear.

Group Gear

The group-gear duffel is the community catchall. It is always carried on a toboggan in the open so that it can be accessible all day. It holds the first-aid kit, repair kit, toilet paper, spare saw blade, candles, rope bag, bungee cord bag, trip library, maps, spare moccasins, whisk brooms, EPIRB, wax bar, slush scrapers and anything else that is needed and shared by everyone.

Your tools are the keys to your success and convenience under normal conditions, and survival and well-being in an emergency. They exist as a paradox of minimums and maximums. You want to have as few of them as possible, in formats that favor lightness and multifunctionality, yet all the while you ask your tools to perform maximally. In evaluating the shifty balance between weight and usefulness, you might find yourself opting for full-sized items that would drive an ounce counter crazy. In toboggan travel, where necessary items are concerned, efficiency may count more than weight. In all forms of travel, unnecessary things weigh a ton, no matter how light they actually are. Be selective. Don't bring junk. Don't forget anything.

USEFUL ADDRESSES

Ice-Chisel Blades

Empire Canvas sells the Snow Trekker ice chisel. It is five-feet long that weighs four-and-a-half pounds.

Empire Canvas Works
P.O. Box 17
Solon Springs, WI 54873
715-378-4216
www.empirecanvasworks.com

Swedish Trail Axes

Gransfors Bruks axes are made of superb steel, are well-balanced and are quite literally the only commercially available axes of any quality. The Scandinavian Forest Axe model is the best trail axe we've ever used.

Duluth Pack Store
365 Canal Park Drive
Duluth, MN 55802
800-777-4439
www.duluthpack.com

Piragis Northwoods Company
105 North Central Avenue
Ely, MN 55731
800-223-6565
www.piragis.com

Empire Canvas
(see address above.)

EPIRBs (ELTs)

Most marine catalogs carry a number of EPIRBs, most of which are geared for marine use. However, many carry a small waterproof model that weighs only 15 ounces. It is called the RLB-21 "Mini B" class B EPIRB, and it's great for canoeists and winter travelers. Try:

West Marine
P.O. Box 50070
Watsonville, CA 95077
800-538-0775 (800-BOATING)
www.westmarine.com

Hamilton Marine
Route 1
Searsport, ME 04974
800-639-2715 (207-548-6302)
www.hamiltonmarine.com

Wilderness First Aid

These organizations are the best in the country and have set the standard for others to emulate. Both offer a variety of courses ranging from month-long W-EMT training programs to workshops ranging from two days to two weeks.

Wilderness Medicine Institute publishes the Wilderness Medicine Newsletter, dedicated to the "recognition, treatment and prevention of wilderness emergencies." Written by the experts in the field, it contains state-of-the-art techniques and ideas.

WMI sells a fine first-aid kit, the WMI bag, at a very reasonable price.

In the East:
Stonehearth Open Learning (SOLO)
P.O. Box 3150
Conway, NH 03818
603-447-6711
www.soloschools.com

In the West:
Wilderness Medical Institute
P.O. Box 9
Pitkin, CO 81241
303-641-3572

Chapter 6

Provisioning: Food & Menus

PROVISIONING: FOOD & MENUS

*"Dream: Two or three figures dancing in a close formation
to imitate ptarmigan. Ptarmigan. A winter white bird.
They saved our lives."*

—from Alexandra's journal, the morning after concluding a two-month snowshoe journey to Kuujjuaq, 1991

One of the most memorable and nearly prophetic statements we have ever heard was uttered at the outset of a lengthy snowshoe journey traversing the Ungava peninsula of northern Quebec*. David and Susan Swappie, Naskapi elders, and their son Noah were inside our tent sipping tea with us. David had just finished carefully examining our combination guns, axes, snowshoes, tent, stove, ice chisel, anoraks, wind pants and moccasins. He had been showing us the favored Indian route north to Kuujjuaq (Fort Chimo) on our crisp new maps spread around the spruce-bough tent floor.

Now he straightened, a troubled expression on his broad, dark face. He glanced toward the food-filled duffel bags that lined the walls and, in the characteristic gesture of his people, pointed to them by pursing his lips and said, "Long trip. Not much food. Maybe get hungry." He paused and added, "Maybe you die."

Two months and 350 miles plus a return flight later, we were again sipping tea, this time in the living room of the Swappies' reservation home. We were sun-darkened; our clothing, worn and stained from life on the trail, hung sloppily on our frames. We had each lost 15 to 20 pounds, a dangerous drop for bodies that naturally carried little extra weight.

But oh, how David and Susan laughed as they squeezed our stringy arms and poked our bony sides. One generation ago, it was common for people returning from the country to be lean and, in many cases, starving. But if you had not died and returned, it was a time for laughter and rejoicing.

So how do you keep from starving on a snowshoe trip? The most impor-

Alexandra emerges from the willows with five ptarmigan during lean times on the walk to Kuujjuaq. (See Journal insert too.)

tant point to consider is not how much food can you bring or procure, but how can you best save from burning calories. The quick answer to warding off starvation is to have at least two more people with you to save caloric output by their assistance in daily chores. Next thing to consider is food. In our case, food drops were out of the question. We were limited as to how much food we could physically haul, so we had to depend partly on what the land could provide. This was a chance we were willing to take, and we were prepared to accept the consequences. As fate would have it, the caribou, a herd one million strong, did not migrate by us. Our lives then rested with the plentiful but lean ptarmigan. However, had our journey taken much longer, even the ptarmigan wouldn't have saved us, for what our bodies needed was the higher fat content that only caribou could provide. So, if you cannot live partly off the land, it's important not only to bring enough food, but to bring the right kinds of foods.

Fortunately, on most journeys, you will not have to face or even worry about starvation. In the following discussion, living on what the land provides will not be addressed.

Principles

How much food should you bring? Whether provisioning a weekend trip or a two-month journey, you will have to account for an identical list of considerations.

o *How long are you planning to be on the trail?*

o *How many people will you be traveling with?*

o *What are the usual diets of these individuals?*

o *Will you be in mild, moderate or extreme cold?*

o *How arduous do you expect the travel to be?*

o *How accustomed are the participants to this kind of trail life?*

We will address these questions in the context of canvas-tent/woodstove camping with travel by snowshoe and hauled toboggan. If you apply the information that follows to related activities, such as winter mountaineering, dogsledding or sledge-hauling in the high Arctic or to bivouacking you could run into real trouble. Food quantities differ greatly depending on whether or not you travel with an external heat source, such as a woodstove.

On one of our early forays into the wintry wilds, we traveled with just a tarp for shelter. Our only sources of warmth were food and clothing. We weren't traveling in this Spartan way to be tough; it was the only way we knew.

We had camped in New England's mountains, which are notorious for winter extremes, and we thought gas-fired trail stoves and lightweight tents were the only (if grueling) way to travel in winter. We had heard of hand-hauling toboggans on

---

*See the color insert pages for Alexandra and Garrett's account of this epic journey.

the waterways, and this combined with our mountaineering ways seemed to work pretty well.

However, without those hours of body-saturating warmth that a glowing wood-stove provides, we had to consume vast quantities of food to get adequate heat. In fact, on that subarctic, bivouac-style snowshoe trip, we each consumed 3.8 pounds of food per day. In tent/woodstove camping, the average is 2.8 pounds! Each day we each had to carry one extra pound of food just to keep marginally warm. On a trip lasting two weeks, we doubt that an average person could easily stay in good health or spirits under such challenging conditions. Certainly, that person could not relax enough to absorb the beauty and character of the landscape.

How long are you planning to be on the trail?

Generally, people's appetites increase as the trip goes on. Part of this is due to mental and physical adjustments. Experience has shown us that people's pretrip diets don't wear off until day four. Coincidentally, it seems to take the same amount of time to become mentally attuned. Once you are well into a trip, you find that your metabolism functions at a higher rate as both mental and physical exercise affect your body. So, on trips more than a week in length, you will have to pack more food per person, per day, than you would on shorter trips.

How many people will you be traveling with?

Food consumption goes up as the work load increases. If you are traveling with only one other person and it's up to you two to accomplish the varied tasks of setting up the tent, getting wood, chiseling water holes, cooking, cleaning up and making repairs, you will burn a lot more calories than you would if there were more people around to share the work. Also, even though traveling with more people means carrying more food, each person actually carries less weight overall because the weights of tent, stove, ice chisel, etc. are shared. Each person's work along the trail is correspondingly reduced as there are more people to break trail and shuttle toboggans forward.

Expanding the group size to maximize efficiency and food consumption only works to a certain point. The ideal group size for the average trip is probably four to six persons. This assumes that the tent will hold all six people; otherwise, you will need additional tents and stoves and the original purpose will be defeated. Of these four to six, at least one should be the recognized leader. Leadership, or the lack thereof, can greatly affect appetites.

In summary, the smaller the group, the more food each person will need each day.

What are the usual diets of these individuals?

Changing diets can wreak havoc with one's daily functions and moods. Most people are more or less addicted to caffeine and, without their cup of black tea or coffee for the day, suffer day-long headaches and drowsiness. Some people ordinarily do not eat much fat. In the cold, you'll find that your body craves and needs it. Meat, and lots of it, suddenly looks appetizing, as do salamis and sausages.

If in your more sedentary life you are inclined toward light oils and fresh fruits and vegetables, your mind and body initially balk at the heavier diet life on the trail demands. Constipation is a common reaction to moving to a different environment, but this can usually be simply and quickly alleviated by drinking more water and eating dried prunes. Steady exercise also encourages the body to adapt to its new diet and routine.

Before planning the trip menu and supplies, learn each participant's dietary needs and/or preferences. One of the most difficult diets to translate into winter trail fare is that of a strict vegetarian (see sidebar in this chapter). Finding non-animal fats that can match the high heat production of the fats in bacon, sausages, butter and cheese is difficult. Nut butters are calorically similar to meat and dairy fats, but they can be challenging to work into meals three times a day.

Will you be in mild, moderate or extreme cold?

The colder it is, the more calories (heat) you need. Mild temperatures are assumed to be roughly between 20 degrees and zero degrees Fahrenheit, moderate between zero and minus 20, and extreme between minus 20 and minus 40. The wind must be taken into account when considering these ambient air figures, because a seemingly benign minus-ten-degree day with a 15-knot wind blowing affects your exposed skin as if it were minus 45. Skin can freeze within one minute at that temperature, creating significant stress on your system; and in response, your body's need for food increases as your metabolic rate rises. In contrast, after a mild, wind-free morning of easy travel, you will need to eat a lot less to refuel than you would on a cold, windy morning.

Ironically, during the coldest lunchtimes, one is least inclined to eat heartily. You soon get used to this natural reaction and learn to eat a lot of food quickly. Filling your anorak pockets with food for hourly snacking is another effective way to get around cold-day reluctance to eat.

How arduous do you expect the travel to be?

The harder you have to work, the more calories you burn. Since your trip will be on a waterway with little overland travel, you will be traveling on a fairly level surface. The colder, deeper and lumpier the snow is, the harder a toboggan pulls. On a day of hard pulling, you will have gone a shorter distance yet burned more calories than on an average day. And if there were only two of you breaking trail, you will have expended even more energy. All this translates into caloric losses that must be replaced by nighttime.

A look at the extremes illuminates this point. One could project that a group of four to six physically fit people traveling lightly laden on a weekend snowshoe jaunt in mild and windless weather might need 3,000 to 4,500 calories per person per day (roughly 2 to 2.5 pounds). In contrast, a couple on a long journey, traveling in cold, windy weather with a heavy load, might use 5,000 to 6,000 calories per person per day (roughly 2.6 to 3 pounds).

How accustomed are the participants to this kind of trail life?

No matter how physically fit you may consider yourself, you are not fit for snowshoeing unless you have been snowshoeing. Different activities use different muscles. Even if you jog six miles daily, you will find that your legs and other parts of you are sore after a day of snowshoeing and setting up camp.

Similarly, if you are new to traveling with a group and sharing small living quarters, you will have to adapt mentally. Traveling alone or with one companion may likewise require major adjustments. The blazing winter sun, the driving snow, the buffeting from the wind as you snowshoe along the winding waterways all become familiar aspects of life on the trail. Learning how to keep one's face covered in a headwind and bare hands functioning at 20 below Fahrenheit, how to don and doff clothes efficiently for rewarming and cooling, how to avoid preoccupation with the past or projection too far into the future—all are vital skills, the acquiring of which burns up a lot of energy.

The more familiar you are with the physical and mental demands of the winter trail, the less energy you will expend. A winter traveler enjoying the fresh air and landscape at the doorstep of a toasty cotton tent, contentedly sipping tea and absorbing the present, burns fewer calories than someone pensively trudging along in the breezes of the ice field, worrying about what tomorrow will bring.

CHOOSING THE BEST FOODS

Generally, you want to pack foods that are nutritionally balanced, lightweight for travel ease, high in caloric content, aesthetically pleasing and easy to prepare on the trail. These foods can be broken down to percentages of proteins, fats and carbohydrates. Getting a caloric balance between these categories is very important, especially on long journeys.

Consuming too much protein without complementary portions of fat and carbohydrates over the long term can lead to death. This is called "rabbit starvation" in the North. This does not refer to a scarcity of rabbits, but rather to a condition that results from living exclusively on rabbits. These animals are extremely lean at all times of the year. At the end of one week of living only on rabbit, you will already show signs of protein poisoning. Your appetite will be enormous, yet after each meal you will still feel ravenous. The stomach distends, and in about eight to ten days diarrhea begins. Death will result in several weeks unless you secure fat.

Perhaps it is useful to regard the three food types in terms of their ability to generate heat. Your body will burn carbohydrates first, then fat, then protein, based on

VEGETARIAN DIET

Snowshoe-and-toboggan country is not a place where vegetarianism has naturally occurred.

Only the last generation or two has had the luxury of arbitrary vegetarianism. In most cases, this is based on personal preference, ethics, morality, religion and other abstractions. Beyond tropical and temperate realms, a vegetarian diet is only feasible now due to rapid transportation systems, controlled environments and importation of foods and culinary traditions from abroad.

Several of our friends who are committed organic growers and vegetarians have attempted to live throughout the year in northern New England on only local produce and native species. Despite ingenious greenhouses over cold frames that let them grow fresh food all through the winter, most have given up on local produce. It is far easier to import the produce, products and ideas of the tropics, Asia, Japan and the South Sea Islands.

To be a vegetarian in a northern environment requires that you know about nutrition in absorbing detail. If you live in a manner that involves physical labor and outdoor work, this is particularly important. Less knowledgeable vegetarians who live such a life tend to have low energy, little stamina for sustained physical work and susceptibility to colds and flus.

There are dozens of definitions of the term *vegetarian*. What is acceptable and what is not to different individuals is exceedingly complex. Most trip leaders issue questionnaires to elicit specific information on this point, but in some cases leaders need thorough coaching from the individuals who will be on the trip.

We have had no problem accommodating vegetarians on winter trips in Maine, where temperatures are moderate throughout the trip. Occasionally, there are nights of minus 30 or below, but the usual range is from plus 20 to minus ten or 20. Also, our Maine trips are all short, lasting only five days to a week.

In deeper cold, vegetarians experience differences in energy output, level of hunger and feelings of cold as compared to omnivores. Frequently, the only time omnivores mention sleeping poorly due to cold is on the nights when the whole party has had a vegetarian supper. (This may be due in part to a digestive environment that overpowers the sudden introduction of a vegetarian meal.) We have one friend who has been on several winter trips in Maine but has no interest in a Canadian trip specifically because she believes her chosen diet would be inadequate in the deeper cold. Based on our own observations, we agree. It is possible to be a vegetarian on winter trips, but it is not necessarily easy or fun. You must know nutrition and your own physiology thoroughly, and you may have to eat more than three meals a day. Two of the meals can be hot, but a series of lunches and perhaps a night snack should be available at ambient temperature.

From a nutritional point of view, vegetarian menus match the nutrient content of omnivore menus fairly easily. The problems seem to arise from the ease of digestion of most vegetarian fare and the speed with which such fuel is burned. An omnivore is like a stove burning seasoned hardwood, while a strict vegetarian is like a stove burning dry pine and needing to be stoked with great frequency for less heat.

In a mixed group, it is best to plan meals so that the vegetarians can be accommodated without complicating kitchen procedure. Reserve one pan for non-animal oils for frying, and plan main courses so that the making of the vegetarian elements can occur in a separate cooking vessel. It is simple to vary lunch options enough so that those who want to avoid meat or cheese can do so.

Vegetarians who travel in the North should be aware that most northerners, whether settlers or natives, are very generous and love to host visitors. The more remote the setting, the more festive the event when strangers arrive. Feasting is the means of partying on such occasions, and it would be rude not to accept either the invitation or the food. The North is a land of black teas, coffee, fats and meat. To native people, vegetarianism is completely unfathomable. With settlers, you might at least speak the same language and come from similar cultures and could explain things, but the idea would still be basically foreign.

Sooner or later, you will be invited for tea or to eat. Your hosts will not have a cupboard full of herbal teas, nor are they likely to have many, if any, vegetables. If they do, they will have been grown in the South and shipped weeks or months ago and would have the same appeal as a hunk of cellulose. You will want to prepare your responses to such invitations in advance so that your manner will be polite and accommodating. If you wait and are forced to think on your feet, there will be heightened potential for cross-cultural missteps, embarrassments and perhaps unintentional rudeness.

We know a high school student who recently completed a canoe trip in an Inuit community. He is a vegetarian and a supporter of the antiwhaling efforts of the environmental organization Greenpeace. Within minutes of his arrival, a beaming cluster of new friends invited him to partake of some beluga whale muktuk (raw strips of blubber, which is a delicacy). He hadn't anticipated anything like this, but not wanting to offend, he joined the feast. His more timid companions did not, and a distinct coolness was reserved for them. In addition to building trust and friendships, he now has a better understanding of the meaning and ramifications of his personal ethics and of the world's complexity.

On our Canadian trips, participants occasionally decide that they would like to try some ptarmigan if no one is opposed to hunting. Over time, we have ceased to be surprised at this request, but one year, it came from a person whose questionnaire had stated a preference for vegetarian fare and whose habits on the trip were in keeping with that. It turned out that wild meat was acceptable to this individual, and acquiring it was a meaningful event much like that experienced by gardeners who harvest their own produce.

For trip leaders, the best advice regarding the feeding of vegetarians might be to experiment continuously, proceed cautiously and don't be surprised by much, even by vegetarians who would have a bird shot or gobble up muktuk.

ease of metabolism. Fat provides the most energy or heat for its weight (9.3 calories per gram) but releases it more slowly. Carbohydrates and proteins both give 4.1 calories per gram, the former giving energy more quickly, and the latter producing heat more quickly. You can choose food for certain desired effects, as illustrated in the following story.

The red and green caboose lights of the northbound Quebec North Shore and Labrador train winked and wobbled as they wove away from us, disappearing into the Labrador night. We stood in the deep, quiet cold, next to our heap of gear, which had been tossed from the baggage car moments before. It was minus 42 degrees—our first night in a subarctic winter wilderness.

Once settled under the nearby spruces, bivouacked in our sleeping bags on our toboggans, we snacked on cocoa mixed with butter from a small plastic tub. Periodically that night, as the cold deepened and the trees and lake spoke in sharp cracks, we'd waken and snack again on this mixture. In 20 minutes, the calorie-rich food would kick in, and a warmth emanating from the stomach would spread all through our bodies.

This was our most dramatic lesson in the wonders of caloric heat. The cocoa's main contributions were taste and some quick heat, while the fat-laden butter provided the slow-burning warmth we needed.

In a temperate climate, an active outdoorsperson might use 3,500 calories each day. In a cold climate, that same person might need anywhere from 4,500 to 6,000. Since fat is the most condensed form of calories, you could theoretically bring nothing but great slabs of fat and ice cream to reach your caloric quota. However, without the metabolic balancing effects of proteins and carbohydrates and the minerals and vitamins of a more varied diet, you would quickly decline.

A group of college students discovered a mild but disconcerting effect of eating too much fat on a two-week winter outing. In fact, the symptom was so consistent from person to person that we dubbed the condition "butter buns."

We had carefully lectured the students before the trip about how to eat to stay warm. Being aware of society's negative attitude toward fat, we harped in particular on the positive qualities of fat consumption in a winter environment. We suggested adding a dollop of butter to each cup of cocoa. Within a day, all of us were heaping butter globs into our hot drinks.

After a week, each of us developed reddish itchy welts on our buttocks and outer thighs, exactly where one puts weight on first. Although we were winter camping, we were getting only moderate exercise for the diet we were consuming. We could only surmise that our group rash was in response to an overly high-fat diet. This same intake of fat would not have had these side effects if we had been exercising heavily or been in deeper cold, for the fat would have been metabolized rather than stored.

In addition to calories from carried and planned foods are the calories your body can obtain from itself. This occurs during extreme privation and is the body's last fighting chance at preservation. When you burn more calories than you take in, your body will literally begin to consume itself. At first, subcutaneous fat will be burned, then the fat surrounding organs. If things get bad enough over a longer term, the body will start to burn muscle tissue, a serious situation that starts only

FOOD CONSUMPTION & CALORIES

Proteins: Eggs, milk, lean meats, fish, whole wheat, oats, yeast, corn, rye, buckwheat, peas and beans. Approximately 1,800 calories/pound (4.1 cal./gm). Rebuild body tissues, liberate more heat than carbohydrates.

Fats: Butter and margarine, cooking oils, animal fats, cheese, nuts and nut butters. Approximately 4,080 calories/pound (9.3 cal./gm). Long burning; liberate most heat.

Carbohydrates: Sugars, syrups, cereals, pastas, starchy vegetables (potatoes, sweet potatoes, peas, beans, corn and carrots), rice, breads, pancakes, dried fruits and candy. Approximately 1,800 calories per pound (4.1 calories per gram). Quick energy.

Recommended percentage of total calories to be provided by each food category:

	General Diet	*Cold Weather Trips*
Proteins	*12%*	*20%*
Fats	*30-35%*	*40%*
Carbohydrates	*46-53%*	*40%*

Recommended number of calories per person per day for average cold-weather trips: 3,500 to 5,000 calories. Extreme work in deep cold: 6,000 calories per day.

after all dispensable fat sources are consumed. This was what happened to us on the Kuujjuaq trip.

On that journey, as closely as we can estimate, we consumed 460,000 food calories, which included the provisions we brought as well as food hunted en route. As mentioned earlier, we also lost 30 to 40 pounds of weight between us. As each pound of body weight lost releases 3,000 calories, we therefore took in an additional 90,000 calories. Our actual caloric intake was 550,000. Each day, then, we were each consuming approximately 5,000 calories. This figure coincides with the ideal daily intake for a male working eight hours in a polar climate as calculated by the U.S. Navy Medical School. However, the reason we lost weight with this caloric intake was that, with just two of us, our work load was extreme—as were the temperatures to which we were exposed.

It is foolhardy to plan on using calories derived from your own body as an energy source, even if you are overweight. Your body does not need the added stress of sudden weight loss through food denial and is better off adapting naturally to its new environs and level of activity. Furthermore, the body does not even begin to metabolize its own fat stores until it has been subjected to prolonged food deprivation. The body consumes itself reluctantly and only in dire straits. Otherwise, the response would be triggered by false alarms such as missed meals or a few days of hunger.

MENU PLANNING

You do not have to become a nutrition expert and memorize long lists of foods, their components and caloric values to be able to plan a successful winter outing. Rather, you need to become familiar and creative with the basic foods that form the foundation of a healthy winter diet.

The list that follows under "specifics" is derived from our experience guiding or traveling with people of different diet preferences and needs on both short and lengthy snowshoe trips in the boreal and subarctic North. When you plan your own provisions, keep a careful record of the types and quantities of food brought. And, very importantly, keep notes on provisioning and tally up food left over (or run out of) at the conclusion of your journey. This way you will have an invaluable account from which to plan your next outing. After years of planning menus and food lists, all you can be certain of is that the basic foodstuffs are dependable, but quantities and food types will have to be revised for each trip.

There is a difference in the basic foodstuffs brought on a recreational snowshoe trip versus an expedition. When you are traveling at a leisurely pace, or guiding a group whose primary reason for being in the country is to have fun, the menu should naturally have variety and perhaps include fancier fare. Stews, stroganoffs and thick, calorie-rich sauces can be premade and frozen in deep trays. These can then be cut into blocks and stored as individual portions. Similarly, egg-rich doughnuts, brownies, 'lassy teutons (Newfoundland-style ginger cookies) and fruity cranberry cakes can be made and frozen before the trip. On a longer trip, when lightness and efficiency of fare are paramount, you'll find it best to travel with basic staples and a pemmican mix. Your fare will be simple and repetitious, but highly nourishing.

Specifics

Now we're getting down to counting raisins and crackers, and we'll begin with a list that includes the entire range of foods we take on winter trips.

Bacon. Wrap meal-size portions in waxed paper for ease of separation once frozen. Unwrap and place a chunk in a warm frying pan with a lid. Remove the lid once the bacon has thawed and continue cooking as normal. Remove the cooked strips and place them on an enamel metal plate under the stove for warmth. Use or save the drippings for "bunkers" (biscuits), etc.

Baking powder. The best brands contain nothing more than calcium acid phosphate, bicarbonate of soda and cornstarch. Store in durable plastic bottles.

Butter. Margarine and butter contain the same number of grams of fat and have the same caloric value. Margarine spreads more readily in the cold; butter is tastier in baking and cooking.

Candy. Hard candies give quick energy. Remember, however, that strictly sugar candies give a boost but have no staying power.

Cereal. Corn, wheat, rye, oats and bulgur—whether cracked, rolled, creamed or flaked—make excellent and varied morning fare. Oat bran is great, too.

Cheese. Frozen, cheddar cheese crumbles and is therefore best used for cooking. Muenster and Swiss can be thawed in the morning by the stove and used on crackers for lunch.

Chocolate. Bars of chocolate are a wonderful high-energy snack and seem to have no storage problems.

Cocoa. Another high-energy food. A dollop of butter melted into it gives an extra caloric boost that will warm you long after the drink has been consumed.

Coffee. This is not an ideal trail drink due to the side effects of caffeine. Caffeine stimulates your nervous system and causes perspiration as well as dehydration. However, on easy trips in mild weather, there is no reason not to enjoy the pleasures of fine roasted coffees, as their side effects will not be as critical to your well-being.

Crackers. On shorter trips, these are ideal for lunch with salamis, cheeses, nut butters and jams. As bread is moist, it freezes rock-hard and is therefore useless for trailside lunches. Hardtack, Royal Lunch crackers, Sea Rounds and Ryvita Crisps are excellent brands.

Eggs. Bulky on long trips, they are fine for short ones. Simply let them freeze and stay frozen in their shells in the original boxes. Cardboard cartons protect them better than foam or plastic ones. To fry a frozen egg, immerse it in a cup of hot water to remove the shell. Place the egg in a hot, buttered pan. It will defrost and slowly cook, much like an unfrozen egg. To boil, place the frozen egg in cold water and bring to a boil. Continue cooking until the egg is either soft- or hard-boiled.

Flour. Bring 75 percent white flour and 25 percent whole wheat or mixed grains. Whole-grain flours provide more roughage and a bit more fat and protein than white flour, but they are more difficult to bake with. When you can, use unbleached, unbromated white flours for maximum nutritional value.

Fruits. Dried fruits are incredibly versatile and a great source of carbohydrates. They can be eaten with hot cereals, snacked on during the day or stewed with a little sweetener for a simple, hot, fruity dessert. This same sauce can be used on pancakes in place of syrup.

Fruitcake. This is not the usual holiday fruitcake that everyone loves to hate. Rather, it is a rich combination of eggs, milk, vitamin C, honey, cranberries, nuts and chopped fruits—a daily nutrition-packed treat one never tires of (see recipe on page 145).

Grains, pastas, rice. Try to get whole grains and brown rice for increased nutritive value.

Honey. The colder it gets, the stiffer honey gets and it soon becomes useless. It is fine for a mild-weather weekend trip but is impractical on longer trips in sustained cold. If you bring it, use a plastic container that can be dipped in hot water to make the honey flow.

Jams and jellies. Store these in wide-mouthed plastic containers with large-threaded lids. Jams will stiffen somewhat in the cold but are usually spreadable. They freeze below minus 24 degrees Fahrenheit, but by thawing during breakfast, you can usually keep them spreadable until lunch.

Jerky. Dried, seasoned meat (see recipe on page 143) makes an excellent snack while snowshoeing. Being mostly a protein, it releases heat more quickly upon metabolizing than do carbohydrates such as candies.

Juices. Hot fruit juices with a dash of spice make an extremely tasty drink. The most practical way to carry juices is as dry fruit crystals.

Legumes. Grind split peas and lentils in a food mill for quicker cooking on the trail. Beans, if you grind them, are equally good fare. Combined with grains, legumes provide carbohydrates as well as protein.

Meats. On shorter trips, you can get away with the additional weight of frozen meats rather than bringing dried meats. Meat tastes better before it is dried, though it is surprising how delicious a stew made from dried meats and vegetables can be. You can also prepare meat sauces at home and freeze them for the trip. On weekend jaunts, it is most practical to precook meals and freeze them in wide-mouthed plastic jugs such as food service-size mayonnaise or pickle containers. To thaw, simply place the jug in a saucepan of water until you can break the contents into removable chunks. Any meat can be frozen. Sausages and other fatty meats should not be dried, but lean prime cuts dry wonderfully.

Milk. Dried milk can be added to cocoa for a richer taste. It can also be added to other hot drinks, pancake mixes, cakes and biscuits. Nonfat dried milk is most readily available, but milk with the natural fat left in is best. Canada Boy dried whole milk is available in some provinces.

Nuts. Cashews, pecans, walnuts, hazelnuts (filberts) and Brazil nuts are all high in fat content and well balanced in both protein and carbohydrates. They are ideal as snack food, as they do not require thawing and are also excellent added to curry sauces, dessert toppings or cereals.

Oils. Lard (animal fat) and vegetable oils are similar in fat content, but animal fats provide more calories. We have found that animal fats also burn more slowly and thus last longer.

Pancakes. You can get a higher nutritional value from a mix that you assemble yourself than by buying a commercial mix. However, some of the finest mixes available can be found in health food stores and require only water. Just before spooning batter onto the hot frying pan, gently stir a cup of dry, light snow into the batter. This will lighten your cakes, particularly if you are cooking without eggs.

Pemmican. A perfectly nutritionally balanced concentrated trail food. It is comprised of dried meat, dried berries and rendered fat (see recipe on page 143).

Salami and pepperoni. Even though fat doesn't readily freeze, these will need some thawing by the stove at breakfast for consumption at lunchtime. On layover days they can be sliced, fried and added to hot cheese sandwiches.

Seeds. Pumpkin, squash, sesame and sunflower seeds are all rich in calories and are excellent added to any main dish or as a presupper snack.

Seasonings. Herbs and spices weigh so little that it's worthwhile to bring a variety.

Soups. Empty the contents of the desired number of soup packets into a durable plastic bag on which you have written how many cups of water to add. Foil-and-plastic packets add unnecessary weight and leave unburnable refuse that you would have to pack out.

Sugar. This is used primarily in baking, as a drink sweetener and in pancake syrup. You will need more than you think.

Syrup. On shorter trips with fancier fare, real maple syrup is irreplaceable. It takes deep prolonged cold to freeze it, so it is practical to bring, though a bit heavy. Maple sugar is an ideal form in which to carry maple syrup. Just add a little water to reconstitute it.

Tamari. This is a soy sauce without additives. It is salty and can be added to sliced tempeh when frying, or to any other dish that calls for salty seasoning. It won't freeze but isn't practical to bring on long trips due to its weight.

Teas. There is nothing more savored on the trail than a mug of strong, sweet tea. Canadian tea bags hold enough tea for two cups. Tea is a pleasant stimulant with no noticeable side effects save temporarily yellowing your teeth. Fruity herbal teas are delicious in place of a juice drink in the morning. A wide selection of herbal teas will be greatly appreciated for the variety they provide. Tea does act as a diuretic, so make sure you drink enough water during the day to stay well hydrated.

Water. Obviously, this is not something you have to bring on the trip, but it is something you must constantly have. A surprising fact: winter air is as dry as desert air. With each breath, moisture escapes your body in billowy, white clouds. The loss can amount to as much as one cup per hour or six quarts (approximately six liters) every 24 hours. In winter, most water is lost through respiration as compared to summer, when the greatest loss is through perspiration.

Each person will need four to six quarts of water per day. During strenuous or prolonged exercise, the thirst mechanism is not always the first thing to be triggered. More common initial signs that someone is not sufficiently hydrated are a headache and irritability. The importance of making sure that everyone is adequately hydrated cannot be overstressed.

A half-gallon stainless steel thermos provides for rehydration of thirsty walkers. Here a party toasts the trail at a height of land between watersheds in central Labrador, making a small ceremony with a hot cup of tea.

SAMPLE MENUS

Breakfasts
Mixed grains for cereals—oats, bulgur, rolled wheat, bran, cornmeal
Dried fruits—apricots, apples, banana chips, dates, figs, papaya, pineapple, prunes, raisins, etc.
Meats—sausage, bacon, scrapple
Tempeh—tasty soybean patties cooked in tamari
Pancakes—multigrain
Eggs—fried or boiled
Hot drinks—herbal and black teas, coffee, cocoa and hot fruit juices
"Bunkers"—drop biscuits cooked in bacon drippings or vegetable oils (see recipe on page 144.)

Lunches
Fresh-baked yeast breads (for layover days)
Bannock—baking-powder bread cooked in frying pan (see recipe on page 144.)
Crackers—pilot crackers, Sea Rounds, Royal Lunch, Ryvita Crisps
Soups
Cheeses
Salami, pepperoni
Peanut and almond butters
Jams, jellies
Jerky (dried meat) (see recipe on page 143.)
Candy
Fatback 'lassy teutons—ginger cookies high in sugar and fat (see recipe on pg. 143.)
Fruitcake—homemade, rich in butter, eggs, milk, dried fruits and vitamin C (see recipe on page 145.)

Suppers
The meat dishes below can be adapted for vegetarians by replacing meat with nuts, cheeses or soy products such as tempeh, dried tofu and texturized vegetable protein, or by mixing complementary proteins such as legumes and rice. Additionally, all vegetables—except those we recommend you freeze—are dehydrated.
Chicken curry with onions, peppers, carrots, apples, raisins and nuts
    Brown rice with butter
    Biscuits
Beef stew made with potatoes, carrots, onions, dried soup, herbs, etc.
    Dumplings
Sweet and sour lentils with molasses, vinegar, tamari, onions, carrots and celery
    Kielbasa (Polish sausage)
    Cornbread

Spaghetti with hamburger, tomato sauce, onions, peppers, mushrooms and garlic
> *Parmesan and mozzarella cheese*
> *Garlic bannock*

Bulgur-wheat pilaf with Polish sausage, carrots, celery, pepper and onions
> *Cream sauce and biscuits*

Beef stroganoff with egg noodles, sour cream, frozen peas, peppers, onions, mushrooms and garlic

Macaroni and cheese with a topping of toasted sesame seeds
> *Pesto sauce* with pine nuts or cashew pieces
> *Vegetable pasta* (spirals)
> *Parmesan cheese*

Snacks

Popcorn—with butter or sprinkled with nutritional yeast
Fruit leather
Nuts
GORP (Good Old Raisins and Peanuts)—plus M&Ms, chocolate chips, dried fruit and other nuts
Jerky (see recipe on page 143.)

Desserts

Upside-down cake
Apple crisp
Pies
Gingerbread
Pudding
Packaged cheesecake
Doughnuts
Hot, rehydrated fruit sauces

Expedition Menu Ingredients

Fresh (killed locally) or dried meats only
Dried vegetables, carrots, tomatoes, onions.
Dried fruits, as snacks or rehydrated for use on pancakes or as dessert
Grains, pastas, split (and ground) peas and lentils and rice
White and multigrain flours for yeast and quick breads, biscuits, pancakes, dumplings and bunkers
Salami and pepperoni
Pork fatback and bacon
Butter or margarine
Sugar, brown and white

Nuts such as raw cashews or peanuts (actually a legume) for snacking or meals
Teas, black and herbal
Cereal grain beverages & fruit crystal drinks
Dried milk
Fruitcake
Pemmican
Jerky

DEVELOPING A FOOD LIST

Organization and attention to detail are the keys to successful provisioning. For shorter trips, you can write out the daily menu thus:

Day 1

Breakfast: cereal with milk and sugar, dried fruits, bacon, bunkers, hot drinks

Lunch: crackers, cheese, salami, peanut butter, jam, chocolate, hot tea

Supper: chicken curry, brown rice with cashews, dried onions, apples and mushrooms, cheesecake, fruit drinks.

For longer trips, you may repeat several basic menus in rotation. Once your menu is finalized, prepare a master food-supply list. If you go on enough trips, you might even want to alphabetize this list for ease of reference. Next to each item listed, tally the amount brought. Leave space so that, at the end of the trip, you can write in leftover quantities or other notations. A list for the one-day menu above might look like the example on the facing page.

FIGURING HOW MUCH TO COOK

Experience, as with everything, develops your skill in planning and cooking. But you have to start somewhere and it is critical that you are accurate, particularly if you have never prepared meals for hungry groups where resupply is not possible. You can get a good jump on experience by using the following rules of thumb. (Remember, quantities vary depending on length of trip, participants' experience, temperature and work load.)

Quantities (expedition quantities in italic)

Baking powder: 1 oz. per 1 lb. (4 cups) flour
Butter: 1 oz./person/day or ½ lb./person/week, *(1.5 oz./person/day)*
Cereal grains: ⅓ cup/person/meal (3 cups = approx. 1 lb.), *(½ cup/person/meal (½ lb./person/week)*
Cheeses: 1 oz./person/day
Crackers: ¼ lb./person/day
Flour: 1 cup/person/meal (approx. ¼ lb.) Subtract ½ cup per person/day if pancake mixes are brought.

Post Trip Comments	Total Brought	Supplies
		baking powder
		bacon
		cereal
		cheese
		cheesecake mix
		chicken
		chocolate bars
		cocoa
		crackers
		fruits, dried: apples, raisins, mixed
		drink crystals
		flour
		jam
		milk, dried
		nuts
		peanut butter
		rice, brown
		salami
		seasonings: salt, pepper, curry, cinnamon etc.
		sugar
		teas, black and herbal
		vegetables, dried

Sample list for a one-day menu (see text on facing page).

Lentils, split peas: 1/3 cup dry/person/meal *(2/3 cup dry/person/meal)*
Meats, fresh or thawed: 1/2 lb./person/meal
Pancake mix: 1 cup/person/meal, *(2 cups/person/meal)*
Pasta: 3-4 oz./person/meal
Pemmican: 1 oz./person/day
Peanut butter: 1 oz./person/day
Rice: 1/3 cup dry/person/meal *(1/2 cup dry/person/meal)*
Sugar: 1/2 lb./person/week *(3/4 lb./person/week)*

By using this list to decide how much rice you need (for example), you must determine what is required per person per meal, multiplied by the number of people and by the number of times rice will be served. It sounds tedious, and it is at first, but it is the only accurate way to determine adequate provisions.

In preparing your supply list, take into account other forms of flour that you may or may not be bringing. For example, if you are not bringing pancake mixes or crackers but are making everything from scratch, you will have to bring more flour.

Or, you might need less sugar if you are bringing syrup, honey, molasses or presweetened desserts such as puddings and cheesecakes.

MAKING MEALS EFFICIENT

In boreal and subarctic areas, daylight is relatively short, so, whether your trip is short or long, plan trip meals with ease of preparation in mind. For instance, in the morning, while breakfast is cooking, lunch foods such as salami, cheese, nut butters, fruitbreads or doughnuts should be thawing near the stove. After hot breakfast drinks are served, boil another pot of water for lunchtime hot drinks. Be sure to prewarm thermos bottles before filling them with hot water or tea.

Using an old trick developed by winter trailmaster Calvin Rutstrum, pack lunch food and thermos bottles together in an insulated drawstring bag to prevent refreezing. Carefully bungee the bag onto the outside of the toboggan load to make it easy to get to at lunch.

At this point, you are very busy with the simultaneous preparation of breakfast and lunch. The last thing you want to hear is that you must also make that day's lunch bannock. Maybe you can delegate that to one of the hungry watchers. As soon as there is room on the stovetop, the 15-to-20-minute bannock should be cooked, thoroughly cooled to let as much moisture as possible evaporate and then packed.

As much as possible, breakfasts and suppers should be one-pot meals. Stoves usually have two spaces on which to cook. Hot drinks and hot water for cereal can be readied first. When the drink water has boiled, you can remove it and start frying bacon. If there is ever an empty space on the stove, water should be put on for washing or more hot drinks.

Just because you may strive for one-pot meals does not mean you should serve "glop!" For stroganoff, for example, you prepare the meat and vegetables in the frying pan, and noodles in their own pot until *al dente*. Once the pasta is drained, sour cream can be added to the meat and vegetables, which can then be gently mixed with the egg noodles. Very simple, and extremely tasty—absolutely elegant, in fact, if you are eating by candlelight in a toasty riverside tent with good friends.

Special treats such as pancakes or baked desserts take some time and can be reserved for layover days or evenings when you have a little extra time or energy. Probably any kind of baking except popovers can be accomplished in the boxy portable ovens made for use over bottled-gas stoves (or woodstoves). Yeast breads are a nice change from bannock, and desserts such as a surprise birthday cake will make a trip unforgettable.

Dehydrating Foods & Storage

When you dehydrate foods, you remove all of the water content, thereby greatly lightening them. Twenty pounds of fresh meat reduces to less than five pounds dried weight. Enough vegetables to last you a full winter of trips will weigh less than two pounds. Soaking the food an hour before you need it (while you are preparing the rest of the meal) is usually sufficient to return it to nearly original condition.

You do not need to invest in a food dehydrator if you have a place to string up vegetables and fruits above a woodstove. Thinly slice clean, select fruits and vegeta-

bles. Run strong line through a stout needle and simply string the slices onto the line, making sure they do not touch each other. Usually it takes three days to dry foods like apples, onions and meat.

If your kitchen doesn't allow this fragrant and colorful ceiling decor, you might borrow or buy a food dehydrator (the American Harvest FD-1000, made by Alternative Pioneering Systems, Inc., is the best, most versatile available). Dehydrated food can be stored in airtight glass jars until trip

Fresh chunks of caribou sautéed with pepper and rehydrated onions, then baked into a bannock.

time. There are a number of good books about dehydrating food, particularly *Trail Food*, rev. ed., by Alan S. Kesselheim (Ragged Mountain Press, 1998).

There are a number of things to keep in mind when drying foods. Do not dry food using too much heat, or it will become "case-hardened," leaving the inside moist and prone to rot. Some foods require blanching to prevent spoilage later. Refer to a dehydration manual for specifics as to which foods require what kind of treatment.

During trips, keep dried foods in labeled airtight plastic bags. These can be put directly into the canvas duffel bags, organized by meal, day, food type or whatever you prefer.

THE KITCHEN KIT

Since all of your cooking takes place on the surface of the woodstove, lidded pots with wide bottoms for increased surface area are best. Metal plates, cups and utensils are ideal, primarily because they don't melt around heat and flames, can be cleaned better and are most durable. Enamel plates can double as pie tins, pot lids or warming trays. Enamelware cups filled with water can be heated individually on the stove. The additional weight compared with plastic is negligible, as you are not backpacking. Strive to have gear serve multiple functions.

Here are the contents of our kitchen kit:

Baking and bread pans. We carry one or two eight-inch enamel pans that are round, two-and-a-half inches deep and lidded. Apple strudel or yeast breads can both be baked in them, rather than requiring extra pans.

Canvas wanigan. You can fashion a lightweight, durable wanigan for storing your cook kit simply by lining a premade canvas duffel bag with a heavy cardboard bottom and sides. The lining prevents denting and keeps the kit organized. Add some ties to the wanigan's exterior for attaching the utensil pouch so it is accessible.

Cups. Enameled metal cups are best. Plastic and insulated metal cups cannot be placed on the stove and the latter do not warm your fingers, which is critical during lunchtime. For a quick single cup of hot water, simply place the filled cup in the small space near the stovepipe.

Forks, spoons, knives. Wrap the handles of spreading knives with cloth tape for easier handling at lunchtime in below-freezing temperatures. Personal jackknives can be used for cutting meat during meals.

Frying pans. Lightweight, seasoned, sheet-steel frying pans are ideal.

Hot pads. Handkerchiefs are fine, but you might want two small, thick pads for use just around the stove.

Kettle. Wide-bottomed kettles heat water best. They fit well on the stove next to flared cooking pots.

Matches. Strike-anywhere matches should be stored in a small, waterproof bottle with the cook kit.

Oven. Coleman makes a folding boxlike stovetop oven that heats to 400 degrees Fahrenheit easily. You soon learn to regulate its temperature with stove stoking, drafts and dampers.

Plates. Nine-inch enameled metal plates are ideal. They can double as lids and baking dishes.

Pots. Stainless steel pots, slightly tapered for nesting ability, are best.

Scrubbies. Plastic and metal pads for cleaning pot interiors. Exteriors need not be cleaned.

Soap. All-purpose, biodegradable soap is ideal for dishes, clothes and people.

Spatula, kitchen knife, stirring spoon. These are used solely for cooking.

Ladles. One for serving water and one for serving food.

Towels. One is used for drying, another is the cook's "apron."

Utensil case. A custom-sewn canvas bag that has compartments separating utensils from each other and is hung on the exterior of the wanigan.

RECIPES

Pemmican

Recipe fills four 12-oz. tuna cans. Melt together:
2 cups animal fat
1 cup bacon drippings
Pour over:
2 cups finely ground dried meat (jerky)

Sprinkle with salt, pepper. Let harden in tuna cans with lids removed. Loosen pemmican by dipping cans partway into hot water. Wrap in waxed paper. NOTE: Dried berries (2 cups) can be added for carbohydrate content and extra flavoring. However, a true pemmican contains only fat and meat.

Fatback 'Lassy Toutons

(A fat pork and molasses cookie from Newfoundland that does not freeze in the cold.)
1 lb. fat pork chopped fine (use bacon if preferred)
5 cups flour
1 cup sugar
3 tsp. each, ginger and cinnamon
1 tsp. allspice
1 1/2 cups molasses
2 tsp. baking soda
1 1/2 cups hot water
Milk, fresh or sour

Melt the fat pork in the oven and let it cool (or crisp bacon and cool). Put the flour in a large bowl and add sugar and spices. To the molasses, add the baking soda, hot water and rendered pork (or bacon) scrunchions. Add this to the flour mixture along with enough milk to form dough firm enough to roll. Roll out the dough on a floured board to 1/2 inch thick and cut into squares. Bake on a greased cookie sheet for approximately 20 minutes in a 350-degree F oven.

Jerky

1 1/2-2 lb. lean meat (partially frozen to slice thinly)
1/2 cup soy sauce
1 tbsp. Worcestershire sauce
1/2 tsp. each, pepper and onion powder (optional)

Trim all the fat from the meat and slice it across the grain as thinly as possible (pieces will be approximately 3 to 4 inches long and 3/4 inches wide by 1/8 inch thick). Combine all the spices and sauces in a bowl and mix until the seasonings dissolve. Add the meat strips and mix to coat all surfaces. Let stand overnight. String the pieces of meat by piercing them with a large needle. Suspend over a woodstove for three days until meat is dark-colored and dry. Or, dry in an oven at the lowest temperature setting (150 to 200 degrees F) or use a dehydrator. Pat off the beads of fat and store in airtight jars.

Bannock

(eight servings)
4 cups flour
4 tsp. baking powder
1/2 tsp. salt
dash of sugar
1/3 cup oil
Enough water to make a stiff dough

Mix the dry ingredients first, then add the wet ones. Mix well and shape into a large pancake. Put onto a HOT, greased eight-inch frying pan. Cover the pan and cook the bannock over medium heat for ten minutes, then flip over and cook uncovered for another five minutes or until a wood sliver inserted comes out clean. Break apart to eat. (Tradition has it that cutting slices brings bad luck.)

Bunkers

3 cups flour
3 tsp. baking powder
1/2 tsp. salt
dash of sugar
1/2 tsp. nutmeg
Enough milk or water to make a nonsticky dough

Put small spoonfuls of dough into 1/2 inch of hot bacon or sausage grease in a frying pan. Turn the bunkers when bottoms are golden brown. (Cooking the first side with the pan covered helps make them light.) When golden on the other side, remove and drain. Serve hot with honey or jam, or plain alongside eggs, bacon or sausage and hot drinks.

Yeast Bread

(three loaves serve eight)
3 cups warm water
1/2 cup sugar or honey
2 tbsp. yeast
Enough flour to make the dough (2 cups whole wheat and approximately 6 cups white)

Mix the warm water (no hotter than body temperature), honey and yeast. Add the flour, mix and knead thoroughly. Shape the dough into loaves and put into greased, warm pans. Let the loaves rise in the oven, with the door open, in a warm, draftless spot. When the dough has fully risen, carefully close the oven door and set oven on top of a very hot woodstove. Bake until the loaves sound hollow when tapped. You can brown the tops of the loaves after baking by tilting the pans near the woodstove. Cool thoroughly before storing.

Winter Expedition Fruitcakes

These rich, highly nutritious fruitcakes are excellent for cold-weather camping as they are high in fat and quick-energy sugars. Made in advance of a trip, they seem to last indefinitely without refrigeration. Recipe makes three fruitcakes. NOTE: A five-ounce portion of this cake provides 439 calories, seven percent protein, 11 percent fat and 82 percent carbohydrates.

2 sticks butter ($^1/_2$ lb.)
1 cup honey
2 tbsp. lemon juice
3 eggs
2 cups chopped cranberries
3 cups flour
3 tsp. baking powder
1 tsp. salt
1 cup dried milk
3 tsp. ginger (or $^1/_8$ cup candied ginger)
2 tsp. each nutmeg, cardamom, rosehip flour
2 cups chopped dates
2 cups chopped nuts
2 cups chopped apricots
3 cups muscat raisins, currants or a combination of the two

Melt the butter and add the honey. Put the lemon juice, eggs and washed, sorted cranberries in a blender (or chop the cranberries coarsely and mix them with the juice and the eggs). Blend briefly and add the butter-and-honey mixture. Now add these wet ingredients to the remaining ingredients. Pour into greased 1-lb. coffee cans until $^3/_4$ inch from top. Bake at 325 degrees F until a butter knife inserted in the middle comes out clean.

FOOD DEHYDRATOR SOURCE

American Harvest
Alternative Pioneering Systems, Inc.
4064 Peavey Road, Box 159
Chaska, MN 55318
800-288-4545

Chapter 7
Traveling Safely on Ice

TRAVELING SAFELY ON ICE

"*So it is that those of us, white and Indian, who have seen much of the interior, have always turned toward the winter trips. If one goes mainly for the trip itself, for the being out, there is nothing quite like the northern winter. There is the region of the elemental; there the keen air and the flash of the low sun on snow; there the rhythmic crunch of snowshoes under the northern lights and the high winter moon, the long trail that knows no willing ending—i-shipits-nan, the Indians call it— their immemorial winter road.*"
—William Brooks Cabot, from an address given January 17, 1911

The winter trail is a road of ice. The freezing of lakes, rivers, bogs and wetlands opens a network of travel possibilities second only to flying. The wind-driven surfaces of huge lakes are tamed; rapids that would force a canoeist to portage are rendered benign; the swamps and bogs that would stop a summer traveler dead now allow easy traverse. A person on foot upon the ice can travel in gales that would keep a canoeist windbound for days. At ground level, water's habit of freezing at zero degrees Celsius or 32 degrees Fahrenheit provides the gift of ice. In the atmosphere, the same property provides the gift of snow.

These crystalline embellishments upon the land are as complex as life itself. Like fire, snow and ice can provide shelter and ease. And like fire out of control, snow and ice can consume the very lives they otherwise provide for. Successful winter dwellers must learn a great deal about ice, and the winter trail is a fantastic teacher for the cautious and observant.

Most of us have a natural fear of walking on ice, commensurate with our lack of experience. The idea of walking on water, frozen or not, is unnerving. This fear serves us as we begin to explore the nature of ice, keeping us cautious and tentative and our mistakes small.

THE NATURE OF ICE

To speak of ice, we must first look at water. This remarkable substance can exist as a gas, a liquid or a solid. The density and behavior of each form is different. Of primary interest to the winter traveler are the liquid and solid forms, and the transition from one to the other.

If we were on a trip that started in a canoe and was about to shift to snowshoes, we would pick a good spot near a lake for a base camp to await the transition from open water to safe ice. During that time, we would put the canoe on a scaffold and cache all our summer gear with it. While we waited, we would have plenty to do, making toboggans and perhaps meeting a plane delivering winter gear on the last open water. Or perhaps we carried our stove, snowshoes and tent throughout the open-water season. Now we are drying moose meat for the winter and using what we don't dry to see us through the late fall and the transition from open water to ice.

Meanwhile, the water in the lake is doing some major shifting in a manner largely invisible to us. The lake is "turning over." All summer, the coldest water has been at the bottom and the warmer water at the surface. Now, after weeks of dropping temperature, the surface water is radiating heat to the heavens. A few times there has even been a skim of ice in the shallow coves. But out in the main body of the lake the surface is getting colder and colder. During the last weeks of canoe use, the water had even felt thick and sluggish, and indeed it was. Even the waves reflected change. They were huge with long bases during the gales, but few broke or showed white. Surface water was nearing 39.2 degrees Fahrenheit, the point at which it reaches maximum density. At that temperature, surface water began to sink and, as it did so, displaced the water at lower levels. Well-oxygenated surface water moved to the bottom, and the shift stirred up nutrients. Everything living in the lake would need this event to see it through the long winter of darkness and reduced oxygen beneath the ice.

As the turnover occurred, a curious thing happened. The water on the bottom, coldest in summer, was now nearing the surface, radiating its heat away and becoming even colder. The 39.2-degree water now settled at the bottom would be the warmest water in the lake throughout the winter. Near the surface, the temperature continued to drop. The last time the canoe was used, the water seemed less sluggish, and it actually was. The very night the canoe was hoisted to its scaffold, the entire lake froze over in a perfect thin sheet of ice. It had been clear, windless and bitterly cold.

As the water approached 32 degrees Fahrenheit, it became quite fluid again, and light, and then turned into a floating solid. Ice. It would be many months before the lake would reverse the process and turn over once again, some time after ice-out when the water could absorb warmth from the sun.

The behavior of water in its gaseous state is a secondary concern for the winter wanderer. Adequate hydration to balance respiration was addressed in Chapter 6, breathable clothing to accommodate transpiration in Chapter 4. Water vapor's practical impact on trail activity emerges in the form of *sublimation*. Sublimation occurs when a gas changes directly into a solid without passing through the liquid state, or when a solid changes to a gas without first becoming liquid.

Your breath frosting on your hair and scarf reveals a gas becoming solid. Although frosted hair makes longhaired women look like fairy-tale damsels and bearded men like hoary old walruses, it does require some management if you're going to keep your face warm. The air following very cold nights is often filled with fine frost crystals. These create beautiful sundogs but also frost up the toboggan bottoms, which makes them pull hard unless they are brushed off before loading.

Sublimation in the other direction, from solid to gas, also has aesthetic as well as practical ramifications. Upthrust ice at the edge of leads or pressure ridges gets wonderfully sculpted by the ice evaporating in the cold winds until it is smooth, sensuous and fantastic, like works of art in glass or crystal. Laundry hung in the windy sunshine will freeze instantly, yet before the day is out, it will be flapping and totally dry. Sleeping bags airing in the sun also lose a small amount of moisture through sublimation; in the process, they lose accumulated body odor and take on the freshness of spruce and sun.

But what is of most interest here are ice and snow as substrates that can ease or inhibit progress—or introduce danger.

Lake Ice

As ice forms in lakes, odd things begin to happen. For one thing, as ice forms, it expands. If there is no snow on the ice and the cold continues, you'll hear the ice groan as it gets thicker. Stress cracks will occur, in a general pattern. They will cross the mouths of bays, string islands together or develop randomly as pressure builds. Since the edges of the lake cannot be moved, the ice itself will buckle and bend. As sheets of ice expand out of bays toward midlake, they meet expanding sheets from other parts of the lake. At these interfaces, the ice will bend upward and in some cases buckle and crack. Continued pressure will create what are called pressure ridges along these fronts. On a big lake, pressure ridges might be several feet high or more. On smaller bodies of water, they may be visible only as slight swellings in the surface of the ice and not even exhibit the upthrust plates of broken ice.

Suppose the weather gets brutally cold and no snow comes to insulate the ice. After a series of nights that dip to minus 30, the ice does something else. It shrinks. The noises it makes now are not prolonged groans of expansion, but sharp pops and cracks that snap through the cold air like rifle fire. All along the pressure ridges, be they small cracks or 12-foot-high jumbles of ice, the ice sheets retreat from each other. Open water is exposed and refreezes. There are now spots of very thin ice mixed with the thicker, older plates that have contracted in the deep cold. Then it snows.

Suppose the storm is one of those mythic blizzards that occupy conversation for months afterward—say, 22 inches of snow in 15 hours. Out on the ice, things are happening beneath the blanket of white. The ice that seems so brittle and hard when the ice chisel strikes it is actually quite plastic. The weight of the snow causes it to bend ever so slightly. The water beneath the ice was under pressure enough from the downward expansion of the ice during buildup, and now with the weight of the snow pressing the layer of ice further, the open lead at the outlet has expanded a full half mile back into the lake. The water there flows in a glassy stream that looks pure black next to the snow.

The water leaving the lake is close to 39 degrees Fahrenheit, which, relative to the ice, is warm. It took but one day for the pressurized flow of warmer water to melt the ice covering completely away from several acres of lake surface where the current picks up at the outlet. All winter this section of the lake will oscillate between open and ice covered, safe to cross or perilous to tread. At times, snow on top of thin new ice shows discoloration from wicking up water, and this indicates danger.

At other times, the ice may be thin, yet hold a dusting of snow so light that the ice is not depressed and overflow does not occur. The snow is not discolored, nor does it appear shallower than the snow over adjacent thicker ice. There are no signs of danger. You will need to know about outlets, suspect terrain and the whole picture. If the open water of the outlet is nearby, you will need to test the ice before trusting it.

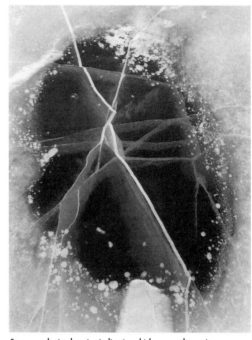

Out in the main part of the lake, nowhere near the outlet, another adjustment is taking place. Thin ice over the water that appeared near the pressure ridges is being depressed by the weight of the snow, and some has actually melted from being pushed down into water that has not dropped to the freezing point. Water is wicking up into the

Stress cracks in clear ice indicating thickness and security.

deep powder all along the pressure ridges and overflow is now expanding onto the surface of the ice well back from the ridge itself. The deep powder is keeping the slushy, water-laden snow from freezing even though the air temperature is well below zero. In some places, snow has slumped in on itself as water has wicked through it. These are visible danger zones, the worst of them discolored from the water and slightly yellowish.

In other places, there are no visual clues to warn of the need for caution. In such areas, a person could simply wander into overflow over solid ice. This would not be dangerous except that you might get wet, which is something you try to avoid in winter. In the event of wandering into overflow, retreat along your track, if possible, since that is known terrain, until you reach an area of dry snow. Such a retreat will automatically be away from the overflow area and any thin ice that may be associated with it.

There may also be dangerous spots along a pressure ridge. There, thin ice that formed just before the storm is still holding up the snow. That ice is less than half an inch thick. There is neither sag in the snow above it nor overflow to discolor the snow. The water below is deep and there is virtually no visual clue to suggest thin ice.

In this case, just as proximity to an outlet makes an area suspect, so does proximity to a pressure ridge. It is knowledge of what might happen in these areas that arouses suspicion, rather than the look of the area, since appearances may reveal nothing. Cross pressure ridges at right angles if you can, and test the ice on both sides of the ridges before committing to a crossing. It is for occasions such as these that the ice chisel and axe are carried with easy access in mind. If you have a grain of doubt, check the situation out.

One inch of ice will hold a person, but this assumes ice fields that are uniform without discontinuities. In this regard the general rules of safety are two inches for a person, six for a horse, eight for a team of horses and on up for vehicles, planes and heavy equipment.

In addition to the areas around outlets and pressure ridges, there may be underwater springs that keep an area free of ice or covered with only a thin sheet. Spring water coming directly from the ground emerges at 50 to 55 degrees Fahrenheit, a full 28 to 32 degrees above freezing. Currents passing through a narrows in a lake often behave the same as a lake outlet and are free of ice or subject to fluctuating thickness. The surrounding landscape as well as a number of visual clues shape one's knowledge. Any changes in snow type, depth or color; an absence of terrestrial animal tracks; or the sudden presence of otter or mink tracks might hint of weak ice and access to open water. And don't be afraid to pay attention to gut feelings and pangs of fear. When in doubt, check things out. It takes mere minutes to check, and hours to recover from a mishap.

Remember, too, that the presence of overflow does not necessarily mean thin ice. It may mean that the ice layer, which builds downward, is pressurizing the body of water beyond the ability of the outlet to maintain equilibrium. In such a case, water might be extruded up through stress cracks that are in three or four feet of solid ice.

River Ice

River ice is more complex because of the current and fluctuating water level. It, too, can conceal dangerous conditions by not revealing any visual clues. As with lake ice, however, basic characteristics can serve as guidelines until you develop first-hand knowledge.

Once winter begins in earnest, watersheds reveal dropping water levels. Springs contribute a small amount of water, but formation of ice and snow prevents major resupplying of water to the system until spring. River and lake levels decline. Ice coverings sag, buckle, adjust and refreeze. Lake surfaces, which one expects to find level, develop some topography. Rivers also reveal the adjustments, as well as introduce their own surprises, such as ice jams that may alter the water level until pressure blows the jam out in a great rush, shoving about pans, boulders and trees and dropping them in peculiar places.

Water that is below freezing may be unfrozen due to the current. If the surface is too fast for the water to freeze from above, ice may form from the bottom of the river upward until the whole river is running on top of the ice.

The erosive force of the water may keep ice thin even if it is cold enough to freeze were the water not in motion. Below lake outlets, where water emerges at temperatures ranging from 39 degrees Fahrenheit to just shy of freezing, it may take water a mile or more to cool sufficiently to allow ice to form over the river again. Often there is shelf ice along the edges, but at times, tobogganers must take to the shore until sound ice forms again.

At other times, open water is not a problem. The river may freeze all the way to the bottom in many places and the channel is not to be found. Many times campers have melted snow or ice chips for water after failing to locate the channel.

Many of the open leads in a river will be in shallow rapids where the speed of the water keeps ice from forming. Deeper rapids and deadwater sections almost always freeze, and may in fact have very thick, solid ice. Occasionally, in huge, high-volume rivers, there will be open leads in deep, strong water. Such places are ominous indeed and look the most like certain black death.

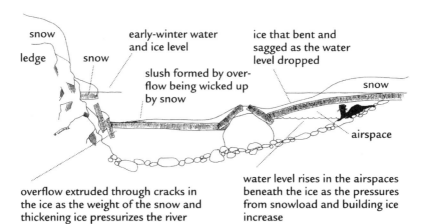

This cross section of a riverbed in midwinter shows not only conditions as they exist at the time of encounter, but also reveals events of the season thus far. The water level dropped as the winter progressed because all but the input of ground springs was suspended in ice and snow. The ice sagged or fractured to accommodate the new water levels. Pressures created by new snow and the thickened, resettled ice fluctuated, and the river continued to adjust and change. Open leads provide the most visible and dramatic examples of equilibrium being established, but there are more subtle things as well. Overflow might be extruded through stress cracks, and the water levels may rise and fall within an airspace beneath the ice. Otters and mink will likewise favor those areas where airspace and access to open water are protected by a roof of ice left over from earlier higher water levels. Very often the speed of the current in combination with the insulating layer of snow on top of the ice will keep these under-ice leads open despite long periods of subfreezing cold in the air above.

Because open leads punctuate a river's length, there is a lot of opportunity for adjustment and resettling of pressure and water levels. This is of concern to winter travelers. The strength of the ice is reduced if the water is not holding it up. If you can hear the roar of rapids from under the ice, the river is telling you that the water level has dropped and there is now air between the surface of the water and the bottom of the ice. You will need much thicker ice to support the weight of your crossing in such a case, and the lead person should constantly be chipping with the ice chisel to make sure there is safe thickness that is uniform enough to trust. In sec-

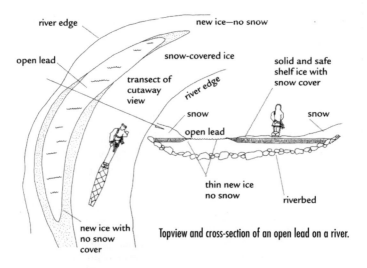

river edge

new ice—no snow

open lead

snow-covered ice

solid and safe
shelf ice with
snow cover

transect of
cutaway
view

river edge

snow

snow

snow

open lead

thin new ice
no snow

riverbed

new ice with
no snow
cover

Topview and cross-section of an open lead on a river.

tions of river that are not rapids, the water is not so loud; it may simply gurgle or chuckle. You may have to stop moving to listen, as the sound of your snowshoes will screen the sound of the water.

At other times, the water does not drop away; it rises. Perhaps a new snow load has depressed the ice, or a cold snap builds ice so quickly that the remaining water is now pressurized enough to come out of the leads and flow on top of the ice. If this occurs on glare ice, the water will quickly refreeze. But often the flow takes place under an insulating blanket of snow. If the snow is deep enough, the water and slush may stay liquid for days or weeks of continued cold without freezing. This is the condition known as *overflow*, and it is the bane of the winter traveler's existence. Overflow often occurs over thick, sound ice, and the danger is not the potential for breaking through, it is the danger of becoming wet while the air is extremely cold. The condition is fairly common on lakes, but you are certain to encounter it on rivers.

To wander into overflow on snowshoes is a terrible experience. Suddenly, apparently dry powder gives way and you wallow in slush that may be a few inches to a foot or more deep. Your snowshoes instantly weigh a ton each, and you stagger helplessly while trying to retreat to dry snow. Once in the air, the slush immediately freezes and must be beaten out of your snowshoes. If your moccasins have gotten soaked, you will need to change into dry footwear. If your toboggan got into the moisture, you will need to scrape the whole bottom clean with the axe as the slush will have frozen fast to the entire running surface. People traveling by dogsled or snow machine have an even worse time of it, and the time lost in recovery quickly becomes measurable in hours.

People on foot have the best chance of recognizing overflow conditions early enough to avoid a full encounter. If you suddenly feel like you are walking on a waterbed in snowshoes, back up—you are about to encounter slush. Animal tracks that are full of water also reveal overflow, and walkers will often notice the tracks ahead of them turning gray as the water wicks up into them. In this case, you can break your own track in fresh snow and perhaps go just fast enough to keep ahead of the water wicking up. In such cases, you will see a single track suddenly fan out into individual tracks, only to merge again when solid snow is gained. Warden pilots in Maine have accurately known our party size from just such sightings as they flew over our trail on the river.

There are other times when the snow over the slush is deep enough so that you and your toboggan(s) can pass above with no hint of the slush beneath until you pass animal tracks full of water or someone steps out of his or her snowshoes and suddenly sinks into glop. The other extreme—complete, drenching, unavoidable wallowing with no hint or warning—is just as likely. In that case, you simply wallow to dry snow and settle in for whatever time it takes to recover.

If you should get your feet wet, cover them quickly with powder snow once free of the slush. This will wick the water away from your footwear and sock systems and, if done quickly enough, may prevent water from soaking into any of your lin-

Traveling on shelf ice next to an open lead.

ers. Frequently, you need not change your moccasins at all.

One way to reduce the possibility of encountering overflow at all has to do with the fact that water always settles in the lowest depressions of the ice, whether the ice is snow covered or bare. On lakes, ice edges near shore are likely to be higher in elevation due to the lake level dropping all winter and the ice settling. In a river, the low spots are often along the shores on the outsides of curves, where the channel is likely to be. If the river has dropped, the edges on the insides of curves are likely to be higher, the ice actually held up by gravel bars and gently sloping banks. Favoring high ice on a river will mean constantly switching sides to seek the insides of curves, and, depending on the steepness of the river and the power of the water, there may be occasions when you will want to check the low spots with the chisel before crossing or at least brush the snow with a mitten to check for overflow. If the river is gentle in gradient and not full of sharp curves, there may be a median ridge down the center where the ice is raised due to expansion toward the center from each shore and to the pressure of the ice plates meeting.

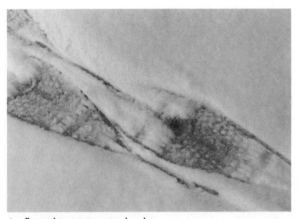

Overflow wicking into just-printed tracks.

You will favor the high spots of river ice for another reason, too. The wind will have removed more snow from these sections than from the lower ones, and the going will be easier. Animal tracks will show you exactly where this high line is. Nobody wastes energy in deep snow.

Not only can you learn from the landscape and the animals on it, but your chiseled water hole can speak to you of the coming day. If you have encountered the waterway at a time when the water level is dropping faster than events (such as continued ice-making or heavy snowfall) can pressurize the underlying water onto the ice surface, then the water level in the hole will be below the surface of the ice. If it is several inches below the rim, your chances of encountering overflow are minimal. If it is just below or at the rim, you will probably need to circumnavigate a few places.

There will be times when water gushes out of the hole and you literally have to jump back to keep your feet dry. If the water flows up on the ice and pools, you are certain to encounter serious overflow at all the natural leads, which will be venting water until equilibrium is established. In avoiding serious overflow, you may have to take to the woods to bypass sections of river, and this is laborious and slow.

Knowing this will help you set expectations for the day and to plan overall. Perhaps you can recover from a slow day getting around overflow on the river by pushing part-way down the long lake just ahead in the moonlight. Or, if it looks like a searing cold snap is coming on the heels of the last storm, you might choose to wait a day or two to make better time in colder snow. If you are really lucky, the overflow will be so bad that the snow is saturated all the way to the surface. This eliminates its insulation value, and the wet snow and slush will quickly refreeze.

Deep powder, on the other hand, can keep an area of overflow wet for weeks of continued cold. For all the misery some ice and snow conditions create, you will be equally rewarded with huge lakes with miles of wind-packed snow so hard

An open lead and a new dusting of six-inch-deep powder. Note the gray overflow seeping over the ice at the tail of the lead.

you don't need snowshoes. Or sections of river that are blown free of snow, and you can trot along for miles with virtually no friction, the sleds clattering along behind. The rest of the time, between the extremes, travel will be relatively mundane, neither grand nor awful.

Never think you know ice. Keep exploring, prodding, poking and testing. There are always surprises, and some of them may jolt a little adrenaline through your cells. These are kind reminders not to become complacent as you gain knowledge and to avoid arrogant assumptions based on the "rules" of ice morphology.

Sea Ice

On sea ice, you must add tides, currents, drift and other special variables to what you have already learned on inland water. Much lower temperatures are required for salt water to freeze solidly enough for travel. Your level of care will have to rise to meet such demands, and it probably will automatically, as the restlessness of the tides presents plenty of eerie noises and strange overflows.

Open water in the sea ice, and in some cases lake ice, can be detected at a distance by observing what appears to be dark air hovering over the ice field.

If your ice-walking companions are Caution, Curiosity and Fear, you should have a fine time weaving trails upon ice. Just don't forget to invite these friends along.

Chapter 8
Finding Your Way:
Navigation

FINDING YOUR WAY

NAVIGATION

In the North, where lakes can be huge, sprawling, confusing, elaborately sprinkled with islands, bays and points and surrounded by low-relief land with few prominent landmarks, you must navigate carefully. You will need a good compass and the knowledge to use it. In addition to compass skills, you will need to develop map and correlation skills. You need faith; knowledge of basic geometry (very basic, such as angles and degrees); and ability to project, deal with abstractions and correlate landforms to symbols in a way that indicates where you are, where you want to go and how to get there. This is so intimidating to many people that they never really get good at or fully understand the process.

The way to get good is to use the skills repeatedly. With repeated success in navigation you will gain confidence and trust and an ability to perform accurately in increasingly complicated situations. Start with some good books, then practice on the trail. If the opportunity arises, travel with a skilled group and learn firsthand in real situations.

Many of the compass companies have done us all a disservice in trying to overcome the intimidation factor by simplifying the process too much. Several basic compasses on the market appeal to the timid because they have fewer features and don't require the user to understand the full picture. Although such compasses may break the ice for beginners, they ultimately strand them at a mediocre level that, at worst, requires some unlearning before the user can progress to higher levels of compass use. It is far better, in our opinion, to get a fully adjustable compass that covers everything. You can use it in the simplest, most basic ways, or use it to its full potential. As familiarity and boldness develop, most people follow this continuum some or all of the way. To be able to do so with a familiar piece of equipment that does not require you to jump ship, change tactics or learn a whole new system is infinitely easier, if a bit more expensive initially.

At the very least, get a compass with a bezel that rotates and contains an adjustable declination feature. The outer edge of the bezel contains the degrees of the circle, and the adjustable declination allows you to compensate for the difference between magnetic north, which the needle will indicate, and true north, which is what your map should be oriented to in the field. The best compass that offers a minimal, yet adequate set of features is the Suunto Leader M-3D, the most compass for a remarkably low price.

If you want to go a step further and get a fully adjustable compass that also has a sighting mirror and in few other features, consider the Silva Ranger, the Brunton Elite Survival or the Suunto Professional MC ID. The Suunto Professional is the most compass for the money. Not only does the sighting mirror perform its navigation-related duties, but it also serves as an all-purpose mirror. On the winter trail, you can check your face for frosting if no companions are near, see if you still have any teeth or comb your hair in the morning.

We assume that you have read *Map and Compass* by Cliff Jacobson in the *Basic Essential* Series and/or *Be Expert with Map and Compass* by Bjorn Kjellstrom, the grandfather of modern orienteering. We also assume that you always orient your map to true north while in the field so that the landscape matches the mapscape and therefore corroborates and checks your assumptions; and that your compass is adjusted so that you get the true north and magnetic readings simultaneously via the instrument rather than by math in your head; and that you are fully capable of taking sightings, figuring your position by triangulation and navigating through thick timber with no views or blowing snow so that you come out precisely at your destination. In addition to all that, you are, of course, the very paradigm of cool-headed wisdom in the face of confusing data and varying degrees of lostness.

Here are some likely realities. Topographical sheets occasionally contain errors. The North has a lot of flat terrain that might not have many features to sight from. Large lakes with fleets of islands, peninsulas and low shorelines are hard to see from the level of the water. A large island might look like mainland. Seen from a distance, dozens of crowded islands blend together and look like mainland or a big island that does not appear on the map. Peninsulas may look like anything. And adjacent water bodies may be so close across narrow necks of land that you might not know if you have crossed into another body of water or are still on the same one. Lakes may have multiple outlets. Maybe a ground blizzard has blown up and you can't see the point you were heading for and now don't know where it is. Even if it is perfectly clear, it all may look the same, even with the map in front of you.

In such situations, good habits help. For complicated areas full of bewildering islands, keep checking your position and progress by lining up, isolating and checking ground features with the map. Predict what you should see next, and feel grateful as your predictions stay true. Stop and locate yourself if your predictions are wrong.

Before heading across large bays or wide crossings, take a bearing on where you want to go from a known position. Do this even in clear weather, when you can see where you want to go. If you have a crossing of several miles or more, it may take a few hours, long enough for the winds to build enough to fill the air with snow (ground blizzard) so you can no longer see. You can't take a map-based bearing on something you can't see if you don't know where you are. You can, however, have your bearing already in place if you take it before starting across.

Suppose you are about to cross a six-mile-wide part of a lake to reach the mouth of a river you wish to ascend. An unskilled person might take a bearing on the mouth of the river, but if it were not an easily discernible inlet, or if blowing or falling snow obscured the view while you were on the way across, you would make landfall and not know whether the river was to the left or right of where you reached shore. Looking for it, you would lose time, at least one person would have to look in the wrong direction, and the group would be fragmented and out of communication with each other. Whoever explored in the wrong direction would then have to backtrack for the proper route.

A skilled navigator would do what is called "shooting off." This means that the bearing would contain a deliberate error of a few degrees to one side of the river coming in. Suppose just to the north of the inlet there is a point sticking out into the lake that would provide a recognizable landmark at close range, which would further verify your position once there. Let's assume the built-in error puts your angle of approach at 242 degrees, which would fall in the southwest quadrant of your compass. Upon reaching landfall, you would know that the mouth of the river would be to the left because your bearing to a point north of the river would land you to the right of the mouth. As you follow that shore south, sure enough, there is a low, wooded point, and the river must be just beyond it. Well, so it is!

When shooting off, you don't need to introduce a big error if the crossing is a long one. You will be more than 92 feet off your mark for every mile traveled with an error of only one degree. In the six-mile crossing above, a one-degree error puts you 552 feet from your destination. The trick is to gauge your deliberate error for the length of the crossing. You don't want to miss by so much that you have a long haul to your destination, but at the same time you don't want to miss by so little that you still don't know which side of your mark you are on. In most cases, shooting off by two to six degrees will suffice. If you want to check, project the line onto the map in pencil and see if you are too close or too far from the objective, and adjust accordingly.

Since tobogganers typically travel single file, a group of three or more can use its own spread of people as a trueing device. If the line is several hundred yards long, a look down the line from the rearmost people can detect even a slight kink in the line. If a kink shows up, a shout or whistle forward could alert the rest of the line. Our signal is for the last person to raise one arm straight up and point with the other arm to the side on which corrective action must be taken. As the leader reaches the true line, the pointing hand rises. When the lineup is reestablished, both arms are straight up and parallel. At this point the lead person simply continues straight ahead as indicated by the line of people. Even in the thickest whirling snow with people only yards apart, a remarkably true line can be held. Compared to the way canoeists are blown and drifted about, snowshoers are laser-straight.

If you carry a watch, there are other means of estimating progress that may influence navigation. Provided you can correlate your progress closely enough with identifiable points on the map, you can gauge the speed of travel for the given conditions.

Once while exploring a route we had figured out on the maps, we found that part of our journey was taking place across a vast expanse of high bog. The maps showed the whole area as a maze of lakes, but we found we were among stunted larch and spruce and only occasionally on small ponds and other bodies of water. There was fairly good wind-pack, and we estimated that the travel rate of the party was about two-and-a-half miles per hour. Off to the west was a long esker that the maps somehow failed to show, and that was the only relief except for a distant low swelling of trees. We were not sure if the rise was enough to merit the only contour line that appeared on that section of our map.

We knew where we had been upon leaving camp that morning on the headwater of a small stream. Now we were on high ground, and it would be a number of miles before we could look for another small stream that would be flowing away from us to westward, and toward a string of lakes we would eventually follow back to Lac Ashuanipi. We assumed such a stream would make a visible notch in the esker provided we kept our visibility, and we continued to scan ahead to look for that notch as the miles accumulated. Unbeknownst to us, some of our guests were fairly nervous with the lack of correspondence between the map and what we were seeing around us.

We paused for a rest and a bit of fruitcake behind a small huddle of spruces, and it was there that the voices of concern piped up. We calculated our mileage based on the passage of time and concluded that we should soon be abreast of the small stream. We scanned the face of the esker, which was about a mile off, and could see no hint of a notch even through binoculars. And indeed, this was cause for some concern. Eventually, one of us moved a few paces past the spruces to get a careful look at our one blind spot. There, sure enough, shadows in the face of the esker revealed a discernible notch. Twenty-five minutes later, our relieved companions chipped through the ice of the stream and noted that the water was flowing in the right direction.

On another occasion, a more complicated use of timing, as well as some projected compass bearings, were applied to the map. We were making a two-mile overland crossing through thick woods from one watershed to another. The contour lines indicated that we could keep the grade to a minimum by starting out almost due south. But then, after the elevation was gained, the map showed a long, gentle slope to the lake we were aiming for. If we just continued south, we would reach the lake, as it was nearly ten miles long. However, observing a slight bay in the lake, we knew that if we altered our course 32 degrees east of south, we could shorten our distance to the shore. The only problem was that we would not know at what point to change our bearing. The whole route was in thick timber with no views, and if we turned too early we would have to climb up and then lose unnecessary elevation where the spur of a ridge made out. Naturally, we wanted to keep to a downgrade.

In the course of packing the float ahead, returning to the toboggans and then moving ahead, we discovered that it took 40 minutes to pack a float half a mile, ten to walk back to the toboggans and 20 to gain the half mile to the end of the float with the loads. At that point we would leave the toboggans and pack the next segment. By factoring rest stops, time elapsed and distance estimates, we made a guess at where to shift our bearing 32 degrees to the east. If we were accurate, we would come out within sight of a small, comma-shaped island.

When we eventually made the lakeshore, we assumed that such a series of estimates would contain a fair amount of error. Neither of us thought to look straight ahead but started scanning up and down the lake looking for the island. We were growing puzzled by the absence of islands, when Carolyn, who was standing with us, asked what was wrong with the little island right in front of us.

Nothing was wrong with it at all. If it were any closer, we'd have stepped on it. We just didn't expect to come out as accurately as if we had shot the final bearing from a known position.

The ideal situation on a trip is to have several people share navigation duties. In this way, each person attending to details independently will show up any discrepancies. Actual navigation also presents great opportunities to teach the skill to the whole group, or the most interested individuals. Unlike contrived navigation, the real thing packs the possibility of a true sense of accomplishment.

Your travels may also take you to lands of sharp relief—ridges, summits, canyons and steep rivers. In such places, navigation is simple due to the ease of correlating landscape to mapscape. With continued visibility, you may not even need the compass. Ease vanishes, however, the minute you lose visibility.

The three most common causes of loss of visibility are darkness, blowing snow and falling snow that may also contain blowing snow. Typically, you will not be traveling after dark, but you may choose to—if you need to make up time—on an open lake by traveling early or late. Or in the deep dark of December, a few hours of twilight may be the brightest part of your day. During moonless conditions, if you are far enough north, the rest of the day can be very dark.

The conditions in which you will experience loss of visibility no matter where you are, even in the blinding sun of late March, are ground blizzards and blowing snow during an actual blizzard. Ground blizzards occur when the wind is strong enough to pick up snow off lake surfaces and whirl it through the air. Typically, such ground blizzards occupy the air to a height of 30 or 40 feet. You can look straight up and see perfectly clear blue sky overhead, but your lateral view may be "blind as a pillow." You may be able to see your companions a hundred feet away or more, but little or nothing else. Landmarks that would normally be available as targets or reference points no longer exist, and you must navigate strictly by map and compass.

The same loss of visibility occurs in regular blizzards. If wind combines a ground blizzard with a falling blizzard, visibility can drop to a few feet. In such a case, you must not only navigate by map and compass, but also pay very close attention to keeping the group together and in contact.

Under normal conditions, a well-led, considerate group will adjust its pace to the slowest member. The best thing to do if you get caught in an unavoidable storm is to put the slowest person first in line if he or she can navigate, or second if not. In this way, normal stride and pacing will keep the group bunched up on each other. If the person is second, the leader will have to be constantly aware and not get too far ahead.

Each person in the line must be responsible for keeping at least one person behind and ahead of them in sight. This sounds simple, but it can be difficult in practice. Something as brief as a pause to relieve oneself or to adjust a hood or scarf can break the sight link. It is up to the front people to stop and wait if the vision link gets stretched or broken. No one should move until the last or "sweep" person is within sight of the second to last, and so on up the line. When each person is in sight of the next, then the whole line can continue to move. Following this rule, the line functions even when conditions are so thick that each person can discern only one other person in each direction.

The entire trick with sight links is to maintain them continuously so that the distances between walkers are kept to an absolute minimum. If forward people stop the instant sight contact is lost with the person behind, those following will almost instantly come into sight and the party will stay bunched up. If everyone stays close and moves only when each member is accounted for, the party never gets separated or out of communication, and the possibility of dangerous complications is reduced. If you must conduct a search, use the same system and series of sight links to make a careful sweep in a circle around the final stopping point. No one should introduce independent elements that could compound the emergency.

Should a lapse in vigilance create a real separation between members, the chances of locating everyone will vanish, and a full emergency will exist. Probably the group will not be able to reunite until the weather clears. In such a case, the main group will have to camp as usual, and the missing members may have to bivouac. Each member must keep a clear head and do nothing without thoughtful consideration.

If you can keep your group together and on course in such conditions, you will have demonstrated admirable navigational skill. The usual going in clear weather, with splendid long views, will then be all the more delicious, and as you gain confidence in your route-finding and location skills, "staying found" will consume considerably less physical and mental energy. Instead of wondering where you are, you can keep a roving eye out for wolves or gyrfalcons or distant caribou.

Global Positioning System [GPS]

GPS, or Global Positioning System receivers, are small battery-powered devices that rely on a fleet of orbiting satellites that beam all sorts of data and position-fixing calculations to each unit. Since their first introduction to the consumer market in the 1980s, GPS units have become smaller, lighter, incredibly sophisticated and amazingly inexpensive.

The past few years have been witness to very aggressive marketing campaigns that have basically pushed GPS units out of the realm of tools to one of must-have toys, for those vulnerable to gadget accumulation.

Be cautious. These things are exciting and very fun. You might even have a real use for one. However, you still need all your map, compass and navigation skills for most of the complexities of bush travel. The GPS is an extra thing to pack, and since it runs on batteries, it can fail.

We know of some geologists, botanists and a few surveyors and soils folks whose work is vastly augmented by having a GPS. But among our acquaintances who are serious bush travelers, few seem to show a serious interest in them, and none are willing to rely on them as anything but an interesting corroboration of what they've already figured out with their brains, maps and compasses.

Michael Peake, a very experienced northern canoeist, has an opinion worth paying attention to. In no way can he be confused with a curmudgeonly Luddite, as he has proudly carried a battery charger, laptop, digital camera, satellite phone and solar panels to maintain an active website for several of his expeditions. He regards GPS units as "the most overrated piece of equipment of the twentieth century."

Tool or toy? It's up to you. As for us, we already begrudge the batteries we carry for our headlamps and cameras, gear that gets hard use all the time. We remain content without any unnecessary equipment that requires batteries.

SOURCES FOR TOPO MAPS

The U.S./Canadian Map Service carries many different formats and scales, as well as the index maps from which you order specific quadrangles. This outfit is fast, courteous and professional, and delivers the goods within weeks. To order through the government offices of either country is to endure a wait of several months.

The U.S./Canadian Map Service
1919 American Court
Neenah, WI 54956
920-731-0101
www.uscanadianmap.com

Chapter 9
Caring for Mind & Body

CARING FOR MIND AND BODY

HYGIENE

The extremely low temperatures encountered on the winter trail inspire most people to plan when and how bathing will take place and to figure out the best times and places for excretions to occur.

We carry a plastic basin in the group-gear pack to be used for washing people or clothes. When used in combination with the cooking kettles, it is possible to keep soap and gray water out of the pots of the kitchen kit. Hair washing and whole-body bathing are best reserved for part of a layover day to ensure enough time for hair to dry completely, and so that you can have a whole tent to yourself while the others are on a day hike or in another tent.

Many people take abbreviated "cat baths" almost daily, and as the trip goes on and inhibitions fall away through familiarity, many aspects of hygiene that are usually conducted in private become a little more public. In the absence of walls, simply turning away or using an adjacent person as a screen are tricks that almost always evolve on trips. And in the close quarters, companions quickly learn to turn away at just the right moments to preserve modesty and allow private space. You can also pin up a temporary screen made of a sleeping bag liner. A nightly wash is accomplished simply and quickly by heating a cupful of water on the stove. Pour the warmed water on your washcloth, taking care to wring out the excess in the bough pit next to the stove, and clean up with minimal fuss.

The best wash kit contains a washcloth and a small towel. The ultra space- and weight-conscious often carry two washcloths, the second serving as a towel. In the heat of the tents, you will evaporate dry after a full bath and only need the towel for fluffing washed hair or occasionally drying after a cat bath.

For an extra-fast cat bath that does not even require pouring a little hot water onto a washcloth, make a snowball from the moist snow near the stove, give your critical areas a quick swipe and then throw the snowball away as if it were a primitive disposable towelette. You can also manufacture toilet paper snowballs the same way.

Trips to the bathroom are made in a number of ways. Some people manage to go while underway during the day. This way, they are warm from walking, can take a break before they cool down and be back in harness in a matter of minutes. Those who have thought ahead will carry toilet paper in their pockets, as well as matches to burn the toilet paper after use. (There is, of course, no fire danger on top of the snow.)

Others must go behind the campsites, and this area must be treated a little more elaborately. In all cases, you want to go over land, if possible, and on ground that is not low or boggy. This will keep sewage out of the water system when everything melts in the spring. Our euphemism for the bathroom-going grounds is the "cemetery," because after going and covering the spot with snow, everyone is trained to mark his or her spot with a spruce stick or dead branch. Once covered with insulating snow, feces may stay unfrozen, and if some other person uses your track and starts to dig a small hole in the snow only to find someone has already been there, he or she will not be amused. A marker in the snow serves as a signal to move over a little and create a new stall. After a few days at a layover camp with a big party, the number of little monuments in the "cemetery" is quite amazing.

If you need to go at night but don't want to go snowshoeing off into the distance, you can simply go in the open at the edge of the packed area in camp.

Many people from the land of chairs and couches have a limited range of motion and find it hard or impossible to assume a full squat. This is too bad, because not only is the full squat very convenient, but the resulting compression of your lower abdomen greatly speeds evacuation and reduces your exposure to the cold. Nonsquatters are advised to find a tree that they can face and use to hold themselves up by hooking one hand around the trunk. This improves balance, precludes the possibility of falling over backward into deep snow and should suffice for the needs of the moment.

Everyone, without fail, must remember to scoop out a large deep hole to go in and splay their snowshoe tails out behind them during bowel functions. It is always embarrassing to be followed home by what you thought you left behind.

Although some people can sleep all night without needing to urinate, many can't. Shy folks with bashful bladders get all the way up and go out into the tent yard at night, but others take full advantage of the tents not having floors. It is a simple matter to peel back the groundsheet at the rear or edges of the tent and kneel or squat for relief. The distance is not far, and the warmth of the sleeping bag remains close at hand. Usually, the sound of a sleeping bag zipper or the telltale hot hissing wakes others and inspires them to follow suit. Those who don't may wake to find half the group giggling and chatting at the back of the tent.

If you have to go, get up and go. You will immediately warm up if you do and will be unable to sleep if you don't.

Basically, with a bit of forethought given to timing and location, and perhaps some compromises with regard to modesty, hygiene on the trail differs little from hygiene at home. Life goes on. You stay clean.

On a more serious note, if you observe your urine stains in the snow, you can monitor your level of hydration. A clear light yellow is good. As you become more and more dehydrated, the color will darken. If it reaches dark yellow or orange, you had better increase your intake of liquids significantly.

PSYCHOLOGY

We cannot speak of living in physical comfort on the winter trail without addressing an equally important element: the landscape and weather of the mind and emotions. On a good trip, you experience the rare wonders of the wild landscape as well as the harmony within yourself and with your companions. The emotional and philosophical approach to wilderness determines, to a large extent, the quality of the trip.

In a mode typical of Western culture, stories of outdoor exploration are usually recounted largely in terms of derring-do. Creative and determined exploration has historically turned all too often into exploitation, turning discoveries to economic advantage. Often the literature and journals of adventurers becomes a barrage of stories of self-aggrandizement and conquering, whether it be of nature or people.

Perhaps in direct response to this approach, in a world with less and less wild land, evolved a culture of outdoors worshippers frequently lacking in basic physical skills but proficient in identifying and engaging with their own and others' emotional worlds. The inner world became the dominant landscape. The glory of a new day emerging in the slanting rays of the sun became of secondary importance to whether you had greeted the day having processed how you felt about yourself and your companions and any fears you might have concerning that day. Ironically, in this introspective quest for dealing with the natural world in a less invasive fashion, we find that we have lessened our ability to let that world touch us deeply. We are possibly as estranged from the natural world as aggressive explorers may have been. For without engagement, there can be no lasting relationship. If nature becomes a place to wage either physical or emotional battle, its voice cannot be heard.

Perhaps the most skillful explorers of the physical and cultural world, then, are those who equally nurture skills involving both mind and body. For without the knowledge and physical skills needed to live in comfort in the wilds, we are limited to brief journeys that depend largely on technical support. As a result, we miss the profound understandings gained from physical dependence on, and engagement with, the land. And without understanding of human emotions and spirit, both our own and others', we never experience that vital interaction between ourselves and the landscape.

This book primarily imparts information to help you develop technical skills for winter living, but only as part of a process to enable you to feel at home in the woods. Our goal is to encourage competence through experience so that you can enter a realm of realities not knowable through science or through a visitor's perspective. It is at this point that you begin to perceive and yearn to explore wilderness on a deeper level. This terrain is difficult to write about and best left for each of us to discover privately. In the meantime, we will discuss some of the more common emotional or psychological situations that can evolve on the trail.

People go on trips for many reasons, some of them unknown even to themselves. Sometimes it is for the sheer love of traveling in wild places or for a chance to get a change of perspective on your life through a change in scenery. For others, the physical demands of outdoor living represent a welcome balance to a more cerebral life. And, as mentioned, there are people who need to combat themselves or others in an attempt to face inner fears or make a name for themselves. Whatever our reasons are, they greatly affect our behavior and the people we travel with. It pays to look at why we want to go on a particular trip as well as what our expectations are. Then, compare notes with potential companions. This can be one of the most important of preparations and the most influential of the factors governing the ultimate success of the trip.

Expectations, of yourself, of others and of the trip itself, can set the stage for complete disappointment or unparalleled satisfaction. For instance, if you inadvertently set unattainable goals, you will have to deal with this problem during the trip, perhaps at a critical juncture. In unsuccessful expeditions, the trouble frequently lies with incorrect or uncommunicated expectations. The fatal flaw in many of these trips is that the leaders did not adapt to changing circumstances, and instead clung to original goals and expectations.

It is often assumed that a certain amount of ground can be covered, without giving thought to the multiple variables that present themselves on any trip, particularly long ones. For instance, on snowshoeing trips, a long storm with deep snow markedly slows travel, and knee joints, arches and Achilles tendons commonly become inflamed from overuse requiring restful layover days. Such delays can eat into a schedule sufficiently to make travelers risk injury or worse in an attempt to meet their original goal. Yet the often overlooked, safest solution to being "behind schedule" is simply to revise expectations.

Nearly all of the most notorious expedition disasters were in large part due to the unwillingness of leaders to abandon their original itinerary. There is a natural tendency to equate changing trip goals with overall trip failure. For instance, if you did not reach the peak of the mountain but turned back, then the whole endeavor is considered unsuccessful. This sort of summit-questing-at-any-expense seems to pervade the thinking of most outdoor adventurers initially. It must sooner or later be outgrown to avoid accidents or tragedy, which are worse than any imagined failure.

The key is to be aware of your goals and expectations and have alternative plans in mind so you won't be surprised when things don't go as planned. By practicing discipline in planning and during the trip yet maintaining flexibility, you will see each trip, regardless of outcome, as rich with experiences that have taken you to places previously unimagined.

On the snowshoe trip that eventually took us across the Ungava peninsula, our primary goal was not necessarily to reach Kuujjuaq. It was to see as much of the land and of the major rivers draining to that Inuit settlement as possible given time and supplies. If that meant turning around once half of the food was gone and we hadn't covered half of the distance, that would be fine. Our plans included retracing our trail if necessary.

Of course, we knew it would be exciting to arrive at Kuujjuaq having hand-hauled toboggans on the same rivers and in the same way as indigenous people did up until the mid-twentieth century. As it was, at the end of the trip we experienced profound joy, not so much from having gotten to Kuujjuaq as from having spent extended time in some of the wildest country left on earth. One of the best and unexpected gifts was that we gained a rare rapport with older native people who could still remember life and travel on the land.

Our sense is that the trips richest in profound experience are based in joy—joy in being at the mercy of a natural order that is at once part of you and greater than you. With this outlook, you are prepared for predictable contingencies and also open to the unexpected. Essential to such journeys, however, is complete fluency with the skills of the trail, a fluency that lets you feel at one with the landscape and the life around you. These, then, are trips to strive toward. In the meantime, there is no lack of joy in the forays you make as you accumulate skill.

Difficulties in outdoor travel can be both physical and psychological in nature, and the longer the trip, the more necessary is timely response. Psychological problems can be lumped into several categories.

Fear of oneself, the landscape or of others:

"Can I keep up?"

"Will I be cold?"

"Will there be enough food?"

"Will the others like me, or will I like them?"

"What if we can't pull this trip off the way we said we would?"

One of the best antidotes to fear is awareness of it. And once you understand that your fear is not unusual, you can replace it with confidence based on skill. Under controlled conditions and with the support of knowledgeable companions, expose yourself to the things that make you fearful.

A common fear in winter snowshoeing, for example, is that the ice is not safe to walk on. We all can frighten ourselves with images of falling through the ice and bobbing along underneath until we succumb. If you are the trip leader, show the most fearful person in the group how to check ice thickness with an ice chisel. Have that person lead the group. Maybe you will travel only a few feet in several minutes, but after half an hour of constantly checking the ice thickness, the person is going to gain confidence commensurate to the fear he or she loses.

Anxiety is often reflected in overeating or undereating, so be attentive to fluctuations in group members' appetites. It is quite natural to wonder and maybe even worry a bit about whether there will be enough food to go around unless you have been in charge of provisioning the trip. If you are a leader, make sure everyone gets a personal supply of snack food to last the entire trip, and see that there is more than enough food served, especially at the first meal. You may also choose to encourage participation in meal preparation, which familiarizes the group with the food supply.

Fear of the landscape is often unconscious fear, so you will have to watch carefully for its symptoms. Many people do not realize how estranged they have become from nature and will not encounter this realization until they are without civilization's amenities. As with many fears, this one falls away with increasing skill and understanding of how to take care of yourself in a world not dominated by humans.

Gather as much information as you can about the area you are to travel. How cold can you expect it to get? Will you come in contact with another culture? What are your points of emergency access and egress? Have you given yourself adequate time to complete the journey? Ask yourself as many questions as possible before the trip and make sure you have answers, or at least informed attempts at answers, before you leave.

Go on shorter trips that mimic longer outings you want to take. A brief journey entails nearly all of the physical skills you need to have in your command, and you may encounter some of the mental challenges that are a part of longer trips. You can be sure that trips never go precisely as planned. So, expose yourself to the dynamics of the landscape until you become fluent in your ability to adapt to new circumstances.

Spend time alone. Distractions such as pets, friends and activities perceived as obligations keep us from honing the ability to listen to our own wise counsel.

A tendency to put things off or lack of discipline:

"I won't say anything now, maybe they'll change."

"I'm too hot. I'll stop when the rest do and change clothes then."

"I'm not sure we're in the right cove, but I can check the map at lunch break when it's convenient."

"I'll just stuff my daypack here until I have time to tie it back onto the toboggan."

"I'll lie in bed just a little longer and dry my stuff tonight instead."

There are, no doubt, many reasons why we procrastinate: it's habitual; we fear change, success or failure; our energy is low; etc. The great thing about the outdoors is that you instantly pay for any indecision or laziness. If you haven't cut enough wood for the night, you will have to go without and be uncomfortable. Or you will have to cut more in the dark and be inconvenienced. If you can't decide whether to adjust your hood and scarf better against the wind, you soon will be forced to as your nose and cheekbones start to freeze.

Similarly, any lack of discipline is summarily corrected by the elements, sometimes none too gently. If you do not always tie loose items completely onto the toboggan, sooner or later you will lose something critical in the snowdrifts.

One morning, in an effort to get on our way quickly, we hastily tied our lunch and thermos onto a poor spot on the toboggan. At noon, there was neither lunch nor thermos to be found. A mile-long backtrack on a windswept lake finally located them, almost hidden in the drifting snow. A lost axe or ice chisel would have had more serious consequences.

In the tent, develop a system whereby every item has its "home" and is always returned to that place regardless of inconvenience. When damp clothes have dried, remove them from the lines and pack them away. On the trail, take the time to do things right the instant they need doing, or you will have to take more time later to correct the situation. If your toboggan lines are loosening, tighten them now, before gear falls off. Readjust your hood and scarf before your face starts to freeze.

Such attention to detail makes the difference between a haphazard journey begging for confusion and trouble, and a smooth trip characterized by free minds and lots of free time.

A tendency to be unduly influenced by the past and preoccupied with the future.

"I was never good at that, you do it."

"Are we going to get there in time?"

"What if the weather stays like this for days?"

"Are we having fun yet?"

Everyday life requires that we become proficient at projecting into the future so that we will be able to look back on a successful past. What attention need we give to the present? Only enough to allow us to plan for the future.

Life in the outdoors demands that we focus on the present. Our needs are immediate and compelling. We need food and shelter and fire. If we do not address these needs, our future is in jeopardy. Trips are recalled vividly in later years, probably because so much attention is given to the present.

Beginning outdoorspeople are often preoccupied with goals: Will we reach our destination? Will we get there in time? Miles are measured, days dissected, food quantities analyzed and reanalyzed. To a degree, all of this attention is necessary until you become familiar with the basics. However, you soon learn that conditions constantly change and most questions can be answered only in the loosest terms.

People often hold back from new activities because of beliefs about what they have or haven't been able to do. Once you abandon those paralyzing notions, try something new and come to recognize what you can do, you suddenly feel like a participant, not a visitor or observer.

Once you are confident with winter camping, it is easy to become lost in thought. For those who are comfortable with themselves and have spent a lot of time thinking quietly, this can be truly illuminating. However, for many people, being inside their thoughts for extended periods leads to upsetting emotions and memories. These thoughts and feelings will not go away without proper attention. Sometimes, a person can think things through privately; many times they cannot, and the whole group may be affected.

Mostly, the person needs a trusted listener. The entire group need not become involved, no more than it would with one member's minor physical problem. And with experience, people's mental and physical problems fall away, enabling deeper engagement with the natural world. It is this engagement that reveals the true riches of the landscape.

Enslavement to quantitative or qualitative goals.

"I think we can include that river system, too, if we just push a little harder."

"Our trip is going to be the first snowshoe crossing of 'terra incognita'."

"Let's go to the Thelon. We need to get a musk ox on our life list."

"I could really make some progress with my interpersonal skills by going with a group."

Whether you are more interested in covering a lot of ground or delving more deeply into intangibles matters not. Awareness of your predilection, however, is paramount and should be discussed if you are going with others.

There is nothing less enjoyable to a person who is enthralled with natural history than to be tearing along at maximum efficiency, day after day, with a leader bent on breaking his or her private speed record. But if you know in advance that the leader is thus inclined, and it suits your interests, then it can be an exhilarating and satisfying experience.

Also, you must look carefully at your abilities. For instance, your trip focus might be to develop the ability to relate more deeply to the natural world. Yet if you are not utterly proficient in physical trail skills, inspired moments will be few and far between. And, contrary to popular belief, deep experience rarely emerges from contrived situations.

The key, then, is to understand that there are different ways of conducting a trip, and that you should be aware of the styles that suit you best and of the abilities required to achieve desired ends.

The belief that if you go somewhere different, then you will become different.

"My life's a mess. I'm going on a trip where I can forget my troubles."

"I'll go with a group of strangers, since they don't know what I'm like."

"The wilderness is a good and kind place; I can nurse my wounds there."

Frequently, people believe that if they travel to somewhere new, they too will change. You may change, but later and in such tiny increments that it can hardly be called transformational. You are who you are, both flawed and talented, no matter where you go. If you have a need for attention at home, you will likely be extra needy on the trail. If you tend to be helpful with family and friends, you will probably contribute similarly to a group of strangers.

Just keep in mind that personality traits become exaggerated on trips, more so in people who are new to the experience. For instance, many people have an unfounded faith that the natural world is full of justice and goodness. It can be profoundly upsetting when you realize for the first time that you and other beings in the natural world are equally meaningful and equally meaningless.

Many initiates experience profound fear in reaction to this discovery. Often they superimpose their fear onto the indifferent landscape and regard the natural world with dread, even as if it were malevolent. Other individuals find a blissful freedom in the feeling of insignificance while at the same time sensing they are somehow part of a grand and vast order.

All of us possess the aforementioned attitudes to a greater or lesser degree. The main point is to recognize them and understand their effects. Then, as a trip leader or participant, you can deal with the many ways these feelings express themselves in behavior. And these behaviors will appear, in yourself and in those with whom you travel. For in a short time, it becomes clear that the outdoors is an uncompromising place where you are no more or less significant than the snow around you.

LEADERSHIP

We don't know why, but groups of four to eight people generally function best. But this does not mean that groups smaller or larger are unworkable. They just require a little more maintenance. As mentioned elsewhere, at least one person must be the recognized leader. It is preferable to have co-leaders, and even better if the co-leaders are of opposite sexes. This often makes one or the other more approachable by mixed group members.

In any group, people tend to settle into roles: the leader, the clown, the doer, the sitter, the giver, the taker, etc. Blending of roles keeps you learning on each trip. The leader becomes a bit of an orchestral conductor, allowing each member a place in the score but not letting any one, including him- or herself, dominate.

A leader must possess a multitude of abilities, but perhaps most important are a sense of humor and physical adroitness. Keeping spirits up with plenty of fun and good-natured poking at otherwise irritating personalities, the leader helps the group become a temporary tribe with its own myths, stories and private jokes. Of equal importance, group members should have total confidence in the leader's judgment and ability to keep them fed and sheltered.

You'll quickly recognize the importance of group dynamics if you read the diaries of adventurers and explorers. Without exception, they contain comments regarding personalities, conflicts and the consequences that resulted from efforts by the leader or group to handle sticky situations.

Group or individual crises often are not what they initially appear. If one member constantly seems to have trouble with various aspects of winter travel, don't be reluctant to study the matter beyond the specific complaints. Often, the person is unconsciously indicating a need for attention. Once you have attended to the physical problems, you can turn your attention to the underlying psychological problem. In most cases, all that is required is for the person to gain some control over his or her surroundings through skill acquisition and to be included more in the group. Then, the physical problems will evaporate.

It is critical to pay attention to these kinds of problems as soon as they arise. For if they are ignored out of impatience or lack of understanding, they will re-emerge, in many cases exacerbated.

On a bitter cold morning during a two-week journey in an inaccessible hinterland, one of our group complained of cold feet. We were all tying gear onto the toboggans and hadn't yet moved, so we were all feeling a bit cold. We suggested she simply run through the deep snow around camp to warm up. Thinking the problem solved, we went back to lashing on our loads. However, she didn't run enough to generate sufficient heat and started out still feeling cold. Soon she mentioned again that her feet were not only cold but that she couldn't feel them. Given the conditions and the time devoted to trail preparation, we knew that it was highly unlikely that her feet were frozen and therefore numb, but we knew we had to check, regardless.

We formed a tight, wind-protective circle around her, took her mukluk off and put her foot on a group member's hot belly. As her foot went from boot to belly, we noticed that it was pink and flexible. The healthy foot and the woman's reluctance to rectify the initial problem signaled that cold feet were not the problem here. However, out on a windy river with the group standing around was not the place to discuss the real issue. So we returned to the old campsite, re-erected the tent, got the stove roaring and had lunch. By early afternoon, we were back on the trail, with everybody well fed and warm and the person with the cold feet looking more relaxed and open than she had during the entire previous week.

From that moment on she became a confident member of the group, the cold no longer a concern. For what she really needed was confidence that the leaders and the group would take care of her no matter how trying the circumstance.

The psychological emergency in this case was as serious and as important as seriously frosted feet. Careful attention solved both problems. However, an inexperienced or insensitive leader might have been fooled by outward appearances and responded with expediency in mind rather than recognizing and solving the camouflaged problem.

As you gain and refine your skills as a leader, the gulf widens between your level of comfort and expertise and that of guests who are newer to life on the trail. Increasingly, you will make decisions subconsciously and without consideration discernible to your guests or companions. If you co-lead, over the long term much of the communication between you and your partner will seem to take place telepathically because it is based on shared assumptions and knowledge. To unknowing trip participants, you may seem to arrive at decisions and strategies so naturally and invisibly that party members are reduced to blind followers. They may trust you implicitly, but this is not always a comfortable position to be in. Typically, the result is a subtle distancing between participants and leaders, and often a little anxiety results.

Fortunately, when this situation develops, participants generally give leaders a wonderfully blatant cue: endless questions regarding just about everything. Why are we crossing here? Which way will we turn once we reach the lake? Why camp here in the shade when it is sunny over there? Often these questions are literal, and, in answering them, a leader has an opportunity to educate as well as to invite group members into decision-making.

In many cases, however, the questions are the subconscious surfacing of a search for parameters by members who are feeling insecure. The two types of questions call for different kinds of answers. Sensitive leaders must constantly feel out these nuances.

Simple questions are best answered directly. We'll cross here because there may be weak ice or overflow over there where the darker snow is. We'll head left when we reach the lake because there is a grand campsite in a little cove there. It will be dark before we are fully set up, and a campsite here will catch the morning sun. Such short responses simultaneously answer the question, educate and indicate thought and competence. They both inform and reassure.

Suppose now that your party is about to start a four-mile crossing toward a peak on the far shore. You anticipate using the better portion of two hours to make landfall, and the wind is building fast. The most direct route, crossing straight toward the mountain, comes at the cost of a shelterless frontal assault from the wind. If you alter your course at the expense of a few miles, you can wind-shadow islands and thereby take the wind from the side rather than the front. Moreover, you can take a rest on the islands or on the ice in the lee of them. If things get really bad, you can camp on an island while waiting for the wind to change or diminish. It might take a single lakeward glance and a fraction of a second for a leader to see this and opt for the island route. A savvy leader will take a few seconds to group up and explain the why and wherefore to the group; a very wise one might not go into full detail.

There is a fine balance to be maintained by revealing informative detail that is reassuring and educational. In the example just mentioned, sharing information empowers the group and at the same time demonstrates navigational and strategic skills that group members may wish to learn. By refraining from expounding on the contingency reasoning related to the islands, a sensitive leader avoids giving participants something to worry about. Approaching an island that a leader has introduced as friendly is far different than approaching it as a desperate life raft in the midst of a frightful gale.

As the leader, you know that if things were that bad, you would never initiate a crossing. But an anxious participant might not know that about you yet. And if things do escalate while underway, another huddle can take place to decide whether to retreat or push for one of the islands. A leader with aces up his or her voluminous anorak sleeves is not necessarily malevolently deceptive. Perhaps the contingency potential of those islands will never be required. This does not devalue the islands in any way, because if they were needed, the necessity might be great or even desperate. But by not revealing everything he or she knows all at once, a leader does not overwhelm participants and leaves them with points they can make on their own, which will be far more gratifying to them.

Supposing a different leader, out of impatience, fatigue or expediency, started leading the way across the ice without communicating anything. We can guarantee that a question, if not a full chorus of them, would arise. Why are we heading for those islands if we want to go toward that hill? Will the wind get worse? Should I put up my scarf? Anyone seen my goggles? The questions may not call for answers, only contact, for communication, for a share of control and power. You have to respond.

As with everything else on the winter trail, it is easier to prevent such questions than it is to respond to them. Nevertheless, no matter how remarkable a leader you may be, you cannot foresee everything, and you will need to become skilled at the art of response. Often you will hear yourself or other leaders preface an answer with "Hard to say," then follow with a list of qualifiers, alternative plans and perhaps interesting little details. The preface means two things. It acknowledges the fact of multiple possibilities. And it buys the leader a few seconds in which to gauge the meaning of the question in order to give the most considered and considerate answer.

Group members need to be able to give something to the group, too. So, the sooner skills and responsibilities are passed on to participants, the better morale will be. If, by contrast, the leaders guard their power by withholding information and knowledge, the group will naturally react by constantly testing decisions, exhibiting low morale and ceasing to engage with the landscape and the experience of the journey.

Rotating chores such as choosing the trail, float packing, camp pitching, water getting, woodcutting, cooking and cleanup is one way to keep the various roles dynamic and to make sure that everyone is initiated into and appreciative of the skills required. And as confidence improves, so do everyone's spirits.

However, full democracy is unwieldy and ultimately dangerous. Certain responsibilities decided upon in advance of trip departure must be reserved for the leaders. The leaders, for instance, might make the final choice regarding campsites because, having more experience, they recognize the importance of timing when the group is tired. Sharing this decision with the rest of the group in an attempt at fairness only invites problems that can quickly develop into situations that could endanger all group members. In outdoor life, decisions must be timely. There is little room for casualness or mistakes.

If the leaders always reserve the right of final word, they can relax into modified democracy. But circumstances are always changing, and leaders must be ready to jump in decisively if needed. The more power that is given to the group, the more the participants will learn, and grow. But there will be times when solid, reliable decisiveness on the leader's part can rally the group and make it function well. So:

o Be aware of your attitudes regarding wilderness exploration. Why are you going on the trip?

o Understand your companions' philosophical inclinations. What are they contributing to the trip and what do they expect to get from the experience?

o Be prepared to handle common behavioral problems. Are the problems truly what they appear to be?

Keep in mind that groups have a life of their own and that basic issues must be addressed regardless of individual desires. Does each person feel personally involved in the group goal?

ALEXANDRA'S DAY ON THE TRAIL

I pulled my sleeping bag away from my head and strained to listen. "A-whoooaaaagh!" I heard it again. It was still dark, but nearing dawn. The barred owl's courting song had woven its way through my dreams all night, and now it connected me with the beckoning day.

"Oh, all right," I grumbled to myself, as if the owls were the ones forcing me out of bed. I brought an arm out of the sleeping bag and opened the door of the cold stove. The matches, shaving curls and splits were in a handy small pile, where I had put them the night before. I quickly arranged them in the stove, lit a match and in a minute, the stovepipe began its characteristic roar.

I tossed a few larger chunks of spruce into the stove and shut the door. I emptied the half-gallon thermos of last night's hot water into the coffee pot, set it on the stove and slid back into the somnolent warmth of my bag. The growing light was beginning to overpower the jigging, orange dervishes of firelight that escaped around the edges of the stove door to reflect and dance on the tent walls. Soon the tent was awash in a salmon glow, and the entrancing dancers had returned to the realm of night.

Smoke was just beginning to come out of the other tent's stovepipe as I passed on my way to the water hole. Feathery frost crystals formed on the hair that spilled from beneath my hat as I chipped out the half inch of ice that had formed overnight. Before filling the buckets and returning to the tent, I lingered, facing the steady white-gold brilliance of the rising sun, marveling at the perfection of the landscape it continuously transformed. Packed snow squawked underfoot as I returned to the tent, "yes-yes, yes-yes, yes-yes, yes-yes," and I handed the buckets through the tent flap.

"One for the sunshine's golden glow. One for the laughter here below. One for the tracks upon the snow." Garrett was chanting as he dedicated palmsful of coffee into the roiling water. "And another for the barred owls." Sausages were spitting on the stove. Two campers were drying their sleeping bags by the stove while another dug in her duffel bag searching for an elusive garment. The other tent dwellers had joined us. Morning activities in camp had begun.

"Coffee's ready!" and hands shot forward, holding mugs. As hot cereal thickened, we puttered in our longjohns. Sleeping bags were gradually stuffed away, dried clothing repacked, journals updated and hot drinks savored. Just outside the tent, the nasal "yank, yank, yank" of the red-breasted nuthatch mixed with the thin and tinkling song of golden-crowned kinglets feeding in the sunny branches of the trees arched over us.

Eager to join the brilliant day, someone was already taking the toboggans down from where they had leaned in the trees overnight. The bottoms were scraped free of frost, a little paraffin rubbed on and lines laid out neatly. Soon gear streamed from the tent: sleeping bags, pads, duffels, daypacks and now the kitchen wanigan. Some of us laid gear on the toboggans, leaving room for the tent and stove and group gear duffel. After the stove was taken out, the snow cloths were pulled up; the tent was brushed and shaken free of frost and rolled up. The coals and ashes were dumped from the stove

A party heads into the falling snow. The two lead walkers without toboggans are breaking trail.

downwind, and the stove was allowed to cool before being dismantled and packed onto a toboggan.

The tent poles, stove skids and leftover firewood were neatly stacked by a tree for future use. Nonburnable refuse in ashes dumped from the stove was added to the trash bag. (We pack out only nonburnables. The heat of trail stoves is sufficient to burn plastics hot enough so that they are truly consumed.) The first level of loads had been lashed to the toboggans, so now we started securing sleeping bags and daypacks with bungee cords. The ice chisel, axes, shovel and some cross-country skis and poles were woven into the strings and bungees of the outer load, transforming the lumpy toboggans into horned caterpillars.

"Does someone have a good spot for the lunch bag and thermos?" The very tail of one toboggan was empty and the lunch gear was securely lashed there, to be removed later without disturbing the other gear. Finally, we doffed our warm parkas and strapped them onto the loads. Everybody had taken their cameras and binoculars from where we had hung them overnight, and now we looked as bedecked as a serious scientific expedition.

The riverbank was somewhat steep, so we carried our snowshoes onto the river before bringing our toboggans down. Then we headed out, each of us leaning into our traces. The random array of snowshoers and gear pulled smoothly into a colorful, sinuous line, a joyful lilt in each step.

We swung along in single file, stopping periodically to shed clothing. Up ahead a scimitar of green-black water seemed to widen as we neared. The lead still smoked in the early-morning air. We paused, studying our approach, for though leads are usually short openings in the ice field, they are preceded and trailed by a winding path of recently frozen open water. A dusting of snow can hide this newer, possibly thinner, ice.

As the ice field on either side of a lead is usually perfectly safe, we paralleled the open water, edging our way over. When we got within a few feet of the edge, we began to chisel the black ice, testing for thickness. Two inches is considered the minimum thickness for safety, so we watched with interest as we got closer and closer to the open lead.

Finally, we found ourselves standing on ten inches of ice a mere three feet from

A rest pause in a headwind. Travelers are facing downwind in the shelter of their wind gear and hoods. This is a good time to check each other's faces for frosting.

the water gliding by. Surprisingly, the bottom was only about three feet down. We knew from experience that the ice tapered quickly from the thick ice field to nothing in the last few feet of ice. After repeated testing with the chisel, we removed our snowshoes and began walking beside the lead on the smooth icy surface.

Our toboggans pulled easily, clattering along behind us. We made good time along the lead. But after another bend in the river, the current slid back under the ice. Where new ice had formed there were gardens of the characteristic feathery "frost blossoms" across the glassy surface. We were now back on the wind-packed snowfield of the river, back in our snowshoes, and the toboggans pulled harder now that the frictionless glide on glare ice was over.

We took care to avoid sags and hollows, for these are suspect areas where old leads have been or where a spring might keep the ice thin and overflow might settle. Snowcover hides a lot, so we kept exploring what this lump was (a rock with ice buckled around it when the river level dropped) and why the snow over there looked grayer than the rest (the river had leaked over a slightly depressed section of ice and had soaked up into the snow, creating slush). As the sun had just been swallowed by a high cirrus curtain, it was becoming increasingly harder to see the topography of the terrain directly in front of us.

The river widened now, and soon we entered a lake. Out in the middle, whirling columns of snow rose in 20- or 30-foot swirls and tore across the lake surface to dissipate almost as quickly as they had risen. The wind was picking up, and, though it was not snowing, the air was filling with the blinding white crystals of a ground blizzard.

Though we knew that the outlet was to the east, directly across the lake, our view was increasingly obscured. We decided on a prudent step: a prominent softwood knoll rose precipitously on the north shore of the outlet and was still just visible. Taking a bearing on it, we scribbled that number in the snow. The first person in line chose the course, periodically checking her compass, and we all followed. Every once in a while someone farther back in the line would stop and check our progress by compass.

Now the ground blizzard had obliterated the far shore, and we were traveling "blind." We continued to recheck our bearing and also took time periodically to stop, face downwind and check each other's faces for frost spots. On one of the initial checks, we discovered a dime-size white spot on a nose. This was easily brought back to healthy color by placing hot fingertips on the spot. The person was reminded to exhale through his nose. It took about a half hour or so to cross the lake. But despite the wind and swirling snow, the dark shore and the knoll loomed ahead, right on target.

Off to our right, we could hear snatches of falling water as the wind tossed the sounds about. At the outlet of any lake there is open water, sometimes flowing for up to a mile before it cools enough to freeze. This is because the exiting water comes from the bottom of the lake, where the densest, warmest water lies.

"Lunchtime, isn't it?" someone yelled. "You bet," and the group bent over their toboggans, unlashing lunch and donning parkas. Several of us searched for private places to relieve ourselves while we were still warm from hauling. Others snowshoed up into the nearby woods and selected a lunch site among three thick spruces. We treaded the area down with our snowshoes, noting how the wind scarcely intruded upon our protective grove.

The lunch and thermos were put down, and we prepared our ringside seats. Each person stepped out of his or her snowshoes, immediately sinking and making a hole in which to rest his or her feet and keep them warm. Soon everyone was comfortably seated on stacked snowshoes, eyes riveted on the hands slicing pepperoni and cheese and arranging crackers, jams and peanut butter.

"Tea, anyone?" Enamel mugs were filled and passed to their owners, who immediately wrapped their fingers around the warming cups. Cups were balanced on snowshoes or held between hands and knees, for putting a mug in the snow would quickly rob the drink of its heat, plus cover the cup with melted snow.

Warping down a steep incline. In addition to the brakeline direct from the tail, the towline can be used as a second safety brake to slow a descent.

A clear whistle was followed by another across the clearing. Two dark gray jays swooped into the snow-laden branches of the nearby spruces. They cocked their heads, showing the white patch of feathers atop their pates. We tossed the birds some cheese bits, and, with little hesitation, first one and then the other "whiskey jack," or Canada jay, landed, snatched a morsel and left in one smooth motion.

After topping off the meal with some pieces of chocolate, we returned the cups and leftovers to the lunch bag; and snowshoed back out to the lake and our toboggans. It felt colder now, mostly because we hadn't been moving for awhile, so it was difficult to take off our parkas and lash them onto the loads. We eagerly took to the traces, and, in about 30 paces, hot blood was pounding through our veins.

It was good to be back on the river, out of the full blast of the wind. We paralleled the open water of the outlet for a half mile or so until we reached solid ice. Periodically, the lead toboggan would pull over, letting the others pass, and rejoin the group at the rear. So far this day there hadn't been much snow to break trail through, but even a few inches is more wearing than traveling in others' smooth tracks.

We came upon another long, arcing lead that passed through a narrows in the river where the water ran slick and black and sinister in its irrevocable rush to pass us and return to the watery world under the ice. The banks sloped steeply on each side of the open river with no route for the toboggans. We took out an axe, and several of us scouted a route up through the woods, planning a trail, choosing the gentlest grade available and the least clearing necessary to make it passable.

The trailmakers returned from packing the float. A group of us clustered near the first toboggan to help bring it up the initial slope to the more level woods. With one or two people pulling and another pushing, each toboggan gained the bank easily. Partway across the overland trail, a parka stuff sack had pulled free and lay at the side of the trail. One of the tobogganers discovered it and tucked it safely onto his toboggan. The last person in line already had the habit of periodically stopping to peer back along the trail to check for anything that might have fallen off. With no one following, the last toboggan in line is the most likely to lose gear.

The group paused at the crest of the steep slope. From here the trail careened down the bank and out onto the reformed solid ice shelf. It looked too risky with the open water nearby to let the toboggans slide down the hill on their own. And it was too steep to bring them down controllably, even with several people braking. The best solution was to warp each toboggan down.

We attached a 50-foot line to the end of the toboggan and took a turn around the base of a tree at the bank crest. With a couple of people guiding the toboggan up front on either side, the sled was carefully let down until it rested on the flat.

On extremely steep trails, the warping rope takes an additional wrap around the belayer's body, mountaineering fashion. Additionally, the hauling line can take a turn around a nearby tree as the sled is slowly lowered. There is no way to check the momentum of a 100-pound sled in motion, so in circumstances such as these, warping is the only way to go.

Down on the river again, we noticed a narrow, deep trail that wound its way along the edge of the river, disappearing into a cedar grove. Sharply edged rectangular holes in the trail gave it away as a deer trail, for these animals favor the less deep snows of the rivers for the same reasons we do. At dusk they would probably return to the shelter of this grove. Their almond-shaped beds punctuated the snarl of the meandering trailwork among the gray-brown trunks. If we were lucky, we might see the elusive woods dwellers feeding on the tips of the cedars.

Ironically, just when our backs were to the river, an otter came out at the edge of the open water we had circumnavigated. We heard its crackling and crunching as it feasted on shellfish or minnows.

Soon, camera shutters were clicking. Cold-stiffened film must be advanced very gently, or it will break or tear in the sprockets. Moreover, in our excitement to get good photographs, we had to be careful not to breathe on the lens or viewing frame, for it takes several minutes to remove the resultant frost. And of course, we had to don thin gloves as protection from the metal camera bodies.

After the deeryard and the otter sighting, we encountered some deep snow, for the river still ran narrowly, and the wind hadn't gotten in there to pack the snow. The lead tobogganer was having trouble breaking trail and pulling at the same time. So the first two in line dropped their traces and set out packing a float ahead about 50 yards. In the meantime, the rest of us began shuttling toboggans forward, regardless of whose toboggan was whose. The trailmakers snowshoed back to the last two toboggans, and then the next two moved forward to break trail. In this manner we were able to move ourselves and our gear efficiently through an initially exasperating section of the river.

We were working up a lot of heat, and hats and outer layers were all secured to the toboggans. Most of us were down to our first shirt layer, a strange contrast to the hoarfrost whitening our hair. The wind must have been dropping somewhat, for the tops of the trees weren't waving anymore. Another hour and it would be sunset.

We had been scouting the shoreline with camp in mind, even through the deep-snow area, but until now the banks had been abrupt, with an impenetrable tangle of young firs and hazelnut bushes behind. We had to push on a little longer than we would have liked, but it was worth it as we finally came upon an open grove on the north bank with a gentle slope where the beavers had been hauling poplars down to the river.

"It's a race against darkness!" Garrett shouted in mock alarm. In a fake British accent someone retorted, "We're up against it now!" There was laughter and bedlam as everyone dropped their traces and fell to their various jobs.

Before doing anything, though, we established a "hanging tree," where we hung our binoculars and cameras and goggles, safe from being knocked or scratched. Here they would stay for the night, never to be brought into the tent, where heat and moisture would cause damaging condensation. If it snowed, the powder could easily be brushed off in the morning, doing the instruments no harm. However, in case it snowed, nothing was left on the ground.

A few of us went into the grove to stomp down two tenting areas and clear the immediate vicinity of eye-poking twigs and branches. We were so near the rivers edge that we'd be able to unload the toboggans out on the river that night. Sometimes we had to pack a special area by the tents in which to "park" our sleds.

Garrett and I headed into the woods to select standing dead spruce for tent poles and firewood; a few others accompanied us to help haul it back to camp. Down on the river, we could hear the fake British accents in full swing as a group unloaded the toboggans. They stacked like gear with like, carefully coiled the lashing lines and leaned the cleaned toboggans up into the trees. "I say, you call this line prop'ly coiled? It looks like a bloody rat's nest." "What say, shall we stand 'em in the copse over 'ere?"

The ridge and scissor poles were in place, and the two tents hung limply, like laundry drying. Corners were pulled out and tied, snow shoveled onto the snow naps, stove pit dug out and groundsheets spread in the leveled interiors. There is always an unacknowledged race to see whose stovepipe starts smoking first, and the rattle of metal indicated the race had begun.

By now, wood had been hauled back to camp, and the steady, long strokes of an experienced sawyer kept flawless time as a backdrop to the shorter, irregular sawing of someone just learning. Enough wood was cut for both night and morning fires. We moved to the side and began splitting chunks. With a deft twist of the wrist at the end of each stroke, the dry wood flew apart, symmetrically halved. As it was thrown into the growing pile, each stick gave a musical "tok," indicating perfectly dry wood.

The ice chiseler had to go nearly to the center of the river to find water, though frequently the channel is nearer to one shore. More often than not, the water is deepest where the shore is steepest, especially on lakes. But the woods tumbled to the water's edge fairly gradually here, with the exception of the small plateau our campsite was on, so a few test holes had to be chiseled before water was actually struck. At the bottom of one of the holes, the chisel edge was nicked as it struck the cobble. The next hole was chiseled more carefully and the hole abandoned as the first flecks of grit appeared in the ice. The third hole was a success, and the chiseler gave a cry as the pressurized waters leapt and gurgled up through the hole. As water settled just below the lip of the hole, the remaining ice chunks and slush were skimmed off and thrown to the side in an arcing spray that seemed to defy the reality of the subfreezing landscape.

"Yes-yes, yes-yes, yes-yes," whispered snowshoes on dry snow, and a hand reached in through a tent flap. "Buckets?" A blast of hot air and white vapor poured out of the candle-bright tent as the buckets were passed outside. The people inside were stripping off layers of clothing, and the lines under the ridge were already sagging. A cluster of black rubber boots had already formed in the "pit" just inside the door. Someone was still sitting at the edge of the pit, whisking his mukluks and liners free of frost and clinging snow.

From the far tent, voices called in unison: "What's for supper?"

"Stuffed truffles and shrimp," some wiseacre retorted, and laughter muffled the ensuing response of our comrades.

We had the supper pot with water for rice heating on the stove; onions, carrots, apples and raisins were hydrating in a smaller vessel under the stove. Chunks of chicken were thawing in the frying pan for a curried dish. A bag of mixed nuts was being passed around the tent.

A hand appeared at the door and then a flushed face, grinning at the host of faces, upturned in greeting. "Hot drink water is ready." The kettle was passed in to us, and we handed out the snack bag for the other tent group. Though everyone shuttled between the tents during social hours, only two people slept in the "hot drink" tent on this trip. This made it a refuge for those seeking privacy.

We ate together in the "cook tent," making up for the earlier lack of conversation. As we ate, everyone soaked up the heat and recounted stories. Tonight someone chose to read a favorite passage, which we discussed briefly before reading that night's installment of a gripping story set, of course, "in a howling wilderness." One passage left the reader incapacitated with laughter that spread rapidly amongst the punchy listeners. But the tale finally continued, and soon the flickering candlelight on the tent walls began to blur before our tired eyes. It was time for bed.

During the rustlings and contortions of bed preparation, I found a straight-grained piece of spruce and, with my crooked knife, fashioned long, feather-thin shavings that were placed on top of the pencil-size splits for the morning fire. I tossed a small box of matches on top of these so nothing would take thought or effort in the early-morning darkness. The last kettle of hot water was poured into a thermos and placed nearby. I double-checked that all water was emptied from all the pots. The group was settled in now, a gentle murmuring of conversation coming from the other tent.

I stepped outside briefly. To the west, a starlit banner was widening as a clearing cold front approached. The deepening cold made the trees pop and snap, the reports echoing off the opposite shore. I pinched my nose and flexed my nostrils, noticing how slowly they relaxed back into shape. That meant it was already 20 below or so. Hard to believe, having just come from the tent's 80-degree warmth. The woods were an impenetrable purple-green darkness, but the river almost seemed to glow a soft purple-white. Out of the corner of my eye, I caught a silent motion in the thick branches of a nearby white pine. A swift, dark form swooped and then sailed, slightly descending as it crossed the river, then disappeared into the far woods. The conductor of my dreams was taking roost. Nighttime life had begun.

Snowmobiles & Komatiks

SNOWMOBILES & KOMATIKS

They walked like the caribou
They followed the caribou's path
And somewhere within ourselves
We are proud to be of those
Who walked for survival.
—"Nikanish" (My People)
by Kashtin, an Innu (Montagnais) rock 'n' roll band, 1991

SNOWMOBILES

To those who know us as voices of moderate consumption, users of wood-and-canvas canoes, users of natural fibers and walkers of snow, it comes as a shock that we maintain two snowmobiles. Rest assured that the decision did not come easily; there is much we find frustrating and unpleasant about them.

Time after time, native people would cross our snowshoe track and wonder why we were on foot. They would follow our track to see if we were in trouble, and of course be totally surprised to meet a bunch of white people traveling in a manner adopted directly from an earlier tradition of their own culture. We'd have tea, talk a bit if we could and then they would be gone. Their camp was always too far away for us to visit, and we of course could never accompany them because we were without a machine in a land where everybody has one. Nobody hitches a ride on another person's snowmobile except in an emergency.

If we wanted to be among native people, we knew we would have to be as self-sufficient as they were, and not hamper their mobility by being passengers.

During winters when we are not on a long walk, the month of March tends to find us somewhere in the North, somewhere in the warmth of endless invitations, somewhere in the land of learning and reciprocity on trails that are endlessly revealing and greatly fulfilling. To be there, we have had to adopt the machine culture of our hosts. This does not mean we have any intention of abandoning snowshoes and toboggans. We have simply expanded our interests and adapted to the needs of pursuing them. We have had to learn things we didn't know we were interested in, lest our friends and mentors leave us behind.

In context, there is nothing strange about snowmobiles; they are simply the vehicles of winter. Schoolyards are peppered with them in every northern community, parking lots are full of them and they dominate lines at gas pumps, with an odd truck mixed in now and again. Tracks radiate from every home and place of business. Winter is the time of greatest mobility. The longest plowed road in any town inevitably ends at the airport or the dump, but the snowmobile tracks never end.

We have met people on Menihek Lake in western Labrador who have come from

Cartwright on the coast. To get there they have traveled north on the sea ice, turned west to travel 150 miles up Hamilton Inlet and Lake Melville, then crossed 315 miles of land to reach the plateau country. In their journey of more than 500 miles, they have passed only three places that sell gas: Rigolet, Goose Bay and Churchill Falls.

That people from Cartwright would make a round trip of more than a thousand miles for a komatik load of caribou is not at all unusual; no more so than someone from Pennsylvania driving to Freeport, Maine, to get something at L.L. Bean.

A historic parallel exists in the world of snowmobiles. Those parts of the landscape that are the former range of the dogsled are home to the larger snowmobiles built more for speed than power. Areas that were the home range of the widest snowshoes and the hand-hauled toboggan are home to the smallest of the snowmobiles, machines that have great power but little speed.

On the sea ice, where it is always windy, and on the biggest of the rivers farthest north, the bigger machines are fine. In interior forests, where the snow is deep and the timber thick, the smaller machines can make headway in the loopy, circuitous routes of a hunting territory. When a small machine falls off its float and flounders into bottomless snow, a lone person can dig, pack and most importantly, lift things back into order.

Among immigrant miners and hydro-project people, there is a different aesthetic. The biggest, fastest, latest, most powerful machine is unquestionably the choice. The home range of these monster

Final packing of komatiks before departure to the bush. Loads will be covered with tarps in the event of rollovers or rough drifts on the lakes. The gas containers in the foreground are packed outside the box in the event of leakage; each one adds 44 pounds to the load.

machines tends to be in and around mining towns, hydroelectric generating facilities and the field camps of resource developers.

Our choices have predictably mirrored those of the people of the Labrador interior. At the time of our introduction to snowmobiles, the preferred machines were Ski-Doo's smallest offerings. The Elan, Tundra and Tundra Longtrack models were in favor among the Montagnais. Farther north, there has been a tendency more recently to larger machines that still fall into the "working" category. After quite a bit of coaching by Tekuanan McKenzie and a young trapper named Paul Duquette, we selected a Tundra Longtrack. When we wintered up the Kenamu River with the Goudie brothers, Horace, the older one, also favored the Tundra Longtrack.

Northern snowmobilers always retrofit their machines for the extreme cold. Hot grips are installed, and a thumb warmer added to the throttle lever. These electrically heated devices are absolutely essential no matter how magnificent your mitten system may be. People without hot grips must literally stop every half hour or so to warm their hands when traveling in the deep cold. The grips also have an off switch for mild conditions and for use into late spring. In the days before hot grips, people with cold hands would flip up the hood of the machine and warm their hands on the hot muffler pipe.

Users also extend their windshields with a higher piece of Plexiglas, which can be riveted onto the existing windshield or sewn on with wire through predrilled holes. When it is well below zero, the artificial windchill created by the speed of the machine requires that the face be totally protected. The highest of the standard windshields are too low, and the extreme aerodynamic miniature windshields on sport machines would be lethal in the North.

Another modification is to remove the oil-injection feature; you compensate for this by mixing the oil with the gas before filling the machine. This precaution is based on the possibility that the oil-injection feature could fail in extreme cold. When you personally mix the oil with the gas, the viscosity of the oil no longer matters, and you needn't worry about whether the injector pump will function.

Now that oil-injection systems have been around for a number of years and have stood the test of time, fewer people bother to remove them and very few have had problems. Today you can probably rely on the feature, but if you are the suspicious type, an oil injector is still simple to remove.

We carry a tool kit that vastly exceeds our skill. This is because the people we are likely to be with may be far more knowledgeable. People in the North tend to be very inventive and familiar with machinery. Repairs have been made in the field that would boggle the minds of southern mechanics, who can't imagine such a level of accomplishment outside a fully equipped shop. The stories of improvisation and of other parties happening along at just the right moment during emergencies are legion. Don't rule anything out—a full kit is not much bigger or heavier than an understocked one. We had ours assembled by a service mechanic as if he were making his own kit for his level of expertise.

Driving in the bottomless frost snow of the North is difficult. It requires agility, great reflexes and balance. Usually you must keep the machine as flat as possible on the snow. When you carve a turn, you must constantly adjust the lean of the machine and always be ready to throw your weight around while controlling speed and power with the throttle. Doing this while towing a heavily laden komatik in deep, dry snow is anything but easy. Unless you have the benefit of traveling on a well-packed float, a day on the machine will be quite strenuous. Such jockeying is nearly impossible with a passenger. The additional weight is bad enough, but the presence of a passenger on a machine built to carry only a driver prevents the driver from responding to conditions with the necessary speed and finesse.

In deep new snow, you may have to pack a float ahead with the machine and then return for the komatik. This uses a lot of gas, and the amount of gas you must carry for a long trip is truly astounding. But, on a packed track, the 200 miles between Churchill Falls and Goose Bay takes ten to 12 hours, and might consume only the gas in the machine, plus one or two refills from the jerricans you carry with. We once made the crossing on new snow with no track. It took eight days and required all 25 gallons of gas we carried, plus the seven we started out with in the machine. We had virtually no tracks from a few miles out of Churchill Falls until we were within 50 miles of Goose Bay. There were two of us on one machine and we towed a komatik plus two fully loaded toboggans that ran side-by-side just behind the komatik. In this way, we could just unhitch the toboggans and komatik, prepare the track on hills with the snow machine only and then return for the sleds.

The same caution and forethought that you need on snowshoes applies to machine travel. Clothing, backup gear, understanding snow and ice and common sense are the keys to success.

Although you can wear your usual trail clothes as a first layer, you will need more to be warm. Add a heavily insulated, windproof outer jacket, pants, hood and goggles.

At ten to 30 miles per hour, the windchill is substantial; it is very easy to frost an ear, nose, cheek or kneecap on a machine.

This exterior layer should be easily removable. It you are not on a heavily traveled trail, you will be periodically falling off the track. Getting a machine back on the trail is sweaty toil.

Bush travelers seldom opt for helmets despite the wind and noise protection they offer. In deep snow and difficult terrain, speeds are generally slow. Frequent stops for digging out, checking traps or responding to the needs of hunting all render a helmet a nuisance. Head protection is not the major concern it might be among sport riders on groomed trails.

In the bush, never travel anywhere without snowshoes, axe and gun. The speed with which the machine covers ground has the potential to strand you at a distance. A day's drive can be a ten-day walk, longer if you need to hunt along the way and make elaborate shelters because you have no gear. Always have strapped to the machine a daypack, spare clothes, some food and sundries such as matches, compass, snare wire and ammunition.

Paul Duquette, who has spent many winters alone in the Labrador bush, always

Snowshoes, axe and gun are essential survival gear on day trips and forays without a fully loaded komatik. Note the spare drive-belt tied onto the seat frame.

parks his Ski-Doo and komatik at a distance from his cabin or line-tent. He never removes the spare clothes and emergency gear from the machine. "If I ever have to jump from a burning camp at night with not many clothes on and no gear, I want my machine to be far enough away so that it can't be consumed by the fire. It'll give me a second chance on survival."

When you get stuck, burying the machine and komatik, you have to swallow your anger at your bad luck and the delay. You are in for perhaps an hour's work digging out. Calmly remove all the extra clothing you wear to cut the wind and cold. Get your snowshoes on, grab a shovel and begin to carefully and deliberately pack the snow around, under and in front of the machine. Create a large packed area so that you can drive the machine out. Everything you will do requires brains rather than strength.

Sometimes, you will have to unhitch the komatik, drive the machine out and swing back by a few times to establish a solid track so that when you hook up again you can pull the whole load back onto the track. After doing this for 45 minutes, you might find that the komatik still won't budge and that you need to unload it and pack the snow underneath it a little better. Once you are finally back on line and traveling again, you might go only a mile before the whole scene repeats itself. Too bad. Be patient. Work carefully. Don't get mad, overheat or raise a sweat. Winter is six or seven months long; you have time to do things calmly and well. Yelling obscenities at an insensible machine only wastes energy. And frantic physical exertion can lead to a hernia, as we know from personal experience. We have never seen Paul or Tekuanan lose their cool in even the most hopeless situations. Getting stuck is easy to do, and you, too, will soon develop saintlike patience.

As annoying as it is, even the worst cases of rolled and buried machinery are mild compared to the ordeal of getting stuck in overflow. The overflow recognition skills that apply on foot are also useful when traveling by machine, but the speed of travel usually means that disasters are of greater magnitude. You go farther into bad conditions before recognition sets in, and if you can't wallow and "swim" your way out with momentum and careful use of the throttle and balance, you are really stuck.

If the slush is deep, you are going to get wet. Dig out your rubber overboots that are in your daypack on your snowmobile. Take the time needed to cut poles and brush for road building and to pry, lever and cajole that heavy machine out of the diabolical slush. If it is cold, you will now have to chip all that ice out of the track, slides, drive sprockets and the complications of the suspension system. When this is done, you may need additional spruce poles to lay down in front of the machine so that you can get some speed up to try for dry snow and solid footing. Once you reach firm snow, hopefully you will still be close enough so that you can tow the komatik out with a length of rope. Once it is out, free its runners of freezing slush and ice, just as you did with the track and suspension of the machine.

A love/hate relationship with machinery seems to be the norm. When the going is good, you will love your snowmobile for the phenomenal distances it lets you cover with ease. When the going is difficult, you will long for the simplicity of snowshoes and toboggan. When machines work, there is fabulous gain. When they fail, you are abandoned in the crudest and roost complete manner. In accepting technology, you must accept both possibilities. Your most useful tool in reserve will be confidence in your ability to walk home, no matter how far that might be or how few tools you may have to make the journey. If you have your snowshoes, axe and gun, the walk home should be bearable.

KOMATIKS

*K*omatik is the Inuit word for sled, and when machines replaced dogs the word for sled stayed the same. Along the coasts, many komatiks are still built as if they were dogsleds, only heavier to accommodate the greater stresses that high speed introduces.

Komatiks are anywhere from eight to 16 feet long. They have solid runners, topped by crossboards as in the old style, or with a sheet of plywood for a base. Many now have a plywood box for gear, and often these are compartmentalized to keep fuel away from camping gear and food. The runners are shod with high-density plastic, and the towing bars are welded from heavy steel with a solid fore-and-aft spring system that absorbs shocks as the komatik and machine pitch and lurch in drifts or over rough terrain. The sliding part of the hitch where the springs are can also swivel around the axis of the tow bar. In this way, machine and sled can be on different planes, and one or the other can nip or roll without damaging the bar or causing the whole train to flip over.

The tow bars and hitches that snowmobile companies manufacture are far too small and weak for the serious workloads that are part of everyday life in the North. There, most of the hardware and komatiks are homemade. However, ambitious welders are just beginning to supply some hardware and service stores, and you can now find ready-made equipment in many communities. Tow bars are in such demand that a good welder known for making them is easy to locate just by asking around.

Tandem hauling komatiks—slow, but possible, and it may involve several trips on hills or passages through deep snow. In this case, tandem hauling allowed a second machine to haul a broken down third machine and its komatik.

Komatiks are sure to take a remarkable pounding. Logs for firewood or a building project, five or six caribou or an outfit for a month on the land are all big loads. Runners and boxes must be able to take the stress of both the weight and the momentum- and leverage-related factors that are magnified by high speed. To flip over at high speed, or to sideswipe into trees, boulders or blocks of upthrust ice, is to introduce explosive impact and force. You can't overbuild a komatik.

Detail of a towing bar showing hitch pin, swivel and fore and aft springs to absorb shocks in rough terrain.

Runners are made from wide spruce boards, which can split. To reduce that possibility, the top edges of the runners are planed so that the outside edge is an eighth of an inch lower than the inside edge. When the crosspieces or plywood are affixed, the runners splay ever so slightly away from each other and resist the pressures that would otherwise cause them to fold inward. In addition, most builders either drive long spikes vertically through the runners or countersink long lag bolts through them. These can help prevent runners from splitting in the first place, and hold the runners together so that they continue to function even if they do split.

Boxes and crossbars are either bolted or lashed on. Lashings allow for flex and torsion. Bolting or using large wood screws must be done carefully, with the composite stresses in mind. Bolts and screws can shear and break, so there must be enough of them to distribute the stress. Boxes are best attached with an eye toward removability, so that just the flat sled can be used if the box is too small, or the wrong shape for the load at hand. Loads such as logs, caribou or a broken-down snow machine require that the flat sled bottom be uncluttered by a box. Yet the komatik box is a real asset. It contains loose items, is easily covered with a tarp and can keep things such as fuel containers away from the main load. Padded with cushions or soft duffels, a box is a secure and comfortable place for passengers.

Detail of a slat-topped komatik with its cargo box tied on. The slats provide for an infinite variety and placement of lashing points for the load within the box, as well as items such as the trail stove that are tied on outside.

In emergencies, there is another advantage to having a box on the komatik. We planned ours so that it is long enough for one person to sleep in. The plywood sides cut the wind, and a canvas cover can be stretched over the top. In a pinch, the box can be unloaded and moved into for an unplanned night on the trail. Even on a normal day on the trail, people take a mug-up or lunch in the lee of the komatik or, on windless days,

A removable komatik box is handy for accommodating oversized loads, such as a disabled snow machine.

sit on its sunny side, leaning against the box.

There are no rules of thumb for towing weight. Different snow conditions allow different loads to be pulled with varying difficulty or ease. If the machine can't go, reduce the load or pack a float ahead. Unless the drive-belt slips, which you can hear and smell, you won't hurt the machine by exploring its limits. Just don't push it unreasonably. On steep hills, two or three machines may tow a single komatik. Other machines can likewise help tow one that is stuck in slush to firm snow. Think of the combinations and possibilities. Keep up with maintenance and avoid reckless use and mistreatment. A well-treated machine will deliver the best service with the fewest problems for the longest time.

With experience, you learn some of the finer points of driving. You should also learn how to adjust the track so that the skis are weighted fairly heavily. This is done by adjuster blocks in the coil springs of the suspension and by an adjustable stopper-strap that controls the transfer of weight between skis and tread during acceleration. Both these adjustments are outlined and described in any owner's manual. A weight-forward or ski-heavy adjustment will make it easier to turn on hard pack while towing a komatik. A heavy komatik transfers weight to the tread, thus lifting the skis and reducing their ability to hold and carve turns in very hard snow; then, when you ride without the komatik, the skis bear too heavily and you turn too much and too easily. You learn to compensate by positioning your own body weight fore or aft above the tread for the type of snow and conditions. Thus, you can make the skis bear harder or let up a little, despite the track adjustment favoring a heavy komatik.

Like any other tools of the trail, snowmobiles and komatiks have their place. A culture of expertise has grown up around their use and is available to those who would adopt some of it should the need arise.

Noisy (we wear earplugs), smelly and awful as snowmobiles may be, they offer many advantages. For us, they provide contact with the native people we most want to be with—the older people, who remember the days before snow machines and who can bring the gifts of earlier trails to light. We can choose to use a machine or not. But if the older knowledge fades away, it does so by neglect rather than choice. We find ourselves caught in a strange paradox: to learn the old ways of living in the wilds, we have had to adopt some of the newer, more technological approaches. If snowmobiles are required to nurture the incredible friendships we have found in remote places, then so be it.

Afterword

A fox is calling just outside our home tent, in the darkness beyond the pool of lampglow. "Ratch . . ." Here I am. "Ratch." Here. We wait, mouths open, ears reaching beyond eyesight, through the cloth wall. We put our books down carefully and sit motionless, except for our eyes, blinking. "Ratch." Hear? We can hear, but what are you saying? The fox moves down the stream-edge trail. In the distance now, "Ratch." I am going.

I want to get up and follow that fox. Become a fleeting shadow, streaking from tree to tree, hunting each hollow and circling every knoll, trotting sure-sighted along the riverbank until the woods lighten with dawn. I'd pause at the base of the arch-rooted hemlock, sniff the morning air, squint once more at the brightening snow, turn, duck under the roots and disappear into the earth.

What wilderness romantic has not imagined being so utterly at home in the woods? Instinct directing all actions. Understanding how to get food. Knowing where to find water. Recognizing home.

"Ratch." I am Fox. Easy for a fox to say. For people, life is not so straightforward. Unlike Fox, we attach meanings and symbols to everything we sense. Unlike Fox, we have the ability then to disengage from the things we think we know. Unlike Fox, we are left with choices.

Do we let life happen to us by default, or do we engage it with passion? Do we embrace the discipline of keeping an open mind, or do we accept dogma? Do we acquire skills for their own sake, or do we gain them as keys to engagement with a profound and thrilling physical and spiritual world?

It is our great hope that you will sense, be intrigued by and trust the life that lies beyond the acquisition of winter living skills. As with any skills that aspire to the level of art, these techniques must be practiced until they become a natural extension of yourself. Then you realize that the important things you seek are not to be found where the trail takes you, but rather in each step you take along the way. For though the snow walker's companions are snowbirds, curiosity, fear and the fox, the truest of companions is the one within. This one, like Fox, recognizes home.

Appendix A

Equipment List

EQUIPMENT LIST

Below is an example of the equipment list we at North Woods Ways send to our participants in the snowshoe and toboggan trips.

Required Items

Two pairs felt boot liners.

Two pairs of felt insoles, one size smaller than felt liners for easy insertion into liners.

Winter-rated down or synthetic sleeping bag, or two good-quality three-season bags to achieve a minus-20 rating. Mummy bags with closable hoods are best.

Full-length Therm-a-Rest sleeping pad or closed-cell foam pad for insulation. With foam, double pads are best. (Therm-a-Rest pads are expensive but worth it.)

One windproof shell parka with hood. This may be a lined or unlined 60/40-style parka, cotton anorak or synthetic anorak or windbreaker.

Three wool shirts, sized to be worn one over the other without restricting movement. It's best to bring one each of light-, medium- and heavyweight wool.

Two pairs wool pants. No cotton.

One set of wool or synthetic long underwear (two pairs on long trips).

Four pairs or more of wool socks, along with silk or synthetic socks to wear between wool and skin if you can't wear wool directly on your skin.

One wool or synthetic hat that completely covers head and ears, or, better yet, a balaclava-style hat that can cover the neck and part of the face.

One pair wool mittens with leather "chopper-mitt" shells, and one pair of heavy wool mittens for backup. Down- or synthetic-filled mittens may be necessary for people with poor circulation, and are good for backup in extreme cold. Gloves are not adequate.

Eye protection for wind and sun. Ski goggles, glacier goggles or even good dark glasses are suitable. Goggles are best for wind protection.

One down- or synthetic-filled parka. This should be carried in its own stuff sack for easy access.

One scarf long enough to wrap around your face and/or ears in extreme cold or wind.

One pair wind pants. High-count poplin paratroopers' pants can be worn over wool pants in high wind. Skiers' warm-up pants are good also, and many have full-length side zippers so that you can put them on or take them off without removing snowshoes.

Several bandannas (primarily for nose wiping, but they also serve many other uses).

Rain gear of the jacket-and-pants type. It occasionally rains in winter, and it is best to be prepared.

Headlamp or flashlight, plus spare batteries.

Daypack. Camera equipment and small, frequently used items go in here. Also a daypack is good for carrying extra clothing, lunch or anything you might need on trips ranging from base camp.

North Woods Ways supplies the following on all trips:

Snowshoeing moccasins. Canvas uppers and soft leather soles—for when snow temperatures are from 25 degrees Fahrenheit above zero to as low as temperatures go on earth.

Rubber boots. Single-thickness rubber boots—for use in the tent each evening and morning, and during the day should the snow temperature rise above 25 degrees Fahrenheit.

Group gear. Snowshoes, food, toboggans, wall tents, trail stoves, axes, saws, ice chisel, first-aid kit, cooking and kitchen kit, water bottles and, in the case of longer expeditions, an EPIRB and combination rifle/shotgun.

Other Important Considerations

If you suspect foot problems associated with footwear with no structural support, be certain to purchase arch-support inserts to be worn inside your felt liners. These supports are available at most drugstores or can be supplied by a podiatrist.

When fitting for felt liners, make sure to get a pair that is large enough to accommodate two pairs of wool socks and one felt insole inserted into the liner.

A headlamp is a good light for any type of camping, as it leaves hands free for the many tasks that require both hands. In the North, daylight is short in winter, so headlamps see frequent use. A headlamp with adequate replacement batteries (they wear out faster in the cold) is well worth the money.

A little trick: sock cuffs cut from worn-out wool socks can be worn as wristlets to bridge gaps between mitten cuffs and shirt cuffs. They can also be worn over one's knees, as knees are particularly sensitive to the cold.

What about sweaters? Sweaters are fine for a layer or two, but remember that a wool shirt has more fine-tuning potential for thermoregulation because it can be buttoned for more warmth, unbuttoned in the case of overheating.

Dietary & Medical Restrictions or Preferences

At your earliest convenience, and no later than two weeks prior to your trip, we must be made aware of any medical considerations the leaders and, where appropriate, the party should know about.

Also, for the purposes of food buying we need to know if you are omnivorous or vegetarian, and what sorts of hot drinks are most appealing to you. The look of dismay on a coffee drinker's face when confronted with eight pounds of herbal tea is only funny a long time after the trip has ended.

The How, Why & Wherefore of Listed Stuff, and Strategy for Assembling Such Gear

The major consideration regarding clothing is that it be thought of in terms of layers, breathability and, for the outermost layer in some conditions, windproofness. Layering maximizes one's ability to thermoregulate and facilitates drying should anything get wet. As many items as possible should be wool or, if they are acceptable to you, any of the synthetics now available.

Despite the recent infatuation with "vapor-barrier" systems, breathable materials are safer, warmer, easier to maintain and regulate, cleaner and on all counts easier to manage in the field. One should always adjust one's clothing to the level of activity and wind conditions. Overheating to the point of sweating is the first step toward being cold. Maintain warmth without getting hot. If you sweat, you will have wet clothing that will cool by evaporation. Maintain transpiration at a level that passes moisture through your clothing as a gas. In this way, you cannot get cold even if the level of exertion changes, because there will be no wetness in the clothing to rob you of heat. Blocking vapor passage with a material that doesn't breathe or through improper thermoregulation is risky and ultimately dangerous. It is always uncomfortable and inconvenient.

Recognizing that a good winter sleeping bag is a serious investment, we offer these thoughts. First, if winter camping is a serious goal, then it is wise to get a good single-season bag for that purpose. However, if you are new to winter camping, are not sure of your commitment or simply don't have the extra money to invest in a winter expedition bag, there are alternatives. You may be able to borrow a second bag to use double with the three-season bag you may already have. If borrowing is not a possibility, many of the larger equipment retailers have rental bags. This not only reduces the cost, but also allows you to sample several kinds over time and make an informed choice should you eventually purchase one. If you already own a good three-season bag and wish to winterize it for a minimum investment, you can buy a fairly light bag that is intended to be used with a full bag. Many of these serve as hot-weather bags by themselves. This is also a good strategy to pursue if you plan to camp year-round and therefore do not want a single-season, single-purpose winter bag.

Goosedown bags are lightest and warmest, compact the smallest, breathe the best and maintain loft with age and use better than other bags. On the other hand, down is very expensive, difficult to clean and dry and useless when wet. Not much can be done about the expense. However, you can exercise patience and care in cleaning, and you can learn how to keep a bag dry. All things considered, down bags are best.

Synthetic-filled bags solve some of down's disadvantages, but in so doing introduce other failings. The major niceties are that synthetics dry quickly, which means they are useful sooner after becoming wet, and most can be machine washed without special care. In addition, most are half the price of down.

On the negative side are such factors as these: to equal down for warmth, synthetics must be heavier and generally much bulkier. Quallofill has been on the market for years now, and its maker claims to have solved the bulk and weight problems. We don't know whether it has or not, but people who tend to feel cold have suggested that there is a distinct lacking in the warmth department and feel that a bit of bulk and weight might not be so bad. So far, all the synthetic fills we are familiar with lose their loft relatively rapidly after a few years of hard use and must be replaced.

Advertisements for synthetics imply, and in some cases say, that fiberfill bags are "warm when wet." Literalists, beware. This means that fiberfill may be warmer than down when wet, but neglects to say that neither material is usable when wet. Wool advocates are guilty of the same sleight-of-semantics regarding wet wool. It is far simpler to learn how to avoid getting anything wet in the first place. Prevention is the key to comfort.

In the end, you must choose what best fits your needs and constraints. Just remember the limitations of each choice, and comfort should prevail.

When accumulating equipment, bear in mind: natural fibers such as wool have a long life, and tight weaves resist abrasion. Good wool is expensive but may be cheaper in the long run due to longevity. Synthetics can be quite expensive also, and most are subject to solar breakdown and may perform poorly in extreme cold. Also, synthetics retain body odor with miraculous vengeance. Don't expect mere washing to erase the history of trips. Beware of experimental materials or those with a history of consumer complaints. Gore-Tex, for example, works in the short term on infrequent outings, but as yet has not satisfied anyone who requires long-term hard-use gear. (Disgruntled owners refer to it as "leak-tex" for a reason.)

If the prices of Filson wool garments cause apoplexy, head for Johnson Woolen Mill or Bemidji Woolen Mill products (see addresses at end of Chapter 4), and if they are intimidating, try the surplus outlets. A lot of good wool can be found in Armed Forces Surplus stores. Pay attention to the peculiar sizing for which military contractors are famous. Whole armies can't be composed of short, wide people or eight-foot beanpoles; try everything on, and keep digging until you find the right size. Often there is a lot of secondhand gear in good condition. If it is used, check the seams and stitching, and watch for too much patching and repair.

Be cautiously comparative, especially when shopping at catalog stores and major retailers of outdoor gear. Style and gadgetry have replaced longevity and practicality in too many cases. Some catalogs try to teach you to need what they have to sell.

Multifunctional gear is almost always better than single-purpose gear and will simplify and lighten your load. Don't be seduced by fancy advertising. Stuff near the pinnacle of refinement doesn't change much; styles do. Salespeople are hired to sell, not to educate. Be wary and specific and careful when dealing with them.

When we meet before trip departure, we have a complete gear shakedown so that nothing important is left out. With luck, a few things that might be overdoing it can be deleted. Adequate preparation yields a free mind, and a free mind has more room for the special pleasures and rewards of comfortable winter travel. Once we are in a snug campsite with a good supply of wood and the stove humming, cold will not be foremost in our minds. Someone may have to throw the tent flap open to cool the place down, and if a fine display of the aurora borealis lures us outside, we'll go happily.

Appendix B

Literary Resources

LITERARY RESOURCES

The enormous amount of literature available on the North as well as the antipodal regions of Antarctica makes it virtually impossible to offer any useful bibliography. There are numerous institutes of northern studies, specialist book dealers and entire wings of major libraries devoted to the historical writings and continuous accumulation of current scientific, literary and other northern accounts. The best place to start would be the references-and-abstracts section of a major library, which may give an overview of what is available, where the major collections are housed and listings of the many, often obscure, periodicals published by special-interest organizations and the northern studies departments of some universities and museums.

Generally speaking, historical writings of exploration and ethnography are of the most interest to modern recreational travelers. These writings reflect the North's golden era, when the land was truly wild and peopled with indigenous cultures. In addition, many of the writers of that time showed enormous attention to detail and remarkable powers of observation. Current wilderness wanderers can thus get a portrait of the unrecoverable Holy Grail of their favored habitat.

The written record of science, natural history and politics as related to the North is in full swing. As the complexities of maintaining the world's escalating human population steer attention ever farther into the tropics and the North, this trend will continue and accelerate.

Nevertheless, there is a crying need for writings by women, native people, naturalists, observers and doers capable of depth and revelation. The best older books give us a standard for which to strive.

The following list contains selections that we feel broaden the perspective that we have introduced in this book.

Technical, Ethnographic & Natural History Books

Boy Scouts of America. *Okpik: Cold-Weather Camping.*
 Very good information.
 Available through: Northern Tier High Adventure Program,
 P.O. Box 509, Ely, MN 55731.
Gorman, Stephen. *AMC Guide to Winter Camping.*
 Appalachian Mountain Club, 5 Joy Street, Boston, MA,1991.
Halfpenny, James C., and Roy Douglas Ozanne. *Winter: An Ecological Handbook.*
 Johnson Publishing Company, 1880 South 57th Court, Boulder, CO, 1989.
Helm, June, ed. *Handbook of North American Indians, Volume 6, "Subarctic,"*
 Smithsonian Institution, Superintendent of Documents, U.S. Government
 Printing Office, Washington, DC, 1981.
MacDonald, Craig. Exceptional material on wall tents and sledding equipment.
 Available via mail from:

Craig MacDonald, RR 1, Dwight, Ontario, Canada, P0A 1H0.

Marchand, Peter. *Life in the Cold.*
University Press of New England, Hanover, NH, 1987.

Mason, Otis. *Primitive Travel and Transportation.*
Exceptional notes on moccasins, snowshoes, sleds, toboggans and more.
U.S. National Museum, 1894.

Osgood, William, and Leslie Hurley. *The Snowshoe Book.*
Stephen Green Press, Brattleboro.VT, 1971, 1975 and 1983.

Prater, Gene. *Snowshoeing.*
Snowshoeing from the mountaineer's perspective.
The Mountaineers, Seattle, WA, 1974.

Rutstrum, Calvin. *Paradise Below Zero.*
A 1968 classic recently reprinted.
University of Minnesota Press, Minneapolis, MN, 2000.

Steffanson,Vilhjalmur. *Arctic Manual.*
Macmillan, New York,1957.

Vaillancourt, Henri. *Making the Attikamek Snowshoe.*
An absolutely exceptional book on the fancy, square-toe snowshoes of the
Attikamek Indians of central Quebec. The Trust is a nonprofit foundation
engaged in the documentation of northern Native technologies. Among other
titles available is *Beavertail Snowshoes*, a video on the making of these beauti
fully patterned, round snowshoes of the Cree Indians of northern Quebec.
Self-published, 1987. Available from: The Trust for Native American Cultures
and Crafts, Box 142, Greenville, NH 03048; www.birchbarkcanoe.net.

Wilkerson, James. *Hypothermia, Frostbite and Other Cold Injuries.*
The Mountaineers, Seattle, WA, 1986.

General Interest

Anderson, William. *Angel of Hudson Bay.*
The story of Maude Watt, including an account of a snowshoe-and-canoe
traverse of Ungava in 1918.
E. P. Dutton, New York, 1961 .

Macfie, John, and Basil Johnston. *Hudson Bay Watershed.*
A photo-and-text memoir featuring snowshoes and sleds before the coming of
snow machines.
Dundurn Press, Toronto, 1991.

Merrick, Elliott. *True North.*
Exquisitely told tales of toboggan and canoe travel in Labrador in the 1930s.
Reprinted by University of Nebraska Press, Lincoln, NE, 1989.

This list barely scratches the surface. For hard-to-find historic editions as well as
current books about the North, get on the mailing list of Northern Books. George
Luste, a well-known and highly regarded traveler of canoe and snowshoe trails, has

added this book dealership to his already busy life. He knows his subjects, and loves the literature with the same passion with which he pursues the wilderness trail. George's personal library is unquestionably one of the more impressive private collections on the North.

Northern Books
P. O. Box 211, Station P
Toronto, Ontario
Canada M5S 2S7
416-531-8873

Another good source:
The Wilderness Collection
716 Delaware Court
Lawton, MI 49065
616-624-4410
e-mail: wlcobwks@aol.com

Videos & DVDs

The VHS video/DVD titled "Winter Walk to Ungava Bay 2003" is a very creative and often hilarious 50-minute film made by Rollin Thurlow. It is about a 60-day snowshoe trip made by the Conovers and five friends.

Northwoods Canoe Co. (Rollin Thurlow)
336 Range Road
Atkinson, ME 04426
207-564-3667 (888-564-2710)
www.wooden-canoes.com

Contacting Garrett & Alexandra

If you are interested in guided snowshoeing or canoeing trips, CD ROMs of some of the Conover's wilderness travels or instruction articles, please visit their website at:
www.northwoodsways.com
or write them at:
Alexandra & Garrett Conover
North Woods Ways
2293 Elliotsville Road
Willimantic, ME 04443
207-997-3723

Appendix C

Patterns for Traditional Clothing & Footwear

EGYPTIAN COTTON ANORAK

(Drawings and plans by Sally Robbins)

These patterns make a wind garment composed of two layers of light, tightly woven 100-percent-cotton cloth.

The anorak is a men's medium or a women's large.

Yardage:

Egyptian cotton—30-inch width, 9 yards needed for men's medium (women's large)

58-inch width, 6 yards needed for men's medium (women's large)

Interfacing: 1/2 yard midweight iron-on

Notes:

These directions are not suitable for beginning sewers. Please read the instructions before cutting the fabric.

Wash and dry the fabric before cutting. For ease of cutting, make a full-size paper pattern first. Cut double of everything (except the one gusset piece)—one set for the outside shell, one set for the lining. (With Egyptian cotton, use the same fabric for the outer shell and the lining.)

Seams are finished, either flat-felled or French. Use 1/2-inch seams unless otherwise noted. Use a new, sharp needle and best-quality thread.

After sewing the pocket welts on the FRONT and

FRONT LINING, the top side of the FRONT LINING becomes the BACK side of the FRONT and the two layers are treated as one unit, the FRONT.

FRONT POCKET OPTION: This design uses overlapping welts to form pocket openings; directions from a sewing or tailoring book will be helpful. For a simpler pocket, make a patch pocket using a paper guide or a pocket of your own design. However, with a patch pocket, you cannot reach through to the inner garments from the outside of the anorak.

Sewing Sequence: Front & Front Lining

1. Lay out and cut all pieces for the anorak shell and lining.

2. Press the interfacing to the back side of the 8 pocket flaps and the 3 tabs for fastening the sleeves and hood.

3. TABS: Fold the right sides together and, using 1/4-inch seams, stitch the top and bottom. Turn each tab right-side out, press and topstitch along 3 sides; use a zigzag stitch on the open raw edges. For each tab sew on hook Velcro or make a buttonhole. Later you will sew one tab on each of the sleeves and one on the hood.

4. POCKET FLAPS (see Figure 1 on page 216): Fold the wrong sides together, topstitch along the folded edge and zigzag-stitch the raw edges together on the

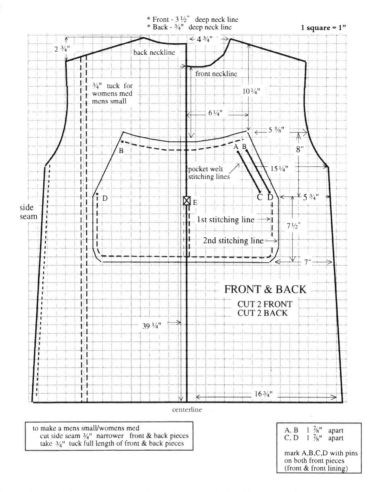

* Front - 3½" deep neck line
* Back - ¾" deep neck line

1 square = 1"

back neckline

front neckline

2 ¾"

← 4 ¾" →

¾" tuck for womens med mens small

10¼"

← 6¼" →

← 5 ⅝"

8"

B

A B

pocket welt stitching lines

15¼"

side seam

D

E

C D

← 5 ¾" →

1st stitching line →

7½"

2nd stitching line →

← 7" →

FRONT & BACK

CUT 2 FRONT
CUT 2 BACK

39 ¼" →

← 16 ¾" →

centerline

to make a mens small/womens med
cut side seam ¾" narrower front & back pieces
take ¾" tuck full length of front & back pieces

A, B 1 ⅞" apart
C, D 1 ⅞" apart

mark A,B,C,D with pins
on both front pieces
(front & front lining)

other three sides. Make buttonholes on two of the flaps, as shown in Figure 1.

5. WELT POCKETS: On the right side of the FRONT LINING mark with chalk or very light pencil the pocket welt stitching lines, using the lines/dimensions shown on the FRONT pattern piece (connecting points AC and BD). On the BACK side of the eight pocket flaps—on the long, zigzag-stitched edge—mark the stitching line, allowing for the presser foot width on your machine (usually ¼ inch). Then with the right sides together, pin the pocket flaps in place along the stitching lines (no buttonhole flaps on the lining), with the folded edges of the flaps facing away from each other (see Figure 2 on page 217. You will use 4 pocket flaps for the FRONT LINING and the remaining 4 for the FRONT. Stitch along AC and BD between points (marked as shown on the FRONT pattern).

From the BACK side, carefully cut between the rows of stitching and at angles to points A, B, C and D (see Figure 3 on page 217), but without cutting into the stitching. From the FRONT, pull the flaps toward each other—they should just

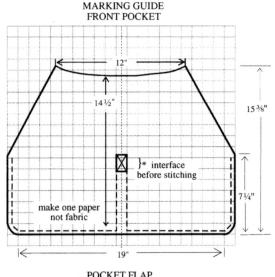

MARKING GUIDE
FRONT POCKET

12"

14½"

15⅜"

}* interface
before stitching

7¼"

make one paper
not fabric

19"

POCKET FLAP

cut 8

4"

fold line

9¾"

FABRIC & NOTIONS		
Fabric	36" fabric	58" fabric
Mens Small	8 yds.	5 yds.
Mens Med	9 yds.	6 yds.

WASH AND DRY BEFORE CUTTING OUT

Toggles - 2
Buttons - 3 or 5 size 32 [¹³⁄₁₆" - 20mm]
  5 if not using Velcro on sleeve tabs
Velcro - Hook - 4 ½" - ¾" wide
       - loop or pile - 10 ½" - ¾" wide
Interfacing - ½ yd. mid wt. iron-on

TIES & LOOPS
Neck Tie   cut 1 - 14" x ¾"
Belt & Neck Loop cut 3 - 7½" x ¾"
Hood Draw String cut 1 - 32" x ¾"

VELCRO
Hook cut 3 - 1½" long
Pile cut 2 - 4" long   } for sleeve
      cut 2 - ½" long
      cut 1 - 1½" long } for neck

INTERFACING
Cut 3 - 1" squares - 2 for hood buttonholes
                     1 for front pocket

cover each other—and pull each piece of fabric to the BACK side (Figures 4 and 5 on page 218). Align the flap closest to the armhole on top. On the BACK side, align the top and bottom zigzag-stitched edges of the flaps and pin them in place. Stitch between points at the base of the welt, through all pocket flap thicknesses. On the TOP side, press and topstitch around all sides of the pocket opening close to the previous stitching lines, being careful not to catch the underside of the flap. On the BACK side, carefully trim away any excess fabric.

6. Repeat step 5 for the welts on the FRONT, placing the buttonhole flap on the armhole (B, D) side and making sure it is on top when aligning the two flaps.

7. Then pin together the FRONT and FRONT LINING, wrong sides together, matching shoulders, neck, pocket flaps, etc. Press and treat both the front shell and lining as one unit from now on.

8, Mark with chalk or light pencil on the FRONT, the stitching line for the FRONT POCKET, using the measurements of the FRONT POCKET GUIDE.

Stitching through both layers of fabric (FRONT and FRONT FINING), sew from D to the FRONT centerline, then up to E, then around to the second D, thus forming the bottom edge of the pocket. Then stitch from B to the second B, forming the top edge of the pocket. Stitch around the pocket a second time, 1/4 inch outside the first stitching (the width of the presser foot) and, this time, go around the armhole edge of the pocket welt.

Hood

9. You will have already cut out 4 hood sides—2 for the outer shell, 2 for the lining. Make a buttonhole on the right side of each outer HOOD SIDE section (shell,

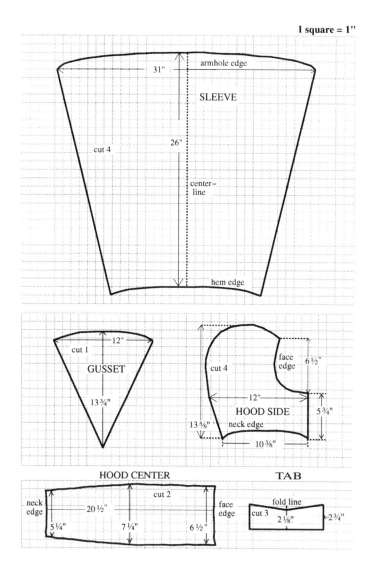

1 square = 1"

SLEEVE
cut 4
armhole edge
31"
26"
center–line
hem edge

GUSSET
cut 1
12"
13¾"

HOOD SIDE
cut 4
face edge
6½"
12"
5¾"
13⅝"
neck edge
10⅜"

HOOD CENTER
cut 2
neck edge
20½"
face edge
5¼"
7¼"
6½"

TAB
cut 3
fold line
2⅛"
2¾"

not lining). Sew the HOOD CENTER and HOOD SIDES together, press seams and topstitch seams. Repeat for the HOOD LINING. With the right sides together, sew the HOOD TOP and HOOD LINING together along the face (curved) edge only. Turn, press and top-stitch 3/4 inch from the edge to make a drawstring casing. The buttonholes are on the outside of the hood.

Joining Front & Back

10. Sew the FRONT and BACK (each is a double thickness of shell and lining, treated as a unit) together at the shoulder. Topstitch, if not using a flat-felled seam.

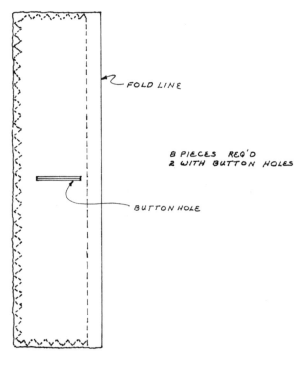

FOLD LINE

8 PIECES REQ'D
2 WITH BUTTON HOLES

BUTTON HOLE

Figure 1

NOTE: IN FIGS. I THRU 5 STITCHES – – – – & ⌃⌄⌃
ARE SHOWN ONLY IN VIEW WHERE STITCH
IS MADE.

Neck Slit

11. Slit the center FRONT to within 1½ to 2½ inches of the pocket stitching line.

Ties and Loops

12. Hem the long edge of the ties and loops, turning in NO ends of the THREE 7½-inch strips that will become the loops, ONE end of the ONE 14-inch tie and BOTH ends of the ONE 32-inch tie. On the BACK, right-side up, pin ONE 7½-inch loop at center neck. Baste in place.

Attaching the Hood to the Anorak Body

13. Starting at center BACK and right sides together, pin the HOOD to the gar-ment at the neck edge. (You may need to trim away extra fabric, if any, at the HOOD SIDES so that the edges of the neck slit and HOOD are even.) Baste. Sew the HOOD to the BODY of the garment at the neck edge and topstitch. I finish this seam using a strip of self-bias or a flat-felled seam.

Gusset

14. Sew a narrow hem on the curved edge of the GUSSET. Along one side, pin the GUSSET to the HOOD SIDE and center front slit and sew, pivoting at the bottom of the slit and continuing stitching up to the other HOOD SIDE section. On the top side, zigzag-stitch at the "V" to reinforce the seam. You may have to trim away fabric at the GUSSET point (check on the wrong side).

Neck Tie & Tab

15. Sew the HOOD TAB to the HOOD SIDE, below the drawstring casing at the GUSSET stitching line. Sew pile Velcro or a button at an appropriate site on the other HOOD SIDE. On the same side as the TAB, sew the 14-inch neck tie at the neck seam. Sew a button on the other side of the GUSSET. The tie wraps around the button to close the neck opening.

Sleeves, Underarm Seams, Hems & Tabs

16. You will have cut out four sleeve pieces, two for the shell and two for the lining. Sew the SLEEVES (double thickness) to the armhole; topstitch if not using a flat-felled seam. With right sides together, sew the underarm and side seam as a continuous seam. Topstitch.

17. Hem the garment bottom and sleeves with a 3/4-inch hem (or desired width). Remember, this garment is made oversized to fit over several layers of outer gar-

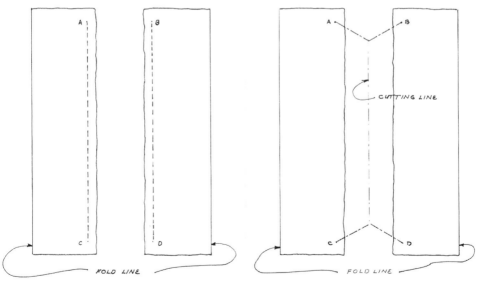

Figure 2   Figure 3

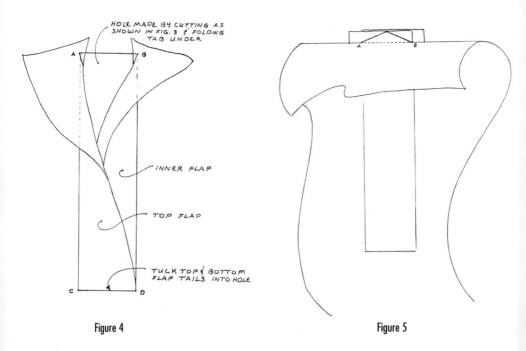

Figure 4   Figure 5

ments and will blouse somewhat when tied with a sash.

18. Sew a TAB to each SLEEVE at the underarm seam, just above the hem. For each SLEEVE, sew a 4-inch piece of pile Velcro, centered on the SLEEVE center-line just above the hem. Sew a 1-inch piece of pile Velcro so that it keeps the TAB in place at the underarm seam.

Tie, Loops, Toggles & Buttons

19. Thread the 32-inch HOOD DRAWSTRING through the HOOD CAS-ING, topstitch the DRAWSTRING in place at both HOOD CENTER seams and thread toggles on each tie end and knot. Sew the remaining two 7½-inch loops at the waist on the side seams. Sew buttons on the FRONT pocket flaps and sleeves if not using Velcro.

WIND PANTS

A garment made of two layers of light, tightly woven 100-percent-cotton cloth, with elastic front, high back waist and tab snaps.

Patterns available from: The Green Pepper, 3918 West First Avenue, Eugene, OR 97402, 800-767-5684 (orders), 503-345-6656 (information). Pattern #147,

Women's Cascade Powder Pants; pattern #148, Men's Cascade Powder Pants. The Green Pepper sells fabric and notions, but they don't sell Egyptian cotton.

Tips from Sally Robbins:

Yardage:

For 60-inch fabric, two layers throughout—3¼ yards.

For interfacing, use midweight iron-on instead of the needlepunch specified in the pattern.

You may omit the side pockets and use snaps at the waist.

Cut at least one size larger than your regular pants size.

SNOWSHOEING MOCCASINS & ATTACHED GAITERS

Materials:

Smoke-tanned deerskin (ideal), split cowhide (okay) or heavy 10-oz. canvas (good for limited use) for moccasins

Waxed thread

Triangular glover's needles

Medium-weight (8-oz.) canvas for gaiters

Decorative rickrack, ribbons and binding tape

Yarn

Moccasins

1. Cut all pieces from the source material.

2. Place the vamp on the sole.

3. Tack the vamp in place. Run thread from A to the vamp, down through both the vamp and the sole at B, then over to the side at C.

4. Attach the vamp to the sole. Begin sewing at D. Whipstitch firmly for 1 inch. Then begin puckering stitches (see "Puckering Stitch," page 225), small at first, increasing in size to A. Continue the puckers, decreasing to 1 inch from C. Whipstitch to C.

5. Remove the tacking thread. Put your foot (with felt or duffel liners) into the partially sewn moccasin. Mark where your heel ends. Trim the end of the sole accordingly. Measure and cut to make the heel crescent. Whipstitch from E to F.

6. Sew the heel crescent over the outside of the seam.

7. Make another moccasin for your other foot. The moccasins are interchangeable, unless the design of the attached gaiter makes them foot-specific.

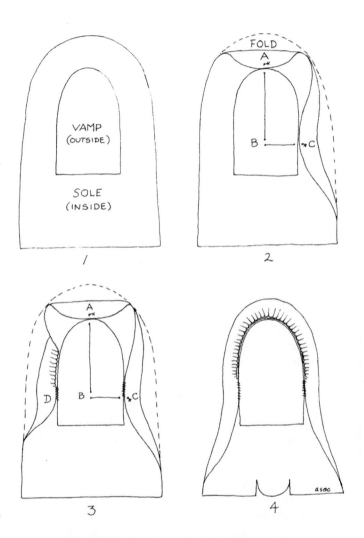

A special thanks to Susan Swappie for showing me how to make this style moccasin.

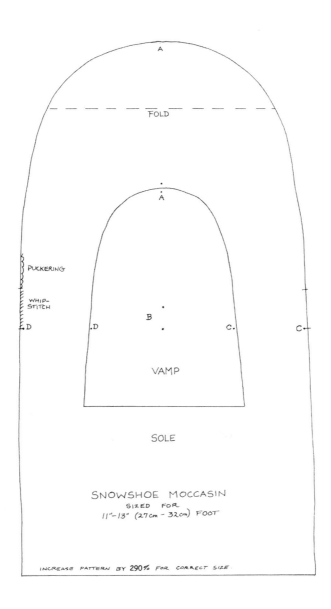

A

FOLD

A

PUCKERING

WHIP-
STITCH

D

.D

B

C.

C

VAMP

SOLE

SNOWSHOE MOCCASIN
SIZED FOR
11"-13" (27cm - 32cm) FOOT

INCREASE PATTERN BY 290% FOR CORRECT SIZE

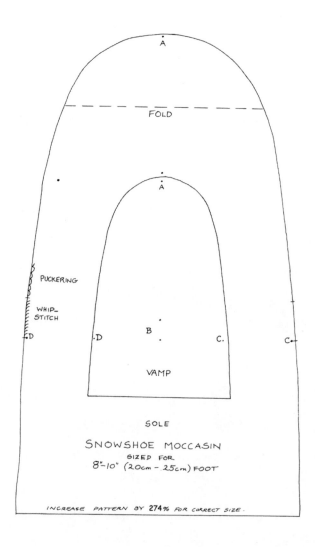

A

FOLD

A

PUCKERING

WHIP-
STITCH

D

D

B

C

C

D

VAMP

SOLE

SNOWSHOE MOCCASIN
SIZED FOR
8"-10" (20cm - 25cm) FOOT

INCREASE PATTERN BY 274% FOR CORRECT SIZE.

Gaiters

8. Lay out the folded canvas. Trace the pattern and cut. Sew on rickrack or ribbon decorations. Bind the bottom edge of the gaiter with colorful binding tape. Turn the gaiter inside out and sew the side seam. Then, turn it right-side out, checking that both the moccasin top and the gaiter bottom openings match in size.

9. Attach each gaiter to its moccasin thus: with both the gaiter and the moccasin inside out, whipstitch them together by joining the top edge of the moccasin with a small pucker taken above the binding tape of the gaiter. This way the binding tape will create a neat trim on the outside of the finished moccasin. Sew the vamp tongue to the gaiter.

10. Turn everything right-side out. Make a 1-inch hem at the top for the braided yarn to go through. Make two openings in outer layer of the top hem. Reinforce the edges with a blanket (buttonhole) stitch. Thread a 40-inch section of braided yarn through the hem holes so that the ends cross and emerge from the opposite holes.

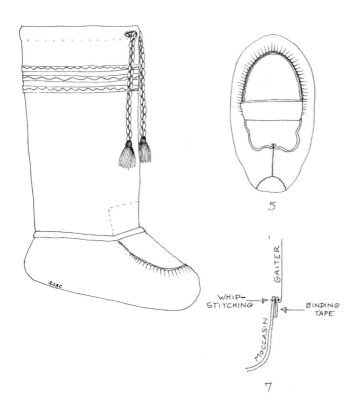

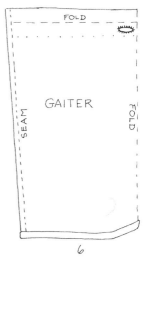

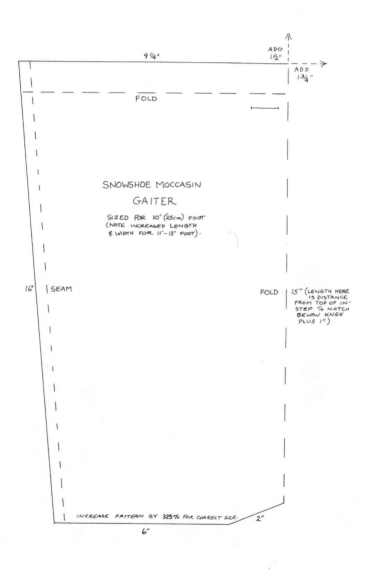

9 ¼"

ADD
1½"

ADD
1¾"

FOLD

SNOWSHOE MOCCASIN

GAITER

SIZED FOR 10" (25cm) FOOT
(NOTE INCREASED LENGTH
& WIDTH FOR 11"-13" FOOT).

16" | SEAM

FOLD | 15" (LENGTH HERE
IS DISTANCE
FROM TOP OF IN-
STEP TO NOTCH
BELOW KNEE
PLUS 1".)

INCREASE PATTERN BY 325% FOR CORRECT SIZE.

2"

6"

Puckering Stitch for Snowshoeing Moccasins

1. Starting at D, whipstitch the vamp to the sole for 1 inch. To begin a pucker, put the needle through the sole only. The width of the stitch determines the size of the puckers. Start with a stitch 1/8 inch or less in length, progressing to about 3/16 to 1/4 inch near the toe area (point A).

2. Crease the middle of the stitch with your thumbnail.

3. Fold the material to create a pucker.

4 & 5. Pass the needle over the pucker. Poke it through the vamp and pull the thread tight.

6. Pull the thread tightly over your index finger, keeping the tension on it with your middle finger. Put the needle through the vamp side, placing the hole near the previous stitch. Now poke all the way through to the sole side, being careful to keep both sides smooth and parallel.

7. When you've completed the puckering on the vamp, turn the moccasin inside out. With the tip of a closed pair of scissors, crease the puckers until they bulge evenly on the inside. This leaves the edges of the outside sole puckers lying flat and neat against the vamp.

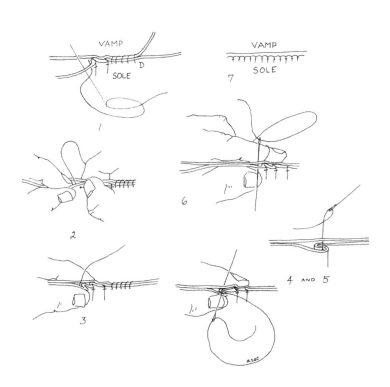

Duffel Cloth Snowshoe Moccasin Liners

Materials:
1 square yard (or meter) duffel cloth (minimum 36-inch width)
Button thread
Yarn

Directions:

1. Trace the patterns, enlarge them to the correct size and cut them out.

2. Pin the patterns to the duffel cloth and cut out the pieces.

3. Butt the edges of the top and heel pieces at A and B and whipstitch them together. Do the same at C and D.

4. Starting at E, sew completely around the sole, joining it to the top and heel pieces.

5. Join either point F on the gaiter with the corresponding point on the top piece.

6. Continue whipstitching up the gaiter seam from F to G.

7. Fold the top edge of the gaiter to form a hem. With colorful yarn, sew it into place, using cross stitching or decorative dashes.

8. With another color yarn, reinforce all the seams with the same decorative stitch.

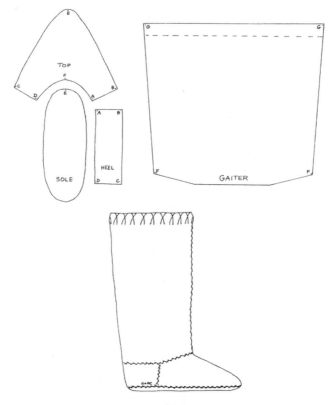

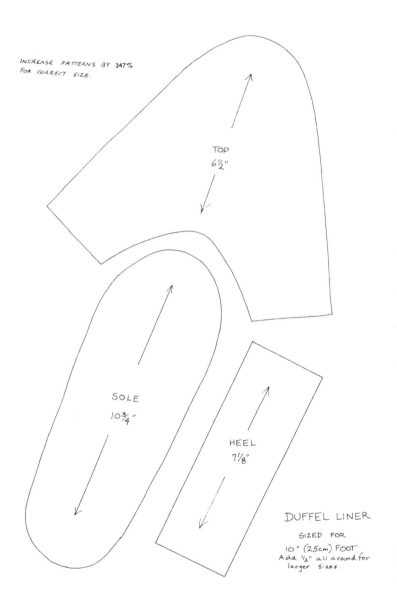

INCREASE PATTERNS BY 347%
FOR CORRECT SIZE.

TOP
6½"

SOLE
10¾"

HEEL
7⅛"

DUFFEL LINER

SIZED FOR

10" (25cm) FOOT
Add ½" all around for
larger sizes.

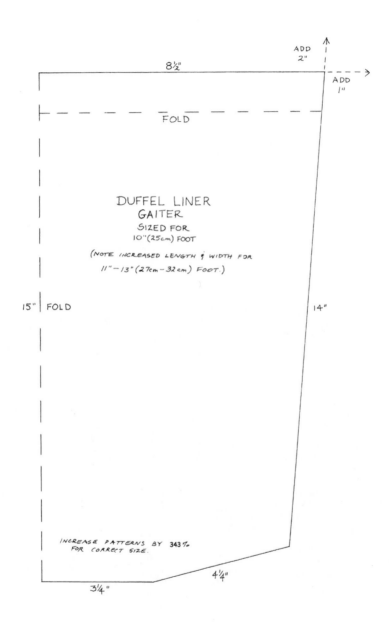

ADD 2"

ADD 1"

8½"

FOLD

DUFFEL LINER
GAITER
SIZED FOR
10"(25cm) FOOT

(NOTE INCREASED LENGTH & WIDTH FOR
11"−13" (27cm−32cm) FOOT.)

15" FOLD

14"

INCREASE PATTERNS BY 343%
FOR CORRECT SIZE.

3¼"

4¼"

DUFFEL CLOTH MITTENS (LINERS & SHELLS)

Materials:
1 square yard (or meter) duffel cloth (minimum 36-inch width), for liners
Button thread
Yarn
½ square yard (or meter) canvas, tightly woven (minimum 36-inch width), for shells
Decorative rickrack or ribbons
Fur for ruffs

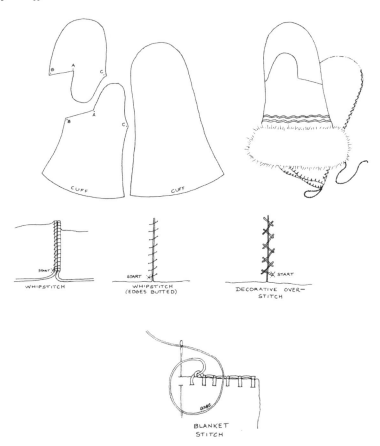

Liners

1. Trace the patterns and cut them out. Mark an **X** on one side of each pattern to identify the outside of the left mitten.

2. Pin the pattern to the duffel cloth, **X**-side up.

3. With the patterns still pinned on, cut out the pieces of cloth.

4. Unpin the patterns and turn them over for the right mitten. Pin them in place

and cut out the pieces.

5. Butt the edges of duffel pieces A and B together so that the seam is flat. In a relaxed whipstitch, sew from A to B using sturdy button thread. Now sew from A to C.

6. Join the outer edges of one mitten, leaving the cuff open.

7. Do the same to the other mitten making sure you have the correct sides facing outward; otherwise, you might end up with two left mittens!

8. Use yarn to strengthen the seams with the decorative overstitch (see illustration). Use the blanket stitch on the cuff edges.

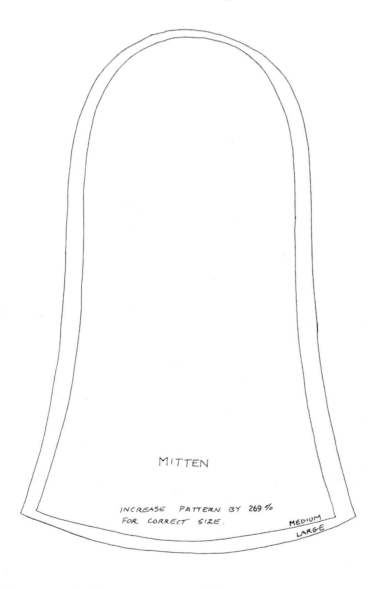

MITTEN

INCREASE PATTERN BY 269 %
FOR CORRECT SIZE.

MEDIUM
LARGE

Shells

Note: To facilitate drying, the shells and liners are not sewn together. Also, you might have to replace one or the other more frequently.

1. When tracing the pattern onto the canvas shell material, add ½ inch all around the edge of each pattern.

2. Sew the pieces inside out, making a flat seam. Turn the shell right-side out. The stitch spacing should be small to make the liners as windproof as possible.

3. Attach fur ruffs around the cuff edge of each shell. (Secondhand stores are an ideal source of fur wraps and collars for cuffs.)

4. Sew a loop of chain-stitched yarn to the liner and a 3-inch length to the shell. In combination, these can be used to hang up the mittens for drying.

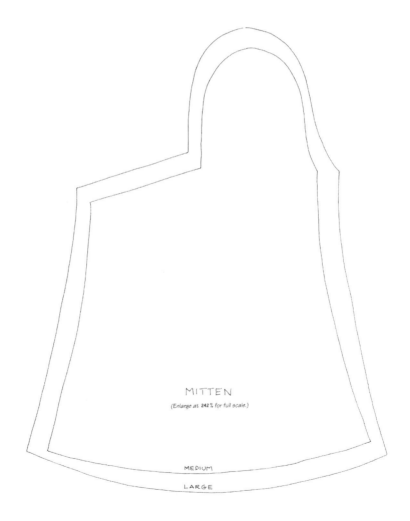

MITTEN

(Enlarge at 242% for full scale.)

MEDIUM

LARGE

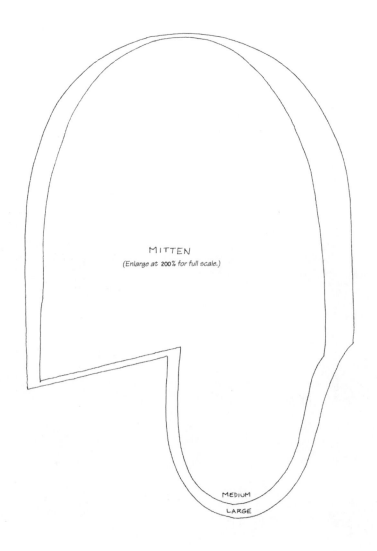

MITTEN
(Enlarge at 200% for full scale.)

MEDIUM
LARGE

Appendix D
Pyramid Tent Plans

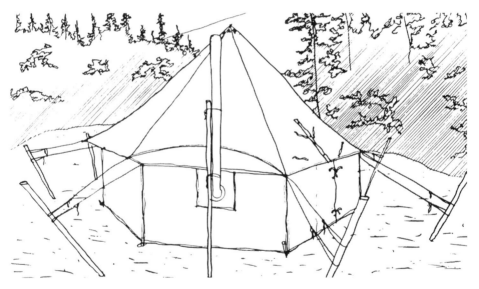

Plans and illustration by David Lewis

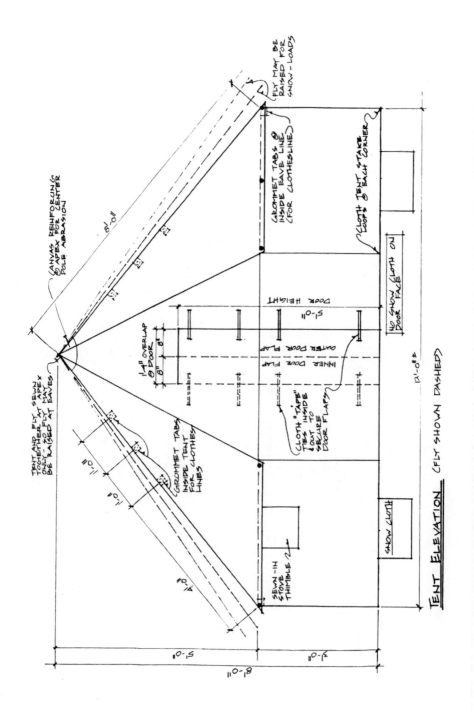

TENT ELEVATION (FLY SHOWN DASHED)

CANVAS REINFORCING @ APEX FOR CENTER POLE ABRASION

FLY MAY BE RAISED FOR SNOW-LOADS

GROMMET TABS @ INSIDE EAVE LINE (FOR CLOTHESLINE)

CLOTH TENT STAKE LOOPS @ EACH CORNER

NO SNOW CLOTH ON DOOR FACE

DOOR HEIGHT

5'-0"

1½" OVERLAP @ DOOR

8"

8"

OUTER DOOR FLAP

INNER DOOR FLAP

CLOTH "TAPE" TIES INSIDE & OUT TO SQUARE DOOR FLAPS

TENT AND FLY SEWN TOGETHER @ APEX SO FLY MAY BE RAISED AT EAVES

GROMMET TABS INSIDE TENT FOR CLOTHES LINES

SEWN -IN STOVE THIMBLE

SNOW CLOTH

8'-0"

5'-0"

7'-0"

11'-0"

9'-0"

7'-0"

9'-0"

5'-0"

7'-6"

11'-8"

12'-0"

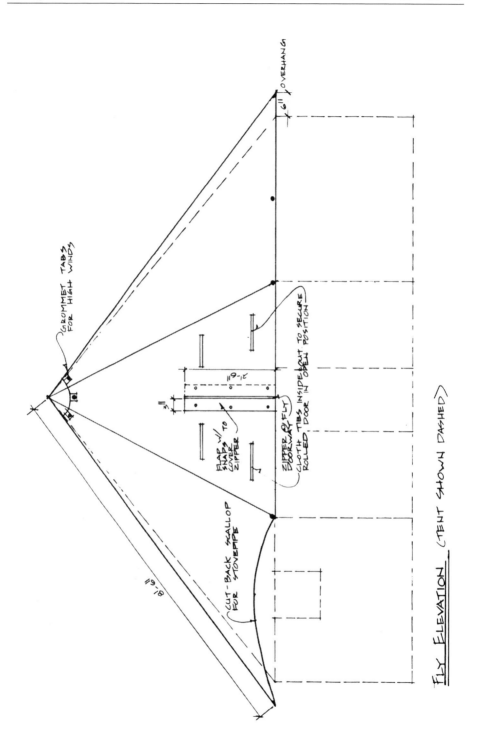

OVERHANG

6"

GROMMET TABS
FOR HIGH WINDS

CLOTH TABS INSIDE OUT TO SECURE
ROLLED DOOR IN OPEN POSITION

ZIPPER ON FLY

FLAP w/
SNAPS TO
COVER
ZIPPER

11'-9½"

3"

11'-9½"

CUT-BACK SCALLOP
FOR STOVEPIPE

11'-9½"

FLY ELEVATION (TENT SHOWN DASHED)

235

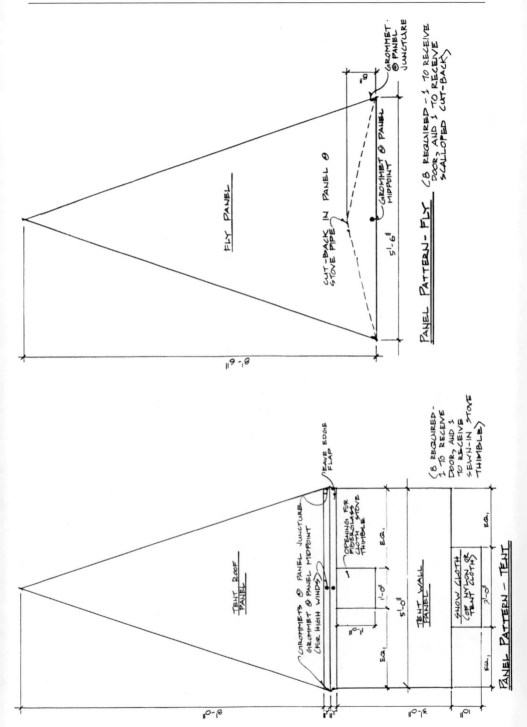

FLY PANEL

CUT-BACK IN PANEL θ
STOVE PIPE

GROMMET @ PANEL
JUNCTURE

GROMMET @ PANEL
MIDPOINT

5'-6"

9"

11'-9½"

PANEL PATTERN - FLY (8 REQUIRED - 1 TO RECEIVE DOOR, AND 1 TO RECEIVE SCALLOPED CUT-BACK)

TENT ROOF
PANEL

EAVE EDGE
FLAP

GROMMETS @ PANEL JUNCTURE
GROMMET @ PANEL MIDPOINT
(FOR HIGH WINDS)

OPENINGS FOR FIBERGLASS CLOTH STOVE THIMBLE

TENT WALL
PANEL

SNOW CLOTH
(OF NYLON OR TENT CLOTH)

1'-0"

1'-0"

5'-0"

2'-0"

EQ.

EQ.

EQ.

EQ.

EQ.

EQ.

11'-0½"

3'-0½"

1'-0"

1"

PANEL PATTERN - TENT (8 REQUIRED - 1 TO RECEIVE DOOR, AND 1 TO RECEIVE SEWN-IN STOVE THIMBLE)

236

Appendix E

Campfire Tent Plans

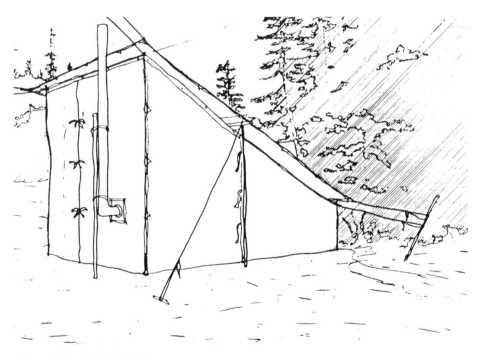

Plans and illustration by David Lewis

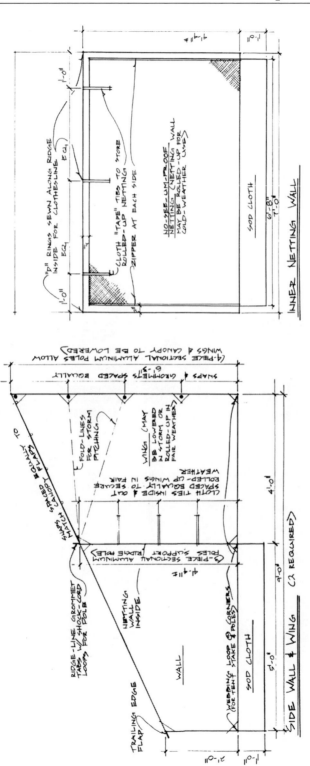

INNER NETTING WALL

"D" RINGS SEWN ALONG RIDGE INSIDE FOR CLOTHESLINE EQ.

CLOTH "TAPE" TIES TO STORE ROLLED-UP NETTING

ZIPPER AT EACH SIDE

NO-SEE-UM-PROOF NETTING (NETTING WALL MAY BE ROLLED-UP FOR COLD-WEATHER USE)

SOD CLOTH

SIDE WALL & WING (2 REQUIRED)

(4-PIECE SECTIONAL ALUMINUM POLES ALLOW WINGS & CANOPY TO BE LOWERED)

GROMMETS SPACED EQUALLY

SNAPS

6'-3"

FOLD-LINES FOR STORM PITCHING

WINGS (MAY BE LOWERED IN STORM OR ROLLED-UP IN FAIR WEATHER)

CLOTH TIES INSIDE & OUT SPACED EQUALLY TO SECURE ROLLED-UP WINGS IN FAIR WEATHER

4'-0"

SNAPS SPACED EQUALLY TO MATCH CANOPY

3-PIECE SECTIONAL ALUMINUM POLES SUPPORT RIDGE POLE

4'-4½"

RIDGE-LINE GROMMET TABS W/ SHOCK-CORD LOOPS FOR POLE

NETTING WALL INSIDE

WALL

SOD CLOTH

WEBBING LOOP @ CORNERS (FOR TENT STAKE @ POLES)

TRAILING EDGE FLAP

7'-0"

5'-0"

1'-0"

2'-0"

238

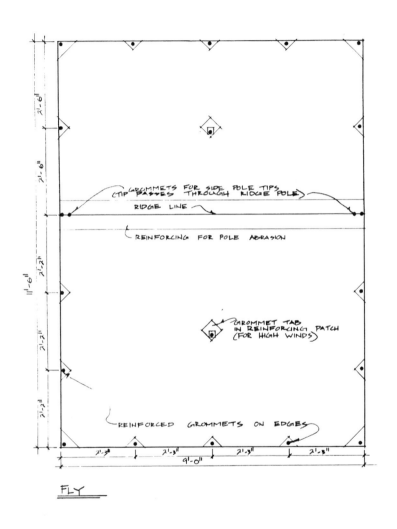

FLY

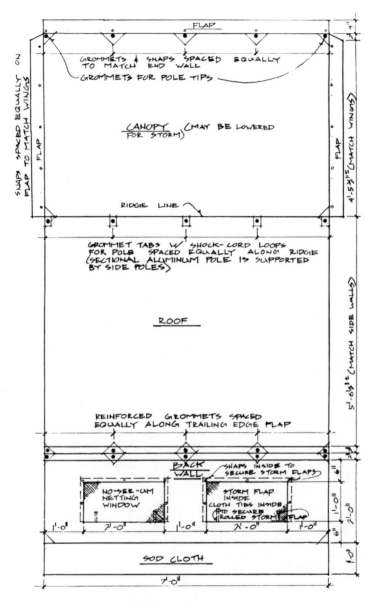

CANOPY, ROOF & BACK WALL

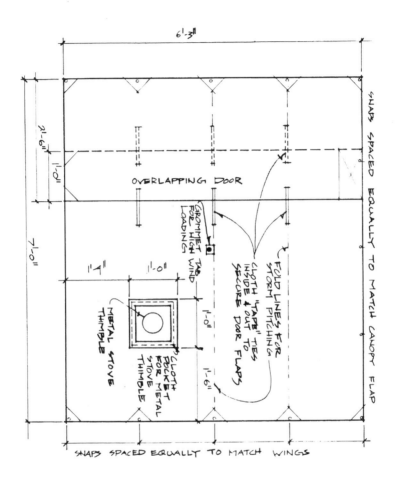

6'-3"

2'-6"

1'-0"

7'-0"

SNAPS SPACED EQUALLY TO MATCH CANOPY FLAP

OVERLAPPING DOOR

GROMMET TAB FOR HIGH WIND LOADING

CLOTH "TAPE" TIES INSIDE & OUT TO SECURE DOOR FLAPS

FOLD LINES FOR STORM PITCHING

1'-4"

1'-0"

1'-0"

1'-6"

METAL STOVE THIMBLE

CLOTH POCKET FOR METAL STOVE THIMBLE

SNAPS SPACED EQUALLY TO MATCH WINGS

REMOVEABLE END WALL (MAY BE REMOVED FOR WARM-SEASON USE)

INDEX

Numbers in bold refer to pages with illustrations

Metric Conversions

Length

1 mile = 5,280 feet = 1.609 kilometers (km)
1 yard = 3 feet = 0.9144 meter (m)
1 foot = 12 inches = 30.48 centimeters (cm)
1 inch (in.) = 2.54 centimeters = 25.4 millimeters (mm)
1/2 inch = 12.7 millimeters
1/4 inch = 6.35 millimeters

Weight

1 ounce (oz.) = 28.35 grams (g)
1 pound (lb.) = 16 ounces = 453.6 grams
2.2 pounds = 1 kilogram (kg)

Capacity (U.S. liquid measure)

1 gill = 4 ounces = 1 cup (c) = 0.1 liter (l)
1 pint (pt.) = 4 gills = 0.5 liter (l)
1 quart (qt.) = 2 pints = 0.9 liter
1 gallon (gal.) = 4 quarts = 3.8 liters

Capacity (British imperial liquid and dry measure)

1 gill = 5 ounces = 142 cubic centimeters (cc) = 0.142 liter
1 pint = 4 gills = 568 cubic centimeters = 0.568 liter
1 quart = 2 pints = 1.1 liters
1 gallon = 4 quarts = 4.5 liters

Temperature

0° centigrade (Celsius) = 32° Fahrenheit (F)
100°C = 212°F
To convert Fahrenheit to centigrade, deduct 32, multiply by 5 and divide by 9.
To convert centigrade to Fahrenheit, multiply by 9, divide by 5 and add 32.